Cities for Human Development

Praise for this book

'*Cities for Human Development* brings an important and much-needed new approach to understanding and acting on urban poverty. Change the lens through which you view it, change who you see and what they need, change your interaction with them ...'
　　David Satterthwaite, *International Institute for Environment and Development, Visiting Professor, University College London*

'This book is a timely and erudite effort that places Frediani among the emerging urban scholars of note. Drawing on practical examples from cities across Latin America and Africa, Frediani artfully applies Amartya Sen's capability approach to city-making. A must-read for urban scholars and practitioners alike.'
　　Dr Jaideep Gupte, Fellow of the Institute of Development Studies, UK

'What are cities for? Are they for making money and creating wealth? Or are they for freeing people to live well? Which goal is fundamental, and which is a mere means? Using the capability approach, Frediani argues that freedom to live well is fundamental. Using a wealth of case studies, he shows how to assess urban decision-making in light of this goal. This is an exemplary pathfinding book for urban theorists, planners, and activists alike.'
　　Jay Drydyk, Professor of Philosophy, Carleton University;
　　President, Human Development and Capability Association;
　　Past President, International Development Ethics Association

'Why not focus on ways of letting the urban world flourish in all its multiple and complex modes of being? And through an understanding of the prevailing circumstances and collective activities that are standing their ground, why not envision new horizons and the project of an urban way of life enjoying greater justice and solidarity? This is the road Frediani invites us to take, founding his approach on the principle of human development as a theoretical and practical counterweight to a cruel economy and monolithic, exclusive, and monetized urban politics. Moving between nine cities and three continents, following the trajectory of action research over more than a decade, the book reveals its lucid, robust structure as it walks the fine line between theory, interpretation of reality, and the reaffirmation of social utopias. Read it with pleasure!'
　　Ana Fernandes, Professor at the Faculty of Architecture, Federal University of Bahia
　　(Faculdade de Arquitetura da Universidade Federal da Bahia, FAUFBA)

Cities for Human Development
A capability approach to city-making

Alexandre Apsan Frediani

Practical Action Publishing Ltd
27a Albert Street, Rugby, CV21 2SG, UK
www.practicalactionpublishing.com

© Alexandre Apsan Frediani, 2021

The moral right of the author to be identified as author of this work has been asserted under sections 77 and 78 of the Copyright Designs and Patents Act 1988.

All rights reserved. No part of this publication may be reprinted or reproduced or utilized in any form or by any electronic, mechanical, or other means, now known or hereafter invented, including photocopying and recording, or in any information storage or retrieval system, without the written permission of the publishers.

Product or corporate names may be trademarks or registered trademarks, and are used only for identification and explanation without intent to infringe.

A catalogue record for this book is available from the British Library.

A catalogue record for this book has been requested from the Library of Congress.

ISBN 978-1-78853-147-4 Paperback
ISBN 978-1-78853-143-6 Hardback
ISBN 978-1-78853-150-4 eBook

Citation: Frediani, A. A. (2021) *Cities for human development: A capability approach to city-making*, Rugby, UK: Practical Action Publishing <http://dx.doi.org/10.3362/9781788531504>.

Since 1974, Practical Action Publishing has published and disseminated books and information in support of international development work throughout the world. Practical Action Publishing is a trading name of Practical Action Publishing Ltd (Company Reg. No. 1159018), the wholly owned publishing company of Practical Action. Practical Action Publishing trades only in support of its parent charity objectives and any profits are covenanted back to Practical Action (Charity Reg. No. 247257, Group VAT Registration No. 880 9924 76).

The views and opinions in this publication are those of the author and do not represent those of Practical Action Publishing Ltd or its parent charity Practical Action. Reasonable efforts have been made to publish reliable data and information, but the authors and publisher cannot assume responsibility for the validity of all materials or for the consequences of their use.

Cover: illustration by Ottavia Pasta
Diagrams: David Heymann

Contents

Boxes, figures, tables, and photos	vii
Preface	ix
1 Towards cities as engines of human development	1
2 Justice, city-making, and the capability approach	19
3 Drivers: Evictions and wellbeing of dwellers in Lagos informal waterfront settlements, Nigeria	33
4 Practices: Experiences and claims for participation in the Euston area of London, United Kingdom	47
5 Aspirations: Re-imagining urban regeneration in Woodstock, Cape Town, South Africa	61
6 Abilities: Housing (un)freedoms in Nova Primavera estate, Salvador da Bahia, Brazil	77
7 Opportunities: Democratizing urban governance through neighbourhood planning associations in Kisumu, Kenya	91
8 Agency: Claiming rights through the occupation of vacant buildings in inner São Paulo, Brazil	105
9 Trajectories: Pursuing buen vivir through participatory neighbourhood planning in Quito, Ecuador	119
10 Learning: Expanding capabilities through knowledge co-production about city-making in Freetown, Sierra Leone	135
References	151

Boxes, figures, tables, and photos

Boxes

1.1 Capabilities	7
1.2 Functionings	9
3.1 Spatial (un)freedoms	39
4.1 Portfolio of options	59
5.1 Adaptive preferences	74
6.1 Conversion factors	86
7.1 Unfavourable inclusion	99
9.1 Cooperative conflict	131
10.1 Institutional capabilities	138

Figures

1.1 Legend for diagrams	16
3.1 Drivers diagram	40
4.1 Practices diagram	55
5.1 Aspirations diagram	71
6.1 Abilities diagram	85
7.1 Opportunities diagram	98
8.1 Agency diagram	113
9.1 Trajectory diagram	129
10.1 Capability map	141

Tables

1.1 Capability elements	15
4.1 Citizens Charter for Euston Area (2015)	52
5.1 Capability-approach methods for identifying dimensions of poverty and wellbeing	70
6.1 Dimensions of housing	82
7.1 Effects of the DMM on wellbeing	95
9.1 Planning and design principles	124
10.1 Capability-oriented urban learning	142

Photos

1.1	Street traders in Kisumu	2
3.1	Sogunro informal settlement by Lagos waterfront	34
4.1	Council housing estates around Euston Station	48
5.1	Resident of Woodstock involved in the Re-imagining Woodstock campaign	62
6.1	Residents of Novos Alagados in the Nova Primavera housing estate	78
7.1	Water kiosk in Kisumu's informal settlement	92
8.1	Residents of Ocupação Marconi in their flat	106
9.1	Los Pinos resident	120
10.1	Residents from the informal settlement of Dwarzack, Freetown	136

Preface

I finished this book in the midst of the COVID-19 crisis. The pandemic has widened social and economic disparities and so raised awareness of the urgent need to address urban inequalities. Many visions of how inequalities should be addressed are emerging. Some argue that we should return to business as usual because we were on the right path before the pandemic. Others emphasize that this crisis is an opportunity to steer away from unjust and unsustainable urban development. The post-pandemic urban recovery agenda will be a contested one, and it is fundamental that care, solidarity, and human development are not set aside in the name of financial recovery. The pandemic reminds us that our past, present, and future depend on what happens not only in places close to us but also elsewhere. Slogans such as 'leave no one and no place behind' and 'we are not safe until everyone is safe' need to go beyond rhetoric and be translated into concrete urban policy and planning programmes. My hope is that this book can contribute to this journey and support reflection on how to put human development, rather than economic growth, at the centre of future urban recovery and development pathways.

While this book speaks to such a wider social–political context, it is at the same time a personal project. It results from collaborations and conversations with many people and collectives who, over the years, have deeply shaped my thoughts and positions. My aim in this preface is to recognize these influences, providing an insight into the relations underpinning this book.

I will start where the book finishes: with learning. Before I encountered urban development planning or Amartya Sen's capability approach, my way of seeing the world had been influenced by critical pedagogy. I am a white Brazilian descendant of Jewish Holocaust survivors and Italian migrants. Brought up in Salvador – capital of the state of Bahia in Brazil and a city marked by deep, intersecting racial and class divisions – I have been acutely aware of privilege and discrimination since I was a child. Early encounters with Paulo Freire's approach to learning and emancipation, both at school and at home, opened a way for me to engage with the social injustices I observed in the city I lived in, as well as those experienced by my family.

A second influence that underpins this book is a particular approach to international solidarity. Since my education in development studies began, I have been embedded in a network of scholars and activists who approach international development critically but also recognize the need for, and transformative potential of, international solidarity. In recent years, my work with the global civil-society network Habitat International Coalition has deepened my understanding of the role that international solidarity can play in advancing local change as well as influencing global processes.

These are, then, the two obvious influences addressed in this book: the capability approach, and urban development planning and practice. I became acquainted with the capability approach in the context of my PhD, which examined a World Bank-funded informal settlement upgrading project in Salvador. In the early 2000s, the World Bank was drawing on Amartya Sen's work to frame its definition of poverty so I decided to apply Sen's concepts to analyse the upgrading initiative. At the same time, I was interested in developing a research methodology based on the principles of participatory action research. While I saw connections between Sen's work and that of Freire, the capability-approach literature was, at that time, dominated by quantitative studies focused on measuring capabilities. Nevertheless, my effort to apply to the capability approach through participatory methodologies was supported by members of the Human Development and Capability Association (HDCA) including Sabina Alkire, Flavio Comim, Severine Deneulin, and Enrica Chiappero-Martinetti. Since then, the HDCA has been for me a key network through which to exchange and cultivate ideas. In particular, I am indebted to Mario Biggeri and Sandra Boni, with whom I have discussed and experimented ways of applying the capability approach in the field of development practice.

My PhD also marked the beginning of my engagement with urban planning and development. During my years at Oxford Brookes University, I became aware of urban development planning as a discipline and this helped me to explore how exclusion and domination can be perpetuated through planning practice. Urban development planning also helped to make sense of the inability of planning thinking to grasp the processes taking place in Salvador, where rapid urbanization is accompanied by deep social and spatial segregation, high levels of informality, violence, and poverty. I remain thankful to my PhD supervisors Roger Zetter and Rod Burgess, whose ideas are reflected in my understanding of the political economy of city-making and of the 'unfavourable inclusions' associated with tenure regularization (see Chapter 7).

From 2007 to 2020, I was based at the Bartlett Development Planning Unit (DPU) of University College London. The DPU was much more than a place of work: for me, it was a place of identify formation. Together with my colleagues at the DPU, I contributed to a joint political project aimed at reconfiguring the field of urban development planning. The DPU has been a place of re-imagining what it means to be an academic, and an urban practitioner, when our positions are infused with notions of social and environmental justice. My interactions with colleagues, students and partners taught me a particular ethos of engagement, one based on principles of co-production, situatedness, emancipation and equivalence (see Chapter 10).

This book has also been influenced by my collaboration with non-profit design organization Architecture Sans Frontières – UK (ASF-UK). Since 2009, I have worked with ASF-UK associates and partners to co-lead a series of action-learning workshops on participatory design and planning. These workshops led to the development of the Change by Design methodology and form the basis of the discussions on democratic city-making reported in Chapters 4, 5, 9 and 10. The Change by Design methodology has been influenced by my reflections on capability thinking as much as ASF-UK's work has shaped the capability approach to city-making presented in this book.

Finally, this book would not have been possible without the generosity and active engagement of the civil-society groups and networks with whom I partnered: Justice & Empowerment Initiatives and The Nigerian Slum/Informal Settlement Federation in Lagos, Citizens UK in London, Development Action Group in Cape Town, Sociedade Primeiro de Maio in Salvador, Practical Action in Kisumu, Movimento da Moradia para Todos in São Paulo, Comité de Desarrollo Comunitario 'Los Pinos' in Quito, and the Federation of the Urban and Rural Poor of Sierra Leone. Their resilience and ingenuity have demonstrated to me the potential of city-making to bring about social and spatial transformations.

At a personal level, I would like to thank a few people that have been fundamental to the development of this book. Margo Huxley carefully edited the manuscript. David Heymann played a key role in the conceptualization of the diagrams. Ottavia Pasta designed a beautiful cover. The manuscript's anonymous reviewers provided helpful comments and useful suggestions. Practical Action Publishing team members, particularly Clare Tawney and Jenny Peebles, provided constructive and encouraging editorial support. I am indebted to Tom Goodfellow and the Department of Urban Studies and Planning of the University of Sheffield, which hosted me as a visiting scholar in 2017 when I was developing the initial ideas for this book. Finally, I am grateful for the support of Beatrice De Carli, with whom I make sense of the world through love, and hope for a fairer future.

CHAPTER 1
Towards cities as engines of human development

Abstract

The thinking and practice around cities as engines of growth has not been able to promote more socially and environmentally just processes of urban development. Inequalities in cities are on the rise and this calls for urgent policy and practice reformulations that are able to address the current trends of uneven urban development. What if cities are approached and recognized as engines of human development and capability expansion? This chapter introduces some of the concepts and methodologies associated with Amartya Sen's capability approach and starts to link this to urban development processes and practices of city-making.

Keywords: growth, inequality, human development, capability approach

Introduction

In the field of urban development, the idea of cities as engines of growth has captured the imagination of decision-makers and played a key role in encouraging public and private investments into cities. This ideal was central to the World Bank's 1990 urban development programmes and, more recently, has found new traction in international development agendas such as the Commission on Growth and Development and the Global Commission for Economy and Climate (Colenbrander, 2016). At the core of this narrative is the assumption that urbanization is a key driver of GDP and part of a wider, linear, trajectory of economic development that requires agglomeration economies leading to increased productivity, innovation, and entrepreneurship. Across the world, such ideals have also been part of many national development programmes that have justified and targeted increased public investment in city infrastructure on the basis of the benefits and returns it can provide to national economies. At the local level, this agenda has generated a series of instruments and approaches to urban planning that focus on enhancing the competitiveness and productivity of cities, making a city more bankable and attractive to national and international investment.

However, over the last 30 years, the world has experienced the urbanization of poverty and inequality. Since 2007, more than half of the world's population has been living in cities, and that share is projected to rise to 60 per cent

Photo 1.1 Street traders in Kisumu (photograph by Alexander Macfarlane)

by 2030 (UN, n.d.). As the world has become increasingly urban, it has also seen an increase in income inequality (Alvaredo et al., 2018). The increasing tendencies for wealth to be concentrated and work to be precarious are deepening poverty and inequalities in cities. Cities have been the epicentre of the massive increase in the gig economy, which various studies have shown produces low pay, job uncertainty, and disconnection from social protections (Kuek et al., 2015). At the same time, similar precarious working conditions are also left unchallenged in the informal economy, which remains a significant and unrecognized economic sector in most regions of the world. While the size of the informal economy has reduced internationally, its share of overall GDP remains significant, especially in Latin America, sub-Saharan Africa, and South Asia (Medina and Schneider, 2019).

Another key facet of the urbanization of poverty and inequality is the growth of housing insecurity worldwide. Recent studies have shown how housing has become increasingly unaffordable as prices grow faster than incomes (OECD, n.d.). According to UN statistics, around 1.8 billion people across the globe lack adequate and affordable housing, and it is estimated that this figure will grow to 3 billion by 2030. This means that we expect two in six of the world's population to be living in poor housing conditions by 2030. While UN agencies have stated that the proportion of the urban population living in slums worldwide declined by 20 per cent between 2000 and 2014, they argue that this trend has recently reversed, with a growth of 23.5 per cent in 2018. At the same time, the absolute number of people living in insecure settlements without access to adequate water, sanitation, and housing conditions grew to over 1 billion, with 80 per cent of this growth attributed to three regions: East and South-Eastern Asia, sub-Saharan Africa and Central and Southern Asia (UN, 2019).

This growing precarity of livelihoods and housing has also translated into inadequate and unequal access to services and infrastructure in cities. According to data collected globally between 2010 and 2018, 2 billion people lived without waste-collection services, and 3 billion people lacked access to controlled waste disposal facilities. In sub-Saharan Africa only 18 per cent of residents had convenient access to public transport (UN, 2019).

Therefore, the ideal of cities as engines of growth has not been translated into increased opportunities for the majority of those experiencing the diverse processes of urbanization across the world. What if cities were approached as engines of human development, instead of pure economic growth? This book explores the implications for examining and intervening in cities if we understand them as places of human flourishing and recognition of social diversity, care, and solidarity. This book draws particularly on the work of Amartya Sen and other scholars advancing the capability approach, which defines the purpose and process of development in terms of the expansion of people's capabilities, rather than pure maximization of income. The capability approach provides a substantive theory of social change focused on people's freedom, agency, and wellbeing, and which has not yet been applied more systematically to contribute to debates about urban development and planning practice. Therefore, this book aims to urbanize the capability approach by drawing on the literature and debates about Sen's idea of development as freedom (Sen, 1999b) to interrogate the purpose and processes of making cities.

Nevertheless, various academics and studies have demonstrated that cities offer great potential for the expansion of material, relational, and subjective wellbeing, and for advancing human flourishing. Colenbrander (2016: 5) argues that, from a material perspective, 'governments can meet many basic needs at a lower cost in cities than is typically possible in rural areas. This is because higher population density reduces unit distribution costs and permits economies of scale.' From a relational perspective, cities have the potential to be engines of recognition of social diversity and contestation of relations of oppression and marginalization. Following the work of Jacobs (1962), Young (1990: 251) develops this point eloquently:

> As a normative idea, city life instantiates social relations of difference without exclusion. Different groups dwell in the city alongside one another, of necessity interacting in city spaces. If city politics is to be democratic and not dominated by the point of view of one group, it must be a politics that takes account of and provides voice for the different groups that dwell together in the city without forming a community.

In this sense, from a more subjective perspective, cities and their urban interactions can open up alternative imaginaries and subjectivities about the nature of the good city and the good life.

> A city isn't just a place to live, to shop, to go out and have kids to play. It's a place that implicates how one derives one's ethics, how one develops a sense of justice, how one learns to talk with and learns from people who are unlike oneself, which is how a human being becomes human. (Sennett, 1989: 84)

Lees (2004) provides a powerful articulation of the debates around the idea of the emancipatory city, which brings to the forefront the role of urban experiences in triggering not just social isolation and alienation among city dwellers but also their critical awareness. These debates on the material, relational, and subjective aspects of cities highlight that processes and activities of making and unmaking the city are key factors in the improvement or diminution of wellbeing. Similarly, Friedmann (2000) argues that cities contribute to establishing the conditions for human flourishing, an Aristotelian concept extremely influential to the development of the capability approach.

The failure to capture and nurture the potential benefits of city-making to advance wellbeing and human flourishing has been made even more explicit and urgent by the international climate, social, and health crises. The climate crisis is a result of interactions between climate change and inequality: inequality makes it harder to tackle climate change, and climate change reinforces inequality. Urbanization has been a key factor in the unequal distribution of environmental risks within and among cities, as the poor are much more vulnerable to the negative impacts of climate variability. The COVID-19 pandemic also exposed the vulnerabilities and inequalities of the urban poor, as inadequate access to water, housing, and health services made them more likely to be infected by the virus. Furthermore, long-term respiratory disorders created by unhealthy living conditions in informal settlements and precarious housing make the urban poor more likely to suffer from the infection. The remarks of Ortiz, writing in 2010, could not be a more relevant summary of the contemporary challenges of city-making:

> The high potential of human development which is characteristic of life in cities – as spaces of encounter, exchange and complementation; of enormous economic, environmental and political diversity; and of important concentration of production, service, distribution and educational activities – is today faced with multiple and complex processes posing immense challenges and problems for social coexistence. (Ortiz, 2010: 115)

As a result of this mismatch between the potentials and failures of cities, the urban question has become central to local and international efforts to advance social and environmental justice. In 2019 and 2020, there were urban protests and unrest in various cities around the world – La Paz, Santiago, Haiti,

Morovia, Paris, Beirut, and Hong Kong, among others. While the protesters' demands were very context specific, mobilizations were driven by general urban experiences of dispossession and discrimination, increased inequalities, climate vulnerability, and lack of trust in existing democratic institutions. Cities have become engines and staging grounds of discontent (Carey, 2019; Weinstein, 2020). By understanding these localized urban unrests in relation to each other, it is possible to see the emergence of a global political agenda associated with notions of justice, sustainability, and care. Meanwhile, through internationally coordinated efforts, transnational civil-society networks have mobilized the notion of the right to the city to argue for global commitments based on a vision of 'cities for dignity, and not for profit' (Global Platform for the Right to the City, 2020). The World Charter for the Right to the City (International Alliance of Inhabitants, 2005), put together by a broad network of popular movements, NGOs, professional associations, forums, and national and international civil-society networks, emphasizes the need to recognize the role of cities in the production of social justice. Harvey illustrates well how the right to the city agenda demands a rethink of the relationship between cities and human flourishing:

> The right to the city is far more than the individual liberty to access urban resources: it is a right to change ourselves by changing the city. It is, moreover, a common rather than an individual right since this transformation inevitably depends upon the exercise of a collective power to reshape the processes of urbanization. The freedom to make and remake our cities and ourselves is, I want to argue, one of the most precious yet most neglected of our human rights. (Harvey, 2008: 23)

Recent international agendas have also highlighted the importance of rearticulating ideals associated with how cities are planned and produced. The UN Sustainable Development Goals (SDGs) include a specific urban goal, SDG 11, which calls for 'sustainable cities and communities'. Targets for Goal 11 include ensuring access to safe and affordable housing, upgrading slum settlements, improving public transport and access to green public spaces, and making urban planning participatory and inclusive. Similarly, the New Urban Agenda led by UN-Habitat articulates a vision of right to the city, 'where all persons are able to enjoy equal rights and opportunities, as well as their fundamental freedoms' (UN, 2017). Underpinning both agendas is an international commitment to leave no one and no place behind.

These efforts and mobilizations bring to the forefront the debates about the questions 'Whose city is it?' and 'City-making for what?' This book engages in a dialogue with these ongoing efforts to shift the idea of cities as engines of economic growth towards articulations that approach cities as engines of equality, emancipation, justice, and sustainability. More specifically, the book aims to contribute to this debate by understanding in practical, methodological, and theoretical terms the implications of approaching cities and urban processes through the lens of human development. The notion of human development draws on the work of Amartya Sen (1992; 1993; 1999a; 1999b), defining development as expansion not of income but of people's capabilities. Sen's work has been key in shifting the international narrative of development away from economic growth towards one that values multiple dimensions of wellbeing and the need to address the uneven distribution of opportunities for human flourishing. This book proposes just such an articulation of cities as engines of human development and expansion of capabilities.

Human development and the capability approach

The concept of human development came into use in the field of international development as a way of departing from income-led definitions of development. According to the United Nations Development Programme (UNDP), human development is about understanding 'people as the real wealth of nations' (UNDP, 1990), indicating that development is about improving people's abilities and opportunities to achieve their aspirations. Understanding cities as engines of human development means approaching urban experiences and changes in relation to how they affect people's freedom to pursue the lives they value.

Many of the theoretical debates underpinning the human development perspective have been influenced by the ideas and practices of the capability approach, a framework initially developed by the Economics Nobel Prize winner Amartya Sen and the philosopher Martha Nussbaum. The capability approach has most often been applied as an evaluative framework, providing analytical elements for exploring how development initiatives affect people's real freedoms. Capabilities are the abilities and opportunities people have to pursue their aspirations. From this perspective, poverty is defined not as lack of income but as deprivation of the capability to pursue a flourishing life. Sen (2009: 16) argues that the focus should be on a 'person's achievements and freedoms in terms of his or her actual ability to do the different things a person has reason to value doing or being'. This approach has played an important role in contributing to a paradigm shift in the field of international development, encouraging a people-centred perspective and addressing poverty as capability deprivation, rather than lack of income.

The capability approach is:

> generally understood as a conceptual framework for a range of evaluative exercises, including most prominently the following: 1) the assessment of individual levels of achieved wellbeing and wellbeing freedom; 2) the evaluation and assessment of social arrangements or institutions; and 3) the design of policies and other forms of social change in society. (Robeyns, 2017: 23–24)

It offers the opportunity to link development actors' theory of change to a substantive theory of justice. Schlosberg explores the contribution of the capability approach to a larger discourse of justice, and he argues that it expands the distributional realm of justice because it focuses 'not just on the distribution of goods we need to flourish, but the processes we depend on for that flourishing to occur' (2007: 33). He also argues that the work of Nussbaum explicitly addresses concerns relating to how social diversity is recognized, as she articulates it as a necessary element in her capability list (Nussbaum, 2000). Furthermore, Schlosberg emphasizes the usefulness of this substantive theory of justice, arguing that 'in addition to distribution and recognition, Sen and Nussbaum's inclusion of participatory rights and freedoms as additional capabilities necessary to transform goods into a good life illustrates the necessity of linking these various conceptions in a larger framework' (2007: 34).

Along similar lines, Frediani et al. (2014a) argued that a capability perspective on development projects would require initiatives to: 1) undertake a deep diagnosis of the context of initiatives, revealing diverse needs and aspirations of marginalized groups; 2) define outcomes in a multidimensional manner, capturing different aspects of people's valued aspirations; and 3) involve project partners as active agents of change, rather than merely recipients or beneficiaries of development initiatives. These aspects lead to the reframing of three key concepts often embedded in urban development planning and practice: capacities, needs, and participation.

From capacities to capabilities

One way to start unpacking the contributions of the capability approach to urban development and planning practice is by reflecting on the distinction between capacities and capabilities. Capacities are normally related to people's abilities or skills to carry out certain activities. For example, entrepreneurial approaches to enhance the income-generation activities of the urban poor have often focused on strengthening the capacities of small-scale entrepreneurs. In these initiatives, urban poverty reduction projects have promoted the development of business skills, vocational courses, and improved access to micro-finance, which particularly benefit street traders. These efforts play an important role in improving access to a diverse set of assets which shapes people's real urban freedoms. However, a capability assessment would require understanding the context and conditions of particular livelihood practices

---

Box 1.1 Capabilities

Amartya Sen defines capabilities as the 'substantive freedoms [a person] enjoy[s] to lead the kind of life he or she has reason to value' (Sen, 1999b: 87). Drawing on the capability-approach literature, I have defined elsewhere (Frediani, 2010) that the concept of capability includes the choices, abilities, and opportunities people have to achieve the things they value. A person's capability is determined by the result of the interaction between these three elements.

and experiences in addition to these issues. It would require understanding the extent to which the new skills and access to new resources could be used and appropriated in equitably improving wellbeing in the city.

When using the capability perspective, the various factors that shape people's freedoms to use and appropriate commodities are called conversion factors. Sen (1993) and Robeyns (2005) define these as personal, social, and structural factors conditioning people's freedom to utilize particular commodities to achieve the things they value. From a capability perspective, city-making requires understanding the factors conditioning the conversion of particular city-making practices into achieved dimensions of wellbeing. In this way, the notion of conversion factors goes beyond people's skills and capacities and opens up a debate about wider issues associated with the structure of opportunities for expanding capabilities in cities. In Chapters 6 and 7, I give more detail about the definition of these factors and their application in city-making processes.

Taking up the example of the livelihood practices of street traders, moving from capacities to capabilities would require understanding the conditions shaping income-generating activities of the urban poor. What are people's real opportunities to use their new acquired skills and finance? How do cities secure and support the economic activities of the urban poor in ways that expand wellbeing? If those supposed to benefit from development initiatives are not allowed to trade in streets, and markets are displaced, criminalized, or gentrified, then conversion factors are diminished and capabilities are limited. Given the diverse social identities of street traders, these drivers of displacement are experienced in different ways and these, in turn, condition and shape people's opportunities to trade. If regulations are unresponsive to the diversity of the needs of small-scale informal entrepreneurs, or if incentives are distributed unevenly among different business actors, simply increasing capacities might not be enough to enhance wellbeing. Furthermore, people's income-generation activities do not have a purely productive role: they influence and are associated with many aspects of wellbeing. Moving from capacities to capabilities means engaging with the multiple purposes and values associated with particular urban practices and experiences. This can be complex as, for example, an initiative that recognizes the right of informal traders to use streets and pavements to conduct their businesses can simultaneously enhance economic opportunities and compromise the mobility of people in the city. A capability approach calls for an explicit engagement with these complexities, interrogating them and creating the conditions to address them through public reasoning.

Beyond needs, towards aspirations

Sen's writings call for development to focus on the many things people value doing and being, which means engaging with the various dimensions of wellbeing. Sen calls the doings and beings that people value functionings.

> **Box 1.2 Functionings**
>
> Amartya Sen (1999b) defines functionings as the various things people may value doing and being. These refer to different dimensions of wellbeing, such as being healthy and well-nourished, being safe, being educated, having a good job. Functionings have an intrinsic value, as they represent fundamental components of wellbeing, and are, therefore, ends in themselves. But they have also an instrumental quality, as achieving one dimension of wellbeing can become a means to achieve another or others.

While capabilities focus on people's freedom, functionings relate to the values and aspirations people associate with wellbeing (for more on functionings, see Chapter 5). This focus on people's aspirations is in direct contrast to the paternalism implicit in 'basic needs' approaches, which predetermine what is a need and what is basic (Fukuda-Parr, 2003). Such approaches risk the danger of assuming that some aspects of life are more important than others. For example, in Maslow's theory of needs, food, water, warmth, security, and safety are prioritized over self-actualization or self-esteem needs. A capability perspective would not approach these dimensions hierarchically but in an interconnected and interdependent manner. In other words, the capability approach calls for evaluative exercises to reveal what people value, and to explore the intrinsic value of each dimension of wellbeing in people's own terms, as well as how these dimensions relate to and affect each other, so revealing their instrumental value.

Sen is preoccupied with the threat of universalizing notions of the good life and so does not identify a list of valued dimensions of wellbeing, instead arguing that this valuation process should take place through public deliberation. Drawing on the open-ended nature of Sen's writings on this, Alkire (2013) and Frediani et al. (2019a) have suggested a variety of methods and processes of public reasoning to reveal and identify valued dimensions.

When considering how dimensions of wellbeing are to be identified, this book draws on the work of Sen, rather than that of Nussbaum, highlighting the need to engage in participatory and democratic processes to identify dimensions of the good life and of the good city. With its focus on aspirations and notions of the good life, the capability approach encourages urban planning not to assume or predetermine outcomes. The focus on revealing aspirations through public reasoning, and encouraging urban inhabitants to reflect critically on them, is a key characteristic of a capability approach to city-making.

Participation as agency

One of the key foundations of the capability approach is the understanding of people as agents of change. Writing in a similar vein to Paulo Freire (1968; 1970; 1996), Sen articulates the importance of individuals and groups playing a central role in the processes of defining their aspirations and the expansion of their freedoms:

> Political and civil rights, especially those related to the guaranteeing of open discussion, debate, criticism, and dissent, are central to the process of generating informed and considered choices. These processes are crucial to the formation of values and priorities, and we cannot, in general, take preferences as given independently of public discussion, that is, irrespective of whether open interchange and debate are permitted or not. (Sen, 1999b: 253)

The capability-approach literature approaches participation not as a means for more effective and responsive development-project implementation, but as a mechanism to expand people's abilities to reflect critically on their values and living conditions as well as to act upon them. The abilities associated with critical awareness and action are understood as agency. This agency-oriented approach to participatory processes requires engagement with the power asymmetries that are played out in practices of deliberation. Not all participants have the same ability to engage in participatory processes and, therefore, the capability approach requires city-making to create strategies to proactively reach out to marginalized voices, thinking about the conditions that would allow them to express and expand their agency.

Debates about participation in capability approaches have often been conducted through the lens of critical and collective learning. Clark et al. argue that participatory practices in a capability-oriented perspective need to promote 'empowered learning systems' (Clark et al., 2019: 395), by *supporting institutions* to ensure open, nurturing, and inclusive environments for participation; *promoting relationships of solidarity and trust* which facilitate long-term partnerships and strategies for development; *enabling critical pedagogy*, which questions the status quo, cultivates critical group consciousness, and disrupts cultures of silence, while at the same time, fostering individual and collective agency; and *striving towards emancipatory outcomes* in terms of intrinsically and instrumentally valuable capabilities for wellbeing and agency (Clark et al., 2019: 395).

Similarly, a capability approach to planning would require making planning practice a process of exploratory discussion and research that helps to expand the agency of participants, changes attitudes related to socially excludent processes, and creates spaces for critical reflection and exposure of alternative practices and norms (Walker et al., 2014).

The capability approach as a framework for urban development practice

In the field of development practice, ongoing debates about particular frameworks for thinking and practising development have shed light on the assumptions, methodologies, and ethics of development. The notion and operationalization of the capability approach has emerged through these debates. Elsewhere, I have argued that the capability approach contributes towards the radicalization of development alternatives by opening up ways of reflecting on the conditions, processes, and purposes of development (Frediani, 2010). This application of the capability approach is in close dialogue with two other prominent frameworks in the field of development practice: rights-based approaches and sustainable livelihoods frameworks. Both of these frameworks have informed thinking and practice about urban development, and the capability approach contributes to them in ways that help the advancement of recent global urban agendas and commitments.

The capability approach is a rights-based approach to development practice: like rights-based approaches, capability thinking and practice have at their core a concern with norms and values, as well as a commitment to address the denial of rights and entitlements. However, instead of taking a solely legalist approach to the definition and protection of rights, application of the capability approach is concerned with the various realms where rights are defined and negotiated. From an urban perspective, this means recognizing that while judicial instruments and procedures are potentially important for the protection and advancement of human rights in the city, they are not the only components.

Rights are also defined, produced, and advanced through the everyday experiences and collective practices of marginalized urban groups. As I argue in this book, collective processes of producing the city can enhance people's access to resources crucial for the actualization of rights (e.g. housing, basic services, public spaces). At the same time, processes producing spaces collectively can enhance critical awareness, promoting better collective understandings about diverse urban needs and aspirations, as well as policy, norms, and regulations affecting urban planning and practice. Collective forms of producing and appropriating spaces in the city enhance social bonds of solidarity and action, helping people to resist violations of rights, to identify pathways for change, and to increase bargaining power to navigate these pathways. The capability approach expands the legalistic applications of rights-based approaches by recognizing various realms of the production of rights. Furthermore, the capability approach provides a substantive theory that explores the connections between the availability, use, and appropriation of resources, and the outcomes associated with the advancement and protection of a set of values, norms, commitments, and/or obligations.

The notions and motivations of a sustainable livelihoods framework (SLF) are also closely connected to the thinking and practice of the capability approach. As with the capability approach, the SLF emerged in the late 1980s from the growing dissatisfaction with income-maximization approaches. Its basic concepts emphasize some familiar features: participation, multidimensional conceptualization of poverty, and empowerment. SLF is also concerned with people's potentials and strengths, and how these are converted into positive livelihood outcomes while addressing issues of vulnerability, risk, and insecurity. The means to combat these hardships are the assets that individuals, households, and communities have. The livelihood literature frequently employs the language of capabilities and acknowledges that it has incorporated some of Sen's concepts. However, a close comparison of the two approaches reveals conceptual and practical differences.

Firstly, the application of Sen's concepts in the livelihoods approach is underdeveloped and limited. The word 'capabilities' is used interchangeably with 'assets' in some places and at other times with 'capital'. Thus, capabilities are related to the capacity to acquire resources. But Sen's concept of capabilities has a broader definition. It incorporates the choice of potential achievements and it is used to explore the process of using resources. Secondly, the livelihoods literature does not consider in detail how livelihoods outcomes are defined and by whom (Kleine, 2010). From a capability perspective, these would be defined in terms of what people value doing and being and are explored in this book as people's aspirations. And, finally, livelihood practices are often limited to productive and reproductive activities, and so are unable to capture other key ways of doing things in the city that can expand people's capabilities in other domains of city-making including mobility, water and sanitation, housing, and participatory practices. In this way, the capability approach enriches the livelihoods framework by making a clear distinction between capacities and capabilities, providing a substantive debate on how aspirations are defined, and by capturing diverse sets of city-making practices, beyond livelihoods, that have roles to play in shaping and advancing capabilities in cities.

Methodology and structure of the book

This book explores the pursuit of human development in cities through engagement with people and places striving for a more just city. It brings together a series of reflections drawing on encounters I have had since 2003. The book follows my journey of applying Amartya Sen's concepts to the understanding of urban development through various action-research initiatives, each undertaken with grassroots organizations of urban marginalized groups and their support organizations and networks. These engagements took place at various times and vary in the extent to which I was personally embedded in the place and involved in the struggle. All of them were shaped by relationships of care and respect for partners. The encounters with each city emerged from shared interests and political synergies with partners similarly aware of the potentials of such collaborations in terms of co-learning and action. They are also conditioned by a personal and collective commitment to advancing struggles that challenge inequalities and injustices in cities. The book refers to these encounters as case studies, defined from a feminist research perspective as thick, contextualized, and embedded descriptions of experiences and systems (Snow and Trom, 2002).

During the course of this journey, it has become apparent that conflicts over the production, use, and appropriation of urban space have played a fundamental role in people's lives. At times, top-down, market-oriented, and physically driven projects have pushed marginalized people into even more vulnerable living conditions, exacerbating urban inequalities and poverty. This is the case, for example, in **Lagos** (Nigeria), where the government's strategy of evicting residents of informal settlements on the city's waterfront has been disrupting the livelihoods of the urban poor and threatening their right to live in the city. In **Cape Town** (South Africa), extremely vulnerable populations living in informal areas in gentrifying neighbourhoods have been forcibly displaced by the state or the private market, being pushed away from areas where they were close to livelihood opportunities, services and where they could access social support systems. In **Salvador** (Brazil), the state relocated residents of a stilt settlement to a nearby housing estate in ways that disrupted social networks and generated new living costs for an already financially challenged population, pushing the poorest to sell the properties they were sent to and move to even more peripheral and marginalized parts of the city.

While internationally there is increasing discussion about the need for participation in the governance of cities so that city-making can be more responsive to citizens' needs and aspirations, in reality we are seeing project-based and tokenistic forms of engagement with urban dwellers. The concept of participation has been often appropriated by urban development projects to justify the inclusion of citizens in processes where they have little scope to substantively influence decision-making. There has been a professionalization of nominally participatory techniques by private firms specializing in the provision of consultation services offering engagements that tend to only reinforce the disillusionment and frustration citizens feel towards processes branded as participatory.

In response to these frustrations, citizen-led practices to enhance the power of urban citizens to influence decision-making about the future of cities have been emerging. This is the case, for example, in **London** (United Kingdom), where people living in the Euston area have been contesting the vision for a proposed new station because they have not been meaningfully involved and because changes will have negative impacts on residents and local small-scale businesses. They have been formulating alternative views and plans for change in their neighbourhood to claim their democratic right to be meaningfully involved in decision-making processes about the future of the place where they live. In **Kisumu** (Kenya), residents of informal settlements have been building water points in their communities so improving their quality of life and creating local livelihoods as well as strengthening local representative structures by setting up neighbourhood associations.

In other cases, civic practices of city-making have gone further than an intent to participate in decision-making and engaged directly in the production of spaces in ways that could make cities better able to meet the needs and aspirations of communities. In **São Paulo** (Brazil), people without access to affordable housing are occupying and transforming vacant buildings into communal living places. On the outskirts of **Quito** (Ecuador), newcomers to the city got together with people who could not afford rents in the inner areas of Quito to occupy a piece of land on the periphery of the city and worked together to develop a plan for their neighbourhood that recognized their diverse needs and lifestyles.

In the meantime, we are seeing growth of knowledge-based institutions interested in critically engaging with processes of urban change attempting to navigate these multiple ways of re-imaging and contesting city-making processes. This interest lies behind the formation of the Sierra Leone Urban Research Centre (SLURC) in **Freetown**, which has been conducting a series of learning, advocacy, and research activities aimed at improving the wellbeing and agency of residents of informal settlements.

It is through the exploration of these cases that this book highlights the role that the production of urban spaces plays in shaping people's freedoms in the city. In each place, the model of cities as engines of growth – encouraging the commodification of urban space and advancing an idea of city-making associated with the logic of market productivity and competitiveness – has been present in a different way. In response, there has been a proliferation of civic-led practices that aim to open up new processes through which the production of space can be a conduit for the enhancement of the capabilities of marginalized urban dwellers and, through this, address inequalities in cities. This book interrogates how human development is being negotiated through these urban struggles, and mediated by the way spaces are conceived, produced, and lived by people.

The chapters of this book are structured around reflections drawn from each of these cases in relation to a particular element associated with the capability approach. These elements are used as devices to explore concepts and debates from the capability-approach literature while also grounding them in the context of urban development and planning practice. Therefore, while the elements are based on discussions and definitions articulated in the literature, they also reflect my interpretation of and proposals for approaching city-making from a capability perspective. The order in which the elements are presented does not reflect a hierarchy or a particular methodological structure but grows from my pedagogical experience and mirrors the sequence which I found most effectively explained the usefulness of the capability perspective when addressing urban development and planning issues.

The brief definition of each element in Table 1.1 emerges from the experiences, debates, and reflections fleshed out in the relevant chapter. Figure 10.1, in the concluding chapter of the book, represents the relationship between these elements as a 'capability map'. This representation has also been informed by the engagements described in the intervening chapters. However, it is important to note that it is not a prescriptive recipe on how to apply the capability approach, but it is rather intended to stimulate debate around diverse ways of using, defining, and mobilizing these capability elements.

Table 1.1 Capability elements

Drivers	Drivers are wider structural trends and processes affecting values and freedoms. They can be understood as conditions in the social, political, economic, ecological/spatial landscape that produce and distribute risks and opportunities, obstacles, and leverages for change in the city.
Practices	Practices refer to the different ways of doing and making things. In relation to city-making, practices bring to light the range of models or ways of operating to produce space, goods and services in the city, described through organizational or governance arrangements.
Aspirations	Aspirations are the motivations and values associated with particular practices. These values refer to policy commitments and obligations as well as to people's ideals, capturing diverse worldviews. In the context of city-making, aspirations are associated with the intersection of the good city and the good life.
Abilities	Abilities refer to people's diverse capacities and skills to draw on practices in the pursuit of their aspirations. These abilities are shaped by people's access to assets. Places where people live and move in the city influence their access to assets. At the same time, abilities condition people's freedom to appropriate and shape the city.
Opportunities	Opportunities relate to the policies, norms, and procedures that shape people's abilities to pursue aspirations. Opportunities highlight the importance of the urban policy and planning environment in shaping people's capabilities, which include formal and informal norms, regulations, and relationships.
Agency	Agency is defined as the personal and collective capacity to reflect, imagine, and act in the city in ways that advance human development. It also refers to the role that institutions as well as spatial arrangements, production, and appropriation have in deepening critical thinking and enhancing people's ability to act.
Trajectories	Trajectories are the pathways people create when pursuing the expansion of capabilities in the city. These trajectories can have different points of departure, and they navigate through the different capability elements to expand personal, collective, and institutional agency to expand human development in the city.
Learning	Learning relates to the co-production of knowledge by documenting, imagining, and making the city in ways that expand capabilities. Learning plays a key role in advancing an approach to city-making that centres on human development.

Before the chapters discussing the elements of a capability approach in detail, Chapter 2 delves into the theoretical debates associated with interfaces between urban development and planning literature and the capability approach, aiming to provide an initial overview of the theoretical debates that this book is in dialogue with.

Each of the subsequent chapters is made up of two sections. The first examines issues and struggles around human development in a particular city. The second section explores one element of a capability approach

16 CITIES FOR HUMAN DEVELOPMENT

Figure 1.1 Legend for diagrams

to city-making as it emerges from that local experience. Each element is illustrated through a series of diagrams. The diagrams include the *components* of each capability element; a set of *qualifiers* that relate to these components; and *examples* emerging from the experience examined in each chapter (see Figure 1.1). The aim of these examples is to illustrate possible links between experience and theory. The diagrams also describe 'spaces of interaction'. These spaces are not those of the spatial production debates addressed in this book but conceptual boundaries that illustrate and explain a set of interactions between components and qualifiers or capability elements. The spaces of interaction represent relationships that generate and/or constrain capabilities; in this sense, they suggest a field within which the capability elements can be put into action.

Chapter 3 focuses on the struggles around tenure security in Lagos to examine the role of **structural drivers** in shaping spatial freedoms and unfreedoms in cities. Chapter 4 examines the experience of grassroots groups trying to influence a particular urban development plan in London. This chapter examines the notion of **practice** in order to identify various ways of expanding human development in cities and using the capability approach to engage in projective thinking and programming, moving beyond its application as an evaluative framework. Chapter 5 interrogates the concept of **aspirations** by reflecting on the lessons learned from a participatory engagement with regeneration aspirations for the neighbourhood of Woodstock in Cape Town. Chapter 6 shares findings from research on the impact of a slum upgrading project in Salvador to interrogate the interactions between spatial arrangements and people's **abilities** to advance wellbeing. In Chapter 7 the analysis of the delegated management model for water management in informal settlements of Kisumu helps to articulate the role of **opportunities** in expanding human development in cities. Chapter 8 documents the experience of occupying a vacant building in the inner-city areas of São Paulo to examine how the process of collective city-making can shape personal and collective **agency**. Chapter 9 draws on the struggles for securing tenure and grassroots planning and developing the neighbourhood of Los Pinos on the outskirts of Quito to articulate the notion of **trajectories** and their use when applying the capability approach in the context of city-making. In the concluding chapter of this book, I reflect on **learning** as a crucial entry point to advance human development in cities by considering the experience of setting up SLURC in Freetown. The chapter also brings the different elements together in an operational diagram and reflects on how useful this has been for facilitating collaborative learning and knowledge co-production processes in SLURC.

CHAPTER 2
Justice, city-making, and the capability approach

Abstract

There is a substantial debate in existing academic literature about the concept, and processes affecting the production, of just cities. In this field, debates about justice are approached through people's urban experiences as well as by analysis of how cities are made. However, there has been limited dialogue between these debates and the notions of development and expansion of people's capabilities. This chapter traces and explores the existing connections between, and entry points into, these debates, as well as addressing misconceptions in the literature about the interface between the debates on the just city and the capability approach.

Keywords: city-making, social production of space, planning, justice, right to the city

Introduction

The relationship between justice and city-making is at the core of many ongoing debates and publications in the field of urban development, planning, and design. In this chapter, I introduce some of these ongoing debates by exploring their interfaces with notions and literature from the capability approach. My objective here is to situate the debates that unfold in the next chapters in the existing conversations in this field. While Chapter 1 has identified some policy and practice motivations for exploring city-making from a capability perspective, this chapter articulates some of the more theoretical and academic motivations for this book. Firstly, I introduce some of the key notions that help to define how city-making is understood here by making links to writings on the social production of space and the right to the city. I argue that the concept of city-making can be used in response to some of the limitations of current theories and practices of urban planning. Secondly, the chapter critically reviews how some authors in the field of urban studies have understood and approached the capability approach. Thirdly, I reflect on how 'the urban' has been articulated in the human development and capability literature. I conclude by identifying the gaps in academic debates that this book aims to address.

City-making and right to the city

In this book, the concept of city-making and its relationship to processes of social and urban change are rooted in the work of French sociologist Henri Lefebvre (1971; 1991a; 1991b; 2003). Lefebvre conceptualizes the production of space in ways that go beyond the shaping and use of physical spaces and sees the production of space as a process of structuring social relations. In his seminal works, Lefebvre identifies everyday life as the site for the negotiation of power, arguing that market forces and post-war capitalism have been colonizing everyday life: affecting people's dreams, desires, values, and mindsets; creating alienation; and generating exploitation. At the same time, everyday life is where social change can occur, 'an inevitable starting point for the realization of the possible' (Lefebvre, 1971: 14). He articulates the role that space plays in affecting the negotiations between alienation and emancipation that take place in people's everyday lives. Purcell (2003: 577) explains this aspect of Lefebvre's work, saying that 'the process of producing space necessarily involves constructing the rhythms of everyday life and producing and reproducing social relations that frame it'.

To reveal the impact of space in people's everyday lives, their values, and relationships, Lefebvre (1991b) argues that it is important to understand three key elements of spatial production: *perceived*, *conceived*, and *lived* spaces.

Perceived space relates to the physical and material characteristics *of* space. This notion emphasizes the descriptive, observable, and material properties of spaces and the human interactions with them. Lefebvre also addresses the perceived space as spatial practice, which highlights the physical characteristics of people's interactions with space: for example, through routes and routines that can be geographically mapped and empirically defined.

Conceived space captures the imaginations, reflections, and conceptualizations *about* space. Conceived spaces reflect discourses, values, and meanings promoted by particular groups, creating power through the ways that spaces are articulated and represented. This aspect of space is articulated through instruments of making meaning of space: for example, through plans, models, and projects that advance particular visions and theories of space and its transformation.

Finally, lived spaces comprise the everyday experiences associated with how people *use and appropriate* space. Uses and appropriations of space can conform, subvert, or contest the purpose for which spaces were conceived. Uses and appropriations of space can also allow people to reconfigure their perceptions about spaces. If, for example, we approach the occupation of vacant buildings in inner-city São Paulo from Lefebvre's perspective, we would need to grasp the power relations associated with the initial conception of that building as well as its ownership and control, then unpack the meanings and understanding people have of that space historically and currently, and, at the same time, reveal the ways that people are living in it in the present. By approaching this triad as a methodology for engaging with space, it is possible to start appreciating the ways in which city-making shapes people's lives and their relations, their freedoms, and wellbeing.

Lefebvre's approach to spatial production elaborates the concept of the right to the city, which aims to contest cities' roles in the commodification of urban life and to open up debate on the potential for cities to enable radical societal transformations (Lefebvre, 1968). When calling for the right to the city, Lefebvre makes a case for processes of city-making driven by the notion of the use-value of urban space, rather than exchange value. Purcell has been key in applying Lefebvre's work to current global urban development challenges, and he articulates the right to appropriation as a key element of the right to the city:

> [The] right to appropriation stands in direct opposition to the private property relation of owner vs. trespassers. Under the property relation the owners of urban space may use and control access to their parcels as they see fit. They have extensive rights as property owners, rights that are fundamental to class relations in capitalism. Appropriation is the right to everyday users: it denies the right of ownership and emphasizes the right of inhabitants to use the space in their city ... the right to appropriation involves more than just the right to physically occupy urban space, it also means that inhabitants have a right to an urban geography that best meets their use-value needs. (Purcell, 2003: 581)

The right to appropriation opens up the possibility of thinking about the expansion of rights through everyday practices in the city, not only by lobbying governments for social and political change, but also by acts of city-making such as occupying vacant land and buildings, incrementally extending one's home, or collectively managing public spaces and services. According to Lefebvre (1996), simply by being in and inhabiting the city, one has the right to the city, and this highlights the role of everyday practices of producing and appropriating the city as a means of advancing citizenship. Holston (2008) has taken this argument further by arguing that informal dwellers' practices of intervening in urban space can be understood as strategies for realizing insurgent citizenship. Therefore, the right to the city and the appropriation of urban space confront market-led approaches to spatial production, emphasizing the use-value and social functions of space. The right to the city opens up the possibility of rethinking city-making with ideals of human flourishing. Lefebvre's work, and that of others further discussing the notion of the social production of space, provide productive methodological and conceptual entry points to better understandings of the role that city-making plays in the advancement of capabilities and expansion of wellbeing.

Exploring these connections between city-making and human flourishing calls for a spatial turn in the capability approach. This concept draws on the work of Soja and refers to the need to recognize the spatiality of human life, social relations, and justice. The focus on space as an object of analysis is crucial, as various injustices manifest in space and they are shaped by spatial production. Spatial turn also relates to the spatial methodologies through which justice is interrogated and expanded. Soja argues that the work of Lefebvre and Foucault has given rise to a new form of spatial consciousness, which he defines as 'a way of thinking that recognized that space is filled with politics and privileges, ideologies and cultural collisions, utopian ideals and dystopian oppression, justice and injustice, oppressive power and the possibility for emancipation' (Soja, 2010: 103).

City-making and the crisis of urban-planning practice

The theory and practice of the right to the city has been at the centre of some of the current debates related to urban planning and city-making. The right to the city narrative has been one avenue through which academics, practitioners, and civil-society actors have addressed some of the current challenges in the field of urban-planning practice. It highlights two coexisting and interdependent processes that have characterized the current limitations of urban-planning practice: 'perverse' globalization (Santos, 2000: 37) and narrow localism.

City-making is facing perverse forces of globalization led by the increasing financialization of land and property and their insertion into global finance systems. Such processes have increasingly removed control and power from localities and governments, increasingly challenging the ability of residents, civil-society groups, and planning actors to influence, shape, and direct urban development processes. As argued in the critical urban literature, 'decisions that shape the city are increasingly being transferred away from democratic citizens and towards corporations' (Purcell 2006: 1923). Discussions of the 'neoliberalization of spatial planning' (Davoudi, 2018: 23) have highlighted how planning practice increasingly prioritizes an agenda associated with market enablement and financial profit rather than social and environmental justice. Internationally, we see the proliferation of planning practices that promote the productivity and competitiveness of cities by focusing on strategies to attract foreign direct investment. These involve, for instance, de-regulation of land use, incentives for large-scale private developments, investments to improve information and communication technology infrastructure in the city, the unbundling and privatization of service provision, and the expansion of airports and convention centres to attract international conferences and events. These initiatives combine to contribute to the making of the 'world city' narrative (Massey, 2013) which situates urban planning as an agent enabling the insertion of 'the city' into the world economy.

Postcolonial urban literature (e.g. Roy and Ong, 2011; Arantes et al., 2002) has highlighted the role played by urban planning that pursues the goal of the global city in the reproduction of coloniality (for more on coloniality, see Quijano, 2007; and Mignolo, 2011). This literature has captured diverse ways in which planning practice has reproduced exclusions, exploitation, and misrecognitions that are historically entrenched, embedded in the legacy of colonization, and are sustained and promoted by current tendency towards neoliberal urban governance. At the same time, the postcolonial urban literature highlights the failure of planning theory and practice to recognize diverse and situated forms of city-making as well as its relationships with processes taking place locally and globally (Roy and Ong, 2011).

One response to perverse globalization is an extreme and narrow localism in planning practice. Recent tendencies in strategic planning constrain practice to localized experiments that have little role in destabilizing – or even interrogating – the wider trends reproducing urban inequalities. Areas in the city are often defined as self-contained units in need of 'revitalization', 'regeneration', 'upgrading', or 'activation'. Planning practice is thus an extremely localized process, with outcomes articulated purely in terms of the benefits it brings to the residents of these areas, rather than challenging wider processes of urban change. When notions of participation and consultation arise in local development planning, they are normally framed as having a consensus-driven motivation that hides the complexity of social diversity and asymmetries of power. Purcell has critiqued the trap of localism in urban development, arguing that 'localizing control over space can produce greater democracy or not, or greater social justice or not, depending on who is empowered by the localization' (2006: 1928). Meanwhile, the works of key thinkers in agonistic democracy are often quoted in planning literature to illustrate how consensus-based planning poses risks to the possibility of deepening democracy. For instance, Davoudi (2018) outlines the link between planning and the writings of Mouffe (2005) and Swyngedouw (2010, 2011) and explains:

> [A] consensus-oriented democracy risks becoming radically undemocratic because the search for consensus risks the evacuation of the political, de-politicization of particulars, elimination of genuine political space for disagreement and contestation, renouncement or displacement of social conflict. (Davoudi, 2018: 22)

This localization tendency frames planning as an instrument of conflict resolution and problem-solving, leading to agreements focused on the low-hanging fruits of urban conflicts and easily solved issues while leaving wider problems and structural issues untouched.

The combination of perverse globalization and narrow localism in planning practice have led to frustration and disillusionment with the transformative potential of planning to foster more environmentally and socially just urban processes. In response, there are efforts to re-invent planning theory and practice in ways that disrupt these tendencies and reconfigure the meaning, purpose, and instruments of planning. These perspectives are analysed in more detail in Chapter 8, and include revisiting planning through the experiences of marginalization and contestation in the city. This has led, for example, to the recognition of everyday practices of use and appropriation of the city as a type of planning practice. Bhan (2019) draws on the literature of Southern Theory (Connell, 2007; Comaroff and Comaroff, 2015) and his own activist work in Indian cities to propose a set of Southern urban practices: to *squat*, *repair* and *consolidate*. The intersections between feminist urban theory and the right to the city show that:

> refocusing upon everyday tactics sheds light on how planning practices might learn to consider space through the prism of everyday life. Through the everyday spheres of life, the gendered and patriarchal nature of cities is more readily revealed and the agency of city dwellers operates to challenge it. (Beebeejaun, 2017: 330)

The emphasis on the experiences of marginalization and resistance in cities has also led to the suggestion that collective forms of resistance in the city can be forms of 'insurgent planning' (Miraftab, 2009). In this sense, collective forms of insurgent practice are not simply as a *response to* planning but are themselves a *form of doing* planning. This calls for an expansion of the idea of what planning is and who plans, recognizing the encounters between 'conflicting rationalities' embedded in planning practice (Watson, 2003). Meanwhile, the notion of agonistic planning allows planning to rethink itself through conflict rather than consensus-building approaches (Pløger, 2004; Gualini, 2015).

These are just some of ongoing efforts calling for new apparatus, lexicons, and methodologies for planning practice. (For more on this, see Frediani and Cociña, 2019.) There is a growing interest in the idea that planning needs to better articulate the connections between structure and agency, to look for ways to operate through multi-scalar approaches without binding itself to a particular scale. There are also increased demands from urban practitioners (in all of their diversity) for urban rights recognized in different international or national agendas to be promoted in ways that challenge current modes for the production of cities. I feel that establishing the connections between the capability approach to human development and the debates on future directions for urban-planning theory and practice can contribute to responses to these demands.

Capabilities in urban literature: initial misconceptions

There have been previous attempts to explore the links between planning and the capability approach. However, I argue that they have taken a selective reading which has compromised a more substantial exploration of the usefulness of the capability approach to address the challenges currently faced by planning practice. As a result, and due to three main misconceptions, discussions in urban development and planning have tended to dismiss the capability approach, arguing that it is too universalistic, too individualistic, and lacks structural analysis.

One of the key discussions of the capability approach in planning and urban development appears in Fainstein's writing about the just city (2000; 2009; 2011). These works make a substantial contribution to the exploration of the links between urban theory and justice by analysing experiences from New York, London, and Amsterdam. To develop a set of principles through which urban policy may be designed and evaluated, Fainstein draws on the 'capabilities approach, originally adumbrated by Amartya Sen (1992; 1999b) and fleshed out by Martha Nussbaum (Nussbaum, 2000), [which] offers a way to devise rules that can govern the evaluation of urban policy and provide content to the demands of urban movements' (Fainstein, 2011: 54). This is an extremely useful and important positioning of capability thinking in debates about urban theory and practice. However, by focusing purely on Nussbaum's work and her list of fundamental human capabilities, Fainstein misses the opportunity to engage in a richer debate about different ways of applying the capability approach. Her interpretation has led others in the fields of urban theory and practice to dismiss the capability approach because of its supposed universalism and lack of embeddedness in local contexts and realities.

> Like the Western liberalism from which it emerges, the capabilities approach largely treats individuals as abstract, universal, atomistic actors disembedded from their social relations and historical and spatial specificities. This account of essential human functionings and rights thus fails to fully come to terms with the importance of the situatedness of both author and subject and the implications that difference has for people's everyday lives, needs and wants. (Connolly and Steil, 2009: 3)

I argue in this book that the work of Sen and many others has generated a very different application of the capability approach to that outlined by Fainstein (2011) and critiqued by Connolly and Steil (2009). My work is positioned in a wider development of constructivist applications of the capability approach, which has focused on the discussion and expansion of capabilities through localized and situated grassroots and participatory practices (Ibrahim, 2014; Frediani et al., 2019a). This approach emphasizes the importance of moving on from discussion of a universalistic list of fundamental capabilities to focus instead on issues associated with the definition and expansion of capabilities through democratic practices. The capability approach has developed beyond the recognition of the need for contextual, situated, and participatory applications of Sen's ideas to tackling issues like adaptive preference (Clark, 2012), power asymmetries (Frediani et al., 2019b), the threat of paternalism (Khader and Kosko, 2019), and epistemic justice (Walker and Boni, 2020). These debates are reviewed extensively in *The Capability Approach, Empowerment and Participation* (Clark et al., 2019), which explores the relationship between participation and capabilities to issues related to situatedness of value systems. I aim to extend this work by demonstrating how the capability approach can navigate between particularisms that fragment urban-planning thinking and practice, and a universalism that homogenizes urban experiences and responses.

A second misconception about the capability approach found in urban development literature is that it is too individualistic (Connolly and Steil, 2009). As a consequence, the critique goes, the capability approach does not provide a meaningful account of the collective processes or social relations shaping diverse experiences in the city. Individualism has been debated extensively by the human development and capability approach community. Some argue that the capability approach is ethically individualistic but this should not be conflated with individualism as such (Robeyns, 2017). Individualism is associated with the idea that human beings can live and flourish independently from others; however, the capability approach can be seen as an evaluative framework focused precisely on social arrangements and relations, while being interested in how they have a direct or indirect effect on individuals (Robeyns, 2017: 57). Others have gone a step further and questioned the ethical individualistic tendency of the capability approach by exploring the relational aspects of capabilities (Uyan-Semerci, 2007) or proposing notions such as collective capabilities (Ibrahim, 2006; Anand, 2007); 'relational capabilities' (Giraud et al., 2013: 9); 'external capabilities' (Foster and Handy, 2008: 4);'structures of living together' (Deneulin, 2008: 110); and 'institutional capabilities' (Frediani et al., 2020: 4). This book aims to continue focusing on this interrogation of social and political arrangements of justice by precisely advancing a relational approach to the understanding and expansion of capabilities. Chapter 5 explores how the capability approach can be applied to the exploration of interactions between spatial characteristics and appropriations, social relations and people's freedom to pursue the things they value; while Chapter 9 explores the concept of institutional capabilities by applying the use of capability thinking to the analysis of, and interventions in, norms and relations within institutions.

The third misconception in discussions of the capabilities approach in planning and development is a lack of structural analysis. The capability approach is seen to place too much emphasis and responsibility on the agency of individuals to address injustices in the city (Amin, 2013), while largely neglecting to focus analysis and actions on the structural conditions that lead to these injustices. It is argued that the capability approach creates a narrative enabling concessionism urbanism focused on punctual, project-based and localized interventions that help the poor to help themselves while potentially leaving oppressors and relationships of exploitation unchallenged (Amin, 2013). I believe Amin's critique relates more to the possible misinterpretation and application of Sen's work by development agencies than to the actual content of the capability literature. Sen's *Poverty and Famines* (1981) is a structural and historical analysis of the causes of famine in India that was fundamental in moving the debate away from issues of food availability and towards a broader economic and political debate about the relationship between colonial legacy, entitlements, democracy, and famine. Since then, important contributions to addressing structural injustices through the capability approach have been made in, for example, *Transforming Unjust Structures: the Capability Approach* (Deneulin et al., 2006). This aspect of how the capability approach captures structural conditions affecting urban development is further addressed in Chapter 3.

I turn now to a more detailed consideration of how this book addresses the notion of human development and capabilities, drawing on the developments discussed above and approaching Sen's writings from a constructivist perspective.

The urban in the capability approach

The literature applying the capability approach to interrogate issues associated with urban planning and practice is fairly limited but there have been some significant contributions which open up a series of important questions. I argue that my work talks directly to these four key contributions: the application of Sen's five instrumental freedoms to approach urban development (Samuels, 2005); the establishment of the conceptual connections between the capability approach and the right to the city debates (Deneulin, 2014); the re-examination of an urban agenda from a capability perspective (Anand, 2018); and the articulation of the idea of 'planning for justice' (Basta, 2016: 207).

Removing Unfreedoms (Samuels, 2005) is focused particularly on the design of evaluations and indicators for use by urban development policy makers. It draws on earlier works (e.g. Khosla, 2002) to propose an evaluative framework based on the use of Sen's five instrumental freedoms: political freedoms; economic facilities; social opportunities; transparency guarantees; and protective security. The book recommends the recognition of the agency of marginalized urban citizens, arguing for the removal of the barriers and obstacles that hinder their ability to bring about change to their social, economic, and physical conditions. The contributors to the book draw on Sen's work to articulate a cultural critique of top-down planning practice and technical rationality embedded in the conceptualization of cities. They mobilize the concept of freedom to argue that universalist solutions to improve the quality of life of urban populations would ultimately result in coercive regulations that restrict freedoms and encourage the replication of a global and monocultural model of the city. They argue that, instead, urban programmes with the objective of enhancing people's freedoms should identify the (freedom-limiting) assumptions underlying the physical designs and forms of the built environment, and address these in practical ways that expand local cultural values of freedom and capabilities.

However, this focus on five instrumental freedoms seems to be a restricted application of the capability approach. Sen calls them instrumental freedoms precisely to emphasize that they are not comprehensive but are points of departure for a more contextualized and situated exploration of capabilities. *Removing Unfreedoms* does not engage in methodological debate on the way these freedoms are approached, and neglects many of the other debates taking place in the capability-approach community, such as discussions about conversion factors (which highlight the various social, economic, and environmental factors shaping people's abilities to use and appropriate goods and services – more on this in Chapters 6 and 7); adaptive preferences (which address potential limitations to processes of participation – more on this in Chapter 5); and structural injustices (which bring to light the connections between structural drivers and people's freedoms – more on this in Chapter 3). As a result, this work creates a 'thin' application of the capability approach, making use of certain ideas present in Sen's work while leaving space for many misinterpretations and limited applications of capability thinking (Anand, 2018: 524).

A second key contribution to the debates about the application of the capability approach to urban planning and practice explores its contributions to the advancement of the right to the city agenda (Deneulin, 2014). Deneulin argues that the capability approach offers a substantial evaluative framework to shed light on how different factors affecting urban life condition capabilities and rights. Using these evaluative qualities to explore how different capabilities and rights affect each other would provide a nuanced entry point for the advancement of the right to the city. The paper proposes the concept of 'just cities for life' (Deneulin, 2014: 7) and articulates the connections between the right to the city and capabilities in an extremely meaningful way.

> the realization of the right to the city critically depends on how urban residents relate to each other and relate to the urban space. And this is a truly collective dimension which does not belong to any resident as such. This is why, the transformation of cities, and the provision of opportunities for all its residents to live well, is bound up with the transformation of relations between people and their relation to land. (Deneulin, 2014: 9)

However, the argument fails to fully recognize the diversity in right to the city theory and practice that addresses many of the limitations outlined in the paper. Deneulin argues that right to the city has mostly been seen as a utopian framework focused purely on principles of direct democracy even though various efforts by civil-society groups and governments propose trajectories advancing the right to the city that endorse democratic pluralism and explore mechanisms of institutionalization that counter the threat of depoliticizing the right to the city agenda. (For more on this, see Belda-Miquel et al., 2016; Frediani, 2019b.) Thus, the paper has limited potential to develop the contribution of capability thinking to the field of right to the city.

In contrast, Anand (2018) makes an extremely important contribution to this field by setting an agenda for future work and identifying how the capability approach can reframe the urban question. Like Deneulin, Anand argues that the capability approach can be useful in the implementation and advancement of rights-based agendas. While there has been a growing recognition in urban agendas of human rights commitments and obligations, in practice 'the urban poor households and communities are forced to choose some rights while they lose other rights. The capability approach offers insights to understand these issues from the perspectives of freedoms and what the basis for evaluation should be' (Anand, 2018: 521). A capability approach helps to highlight the role of 'citizen agency (ability to act) and the use of network-based approaches to resolve complex and large-scale problems' (Anand, 2018: 521).

Finally, the fourth key existing contribution to the debates about urban development and planning in the capability literature argues that Sen's work enables planning to engage explicitly with wider social justice outcomes, rather than focus purely on the 'distribution of spatial goods' (Basta, 2016: 199). I have contrasted the work of John Turner and Amartya Sen elsewhere (Frediani, 2009) and, in the same way, Basta suggests that Sen's work helps planning debates to move from what 'things' *are* to what they *do* to people's lives (an idea explored in more detail in Chapter 4).

> My interpretation of this fundamental passage of the Senian philosophy is that only enhancing this relational condition (intended as the variant effect things can have on varying individuals) 'matters', normatively, at the end of advancing social justice. Without considering the concrete 'space of freedom' that qualifies this relational condition between capabilities and 'things,' 'things' – both tangible and intangible – can be anything but merely possessed, accessed, or even suffered, without necessarily enabling the pursuit of those 'prioritized outcomes' individuals set along their lives. That is why ... capabilities are not in opposition to primary goods; but rather a necessary (and by no means corollary) extension of their conceptualization as means of equality. (Basta, 2016: 1999)

The focus here is on the application of the capability approach as an evaluative framework rather than on its potential use as a wider planning methodology that could also inform processes of the design and implementation of urban-planning initiatives. It is this lack of engagement by the capability literature with the projective elements of planning processes that this book aims to address.

Other, more evaluative, exercises focused on the use of the capability approach to explore urban development issues have evolved in two ways. The first object of study has been how the availability of infrastructure or the characteristics of the built environment might compromise or facilitate individuals' abilities to enhance their wellbeing. These discussions draw on ideas about the functioning of the built environment to explore how diverse individuals make use of particular urban facilities. The capability approach is applied in this context to stress the importance of not only the availability of certain urban infrastructure facilities but also who uses them and for what purposes (see, for example, Lewis, 2012; Oosterlaken, 2009; Talu and Blečić, 2012). The capability concept of conversion factors resonates particularly well with the preoccupations of this field, as it highlights the importance of exploring a range of factors (such as personal, environmental, and social) that mediate the availability and use of commodities (Robeyns, 2005). Such applications of the capability approach have often reduced notions of capabilities and freedom to mere usability of space without sufficiently addressing the wider social, political, and economic conditions underpinning the production of such spaces.

The second area of interest in this field attempts to measure the diverse levels of quality of life across the urban territory. Such studies (e.g. Blečić et al., 2013; Fancello, 2011) address important questions of how public resources are distributed in the city and thus have the potential to generate important evidence on spatial segregation. This is the preoccupation of many urban sociological studies which bring together data on the availability of infrastructure and levels of vulnerability to produce deprivation maps. The focus on measurement means these initiatives run the risk of reinforcing reductionist assumptions about the relationship between the availability of, and proximity to, urban facilities and poverty: these assumptions contradict some of the basic notions of capabilities.

In a similar vein, increased attention is being paid to the wellbeing achievements and failures of residents in informal settlements. The work of te Lintelo et al. (2017) and Woodcraft et al. (2020) is particularly interesting: the authors argue that wellbeing studies can capture dimensions of urban deprivation that are not considered by the current poverty measures focused on income and expenditure. They emphasize the contribution 'local area scale wellbeing appraisals' (te Lintelo et al., 2017) can make to informing policymaking, especially by revealing areas in which policy and programmes are failing to improve the quality of life of the urban poor. 'Connecting grassroots' and city/central governments' wellbeing data collection and analysis can address a major practical challenge in assessing urban poverty: the unavailability of data at the right geographical scale' (te Lintelo et al., 2017: 400). These studies make an extremely valuable contribution by engaging with how urban living conditions affect the analysis of and response to poverty. They propose methodologies that are able to address important silences in current understandings of experiences of marginalization and exclusion. However, the focus is on the measurement of levels of wellbeing and the quantification of achievements or failures of policies rather than the freedoms and conditions that shape these. In this sense, there is little emphasis on how wellbeing is produced, negotiated, contested, and advanced in cities. The conceptual and methodological elements of the capability approach could expand the scope of such studies by shedding light on processes and conditions affecting the advancement and generation of capabilities in cities.

It is to these debates about the urban application of the capability approach that I hope this book will make its main contributions. City-making helps us to capture the ways through which spatial production affects people's lives. It reveals the negotiations of people's imaginaries and freedoms as cities are conceived, perceived, and lived. It offers the possibility of emphasizing the role of cities in advancing rights and the common good rather than simply economic prosperity. The lens of city-making helps us to engage directly with some of the limits of approaches, practices, and thinking currently shaping the ways cities are planned and designed. Therefore, it enables the concepts, debates, and preoccupations of the capability approach to address more directly the concerns of those producing cities – architects, engineers, and city planners as well as social movements, community groups, and urban dwellers. I aim to engage in these debates on city-making in order to urbanize the capability approach.

CHAPTER 3

Drivers: Evictions and wellbeing of dwellers in Lagos informal waterfront settlements, Nigeria

Abstract

In Lagos, forced evictions are adversely affecting the wellbeing of residents in informal settlements by negatively affecting health, disrupting livelihoods, and weakening social networks, so risking further marginalization and social-spatial segregation in the city. This chapter explores some of the key structural drivers associated with the increasing numbers of evictions in Lagos. It then discusses in more detail how these causes and contexts of change are considered in the capability and urban development literature. The chapter argues that a capability perspective on city-making needs to interrogate and address the wider structural drivers shaping the capabilities of people in cities.

Keywords: Lagos, evictions, housing, structural drivers, spatial (un)freedoms

Introduction

On 9 October 2016, the Lagos state governor Akinwunmi Ambode convened a press briefing in Ilubirin, an informal Lagos waterfront settlement, at which he announced: 'We will commence demolition of all the shanties around the creeks in Lagos state and also around our waterways in the next seven days' (Ambode, 2016). Community profiling and enumeration carried out by the Nigerian Slum/Informal Settlement Federation (gathering data about the priorities and socio-economic conditions of communities) show that this threat affected over 40 waterfront communities, inhabited by at least 300,000 persons.

Following this statement, the Lagos state government embarked on a series of eviction processes: on 9 October, New Kuramo, an informal settlement in Lekki, was forcibly evicted; on 15 October, the inhabitants of Ilubirin, a fishing settlement on the shore of the Lagos Lagoon, were evicted; on 9–11 November, over 30,000 people were forcibly evicted from Otodo Gbame and thousands more from Ebute-Ikate, both informal settlements on the Lagos Lagoon.

According to the local NGO, Justice & Empowerment Initiatives (JEI), the demolition of Otodo Gbame was carried out in the middle of the night by the

Photo 3.1 Sogunro informal settlement by Lagos waterfront (photograph by Alexander Macfarlane)

Nigerian police, the Nigerian military, the Nigerian civil defence corps and the Lagos state government task force using fire and a bulldozer to destroy peoples' homes. Evictees fled the fires and the police bullets and teargas, running into the Lagos Lagoon where at least 11 people lost their lives (JEI, 2017).[1] The Lagos State High Court ruled that waterfront evictions constituted 'cruel, inhuman, and degrading treatment' in violation of the constitution of Nigeria (Lagos State High Court, 2017).

These issues threatening the wellbeing of residents in informal settlements were discussed during a participatory video workshop I led in 2017 with my academic colleagues Alejandra Boni and Alexander Macfarlane, JEI staff, and members of the Nigerian Slum/Informal Settlement Federation. Our work explored the roles that participatory video can play in the struggles of informal settlement dwellers to advance their wellbeing. The one-week workshop brought together 30 Federation members who: 1) reflected and prioritized issues affecting their wellbeing; 2) designed storyboards for their films; 3) captured images of informal settlements; 4) collectively edited their films; and 5) screened the films to share their stories with other Federation members and key stakeholders (Macfarlane and Frediani, 2018).

This chapter draws on this experience and debates the central question that was addressed by all the films produced in the workshop: how do evictions and insecurity of tenure affect the wellbeing of those living in informal settlements on the waterfront in Lagos? This chapter examines the contextual drivers affecting informal settlement dwellers' right to feel secure against the threat of eviction or displacement. In Lagos, an estimated two-thirds of the city's 23 million inhabitants live in informal settlements lacking security of tenure. (Security of tenure refers to the protection of one's occupation of a particular piece of land, a structure, or premises, and can be ensured by land law, landlord and tenant law, or similar laws.) Without security of tenure, inhabitants of informal settlements live in constant fear of eviction. Fear and uncertainty make long-term investment risky, in turn limiting both public and private efforts to improve dwellings and upgrade infrastructure.

In a Lagos-wide profile created between 2014 and 2016, the residents of informal settlements identified security of tenure as their number-one priority – above access to water, sanitation, electricity, schools, or health clinics (JEI, 2017). This chapter argues that some of the main causes of insecurity of tenure for the urban poor in Lagos are the combination of political and economic support for large-scale property development and the intertwined ethnic politics. This generates a particular vision of the future of Lagos and determines which residents should have their rights protected. Apart from uncovering drivers of spatial unfreedom, the story of these residents also reveals examples of spatial freedom, as communities link up with international networks of organized informal settlement residents to support their struggles and advocate their rights to live in and shape the cities they inhabit. Drawing on this case study, the chapter reflects on how 'drivers' may be defined, making reference to the experiences in Lagos as well as discussions on the capability approach and critical urban theory.

The case of the informal waterfront settlements in Lagos

According to JEI team, the forced eviction and demolition of Otodo Gbame was carried out in spite of a court order restraining the police and the Lagos state government from carrying out any demolition or eviction of waterfront communities across the state (Lagos State High Court, 2016). At the time this book was published, JEI and the Nigerian Slum/Informal Settlement Federation were arguing that the Lagos state government had still not rescinded its eviction threat but rather, in the face of mass outcry, community organizing, and legal actions against evictions, has reaffirmed on several occasions in public statements its commitment to demolishing informal waterfront settlements.

Evictions have led to decreased wellbeing by negatively affecting health, livelihoods, and social networks as well as increasing low-income residents' exposure to COVID-19, so risking further marginalization and social-spatial segregation. Meanwhile, public justifications for forced evictions and the demolition of informal urban settlements have often been associated with a top-down and exclusionary understanding of wellbeing, based on notions of 'orderliness' and 'cleanliness' (Rigon et al., 2015). Most prominently, these include 'getting rid of criminals', 'city beautification', 'clearing drainages', 'enforcing compliance with a master plan', and sometimes, removing people from 'unsafe conditions/environments,' such as flood-prone areas or areas below high-tension wires.[2]

These justifications are underlined by a series of drivers of evictions which shape the politics of space in Lagos. The interest of the government and large-scale developers in guaranteeing access to well-located and high-value waterfront land and property is intertwined with a long history of Nigerian ethnic politics. In the aftermath of the 2016 forced evictions in Otodo Gbame and Ebute-Ikate, the Lagos state commissioner for information published a statement describing the Lagos waterfront communities as the 'abode of miscreants/street urchins, kidnappers, touts' followed by allegations that they are home to 'Niger Delta militants', 'Boko Haram terrorists', and 'foreigners' (Totaro and Ponsford, 2016). All of these justifications are aimed at rallying public support for evictions and demolitions.

Land in Lagos is increasingly valuable because of its scarcity (more than 30 per cent of the state is covered by water, creeks, and lagoons) and also because it is in high demand due to a population that is rapidly increasing due to both natural growth and significant inward migration. In 2007, Lagos had the fourth-highest population density of any city in the world, after Mumbai, Kolkata, and Karachi (City Mayors, 2018). As a result, contestation for the control of well-located land has intensified, and market-led urban development pressure has become a key driver of increased insecurity of tenure. Large-scale developers, supported by government policy and programmes, have been claiming ownership of land where informal settlements have been located for generations.

Lekki, a city in Lagos state designated for real-estate development, is a key example of this trend. The city has been designated a free trade zone, and its development has included the reclaiming of 10 square kilometres of land for the Eko Atlantic Project. This project is part of a wider tendency in the planning of African future cities to target global property investors seeking new markets after the 2008 financial crisis (Watson, 2013). Such a process of 'world-city making' represents urban governance prioritizing the competitiveness of cities (in an attempt to attract foreign direct investment) over the needs and aspirations of their citizens. This increasing insertion of the real-estate market of cities like Lagos into international investment flows has not led to the promised trickling down of benefits to the urban poor through increased job opportunities and tax revenues. Instead, it has fuelled the dispossession of the urban poor through evictions and denial of political rights. Furthermore, it has the potential to deepen the separation between rich and poor, thus opening up 'the prospect of urban spatial and social inequalities at an unprecedented scale' (Watson, 2013: 229).

In Lagos, these processes are intertwined with national and regional ethnic politics. The urban poor in informal settlements are made up of a multitude of ethnic minority groups (including the Egun, Ilaje, and Hausa) and are frequently labelled outsiders or foreigners, irrespective of whether they migrated to Lagos from elsewhere in Nigeria or from abroad. Many of the informal settlements in Lagos are inhabited by fishing communities that migrated from other riverine areas in Lagos state, other states in Nigeria, or across the border in Benin. Other migrant groups, such as those coming from northern Nigeria, may have lived in Lagos for decades but (if poor) tend to live 'off-the map' holding on to different cultural traditions and communal ways of life in informal enclaves.

Despite a century of multi-ethnic, multi-religious, and multi-lingual coexistence in Lagos, recent megacity development has given priority to wealthy indigenes and used alleged non-indigenous origins and non-citizenship to justify the exclusion of residents of informal settlements. JEI (2017) argues that, as a result, these areas and their largely ethnic minority migrant/immigrant residents are increasingly out of step with megacity planning and excluded from urban development programmes. Local advocacy NGOs have been denouncing the discrimination entrenched in government offices and the judiciary by demonstrating that migrants who attempt to apply for title documents are often denied while courts are prioritizing the land claims of wealthy indigene families. Often these claims rely on re-invented history to make customary land ownership claims to huge swaths of the city – relegating anyone who migrated to the city within the last century to permanent insecurity of tenure. Government and wealthy indigene families (i.e. traditional landowning families) also use alleged non-indigene and non-citizen status of the communities on 'their' land to justify further evictions and displacement, simply pushing already impoverished urban poor populations to the city's further margins.

These drivers are also manifested through more subtle practices of displacement, such as criminalization of the livelihood activities of the urban poor. This process is depicted in two participatory videos (Bartlett DPU, 2017a; 2017b), which explain how government authorities made the business of extracting and selling sand from Lagos waterfront illegal and how this affected a whole chain of people involved in related activities (such as diggers, truck drivers and owners, and food sellers), depleting the main source of the livelihoods of residents of the Ebute Ilaje Bariga community. The films also highlight how reduced incomes have affected school attendance, threatening the sustainability of locally run schools.

Despite these causes of deepening inequalities in Lagos, residents of informal settlements by the waterfront have also been affected by drivers supporting them in securing their rights to the city. Elsewhere in sub-Saharan Africa and other regions in the global South, there has been a growing recognition by city governments of the importance of securing tenure for the urban poor to enable broader inclusion and *in situ* upgrading of informal settlements. Successful examples have generally evolved from the long-term struggles of the urban poor and support networks demanding social, political, and policy change, that have ultimately led to changes in land law and administration as well as broader urban governance. In the Lagos context, the Nigerian

Slum/Informal Settlement Federation is an example of a network whose strategies for increasing security of tenure have been informed by other such regional experiences. The Federation is supported by JEI and is an affiliate of Shack/Slum Dwellers International. The groups from Lagos have been particularly inspired by the work of affiliate members from Kenya (Muungano), and how they use community-based savings and profiling as a tool for social mobilization and partnership-building with government authorities. This growing internationalization of struggles for security of tenure, facilitating learning across communities as well as the emergence of common agendas, has been a positive key driver affecting the urban poor in Lagos.

In Nigeria, grassroots community organizing under the umbrella of the Federation has been supported by professionals from a variety of disciplines, including law, advocacy, urban planning, health, creative media, and architecture. The Lagos Chapter of the Federation is active in over 70 informal settlements (out of hundreds in the city) and supports savings groups in 41 communities; it has carried out community-led profiling and mapping in 53 communities, gathering important data about community priorities and resources, demographics, social and physical infrastructure, etc.

Apart from supporting savings and profiling, the Federation in Lagos has also developed legal empowerment strategies that focus on advocating the rights of the urban poor within judicial spaces. This rights-based approach has been supported by JEI who train community paralegals – women and men trained in law and basic advocacy skills who assist individuals and communities to access justice through both alternative dispute resolution and the formal legal and administrative system.

The Federation has made inroads into establishing important relationships with several local governments, the Lagos State Urban Renewal Agency, and the University of Lagos in working towards broader participation by the urban poor in urban planning and upgrading projects. A key achievement of the Federation and JEI legal empowerment strategy is the January 2017 ruling by the Lagos State High Court stating that forced eviction and demolition constitutes a violation of the right of dignity. This sets an important precedent that can become a turning point in struggles for security of tenure (Ponsford, 2017).

Reflections on drivers

The example above highlights the fact that the capabilities of the urban poor are being conditioned by a series of structural factors driving spatial (un) freedoms (see Box 3.1). It demonstrates that opportunities in cities are affected by historical social, economic, environmental, political, and cultural factors influencing the production of space. The market-led urban development model has inserted Lagos into global networks of property investment, resulting in the intensification of evictions, pushing the poor to peripheral and vulnerable locations far from livelihood opportunities and prone to

> **Box 3.1 Spatial (un)freedoms**
>
> Spatial (un)freedoms are the spatial dynamics that condition capabilities. This concept highlights the role that spatial production plays in structuring opportunities in cities. It relates to spatial dynamics (such as financialization of land and housing, social-spatial segregation, or re-appropriation of vacant land) and underscores their impact on people's freedoms and unfreedoms.

environmental threats. In different geographies and at different times, there would be a different set of conditions at play. Some of these drivers have a global political and economic character that especially affect mega cities like Lagos. However, they interact with other global and local drivers in diverse ways; as we have seen, in Lagos, politico-economic factors are intertwined with ethnic politics rooted in long-term historical processes.

Other types of drivers might include longer-term trends such as demographic changes caused by population growth or/and migration flows. An example of this can be seen in the rapid urbanization of Freetown, which has been triggered by both natural population growth within the city and in-migration caused by the civil war in Sierra Leone (1991–2002), leading to the densification and proliferation of informal settlements in high-risk areas prone to flooding and landslides. Meanwhile, shocks are external factors caused, for example, by humanitarian or health crises. An example of a shock that affected longer-term structuring capabilities in a city was Hurricane Katrina which struck New Orleans in 2005: the aftermath deepened the city's economic and racial segregation (Watkins and Hagelman, 2011). Figure 3.1 illustrates the components, qualifiers, and some examples of structural drivers associated with the case of the informal waterfront settlements in Lagos. The structural space describes how different drivers interact, and how this interaction affects the relationship between city-making and capabilities.

While some drivers exacerbate the inequality of capabilities in cities, others might open up opportunities for redistribution. In the case of Lagos, the consolidation of transnational civil-society networks has inspired local collective action and fostered learning about strategies for securing tenure in cities. Another example of a driver of spatial freedom is the emergence of new technologies and their increasing appropriation by the urban poor and social movements for a variety of purposes from enabling financial inclusion to organizing collective action. Mobile money transfer is playing a role in supporting the livelihood activities of informal women traders in Nairobi, while social media and digital technologies have been key in supporting grassroots groups to coordinate responses to COVID-19 in informal settlements throughout cities of the global South (Duque Franco et al., 2020; Sverdlik, 2020).

The drivers of spatial (un)freedoms may not have simple negative or positive roles in affecting urban inequalities: they can simultaneously both reproduce

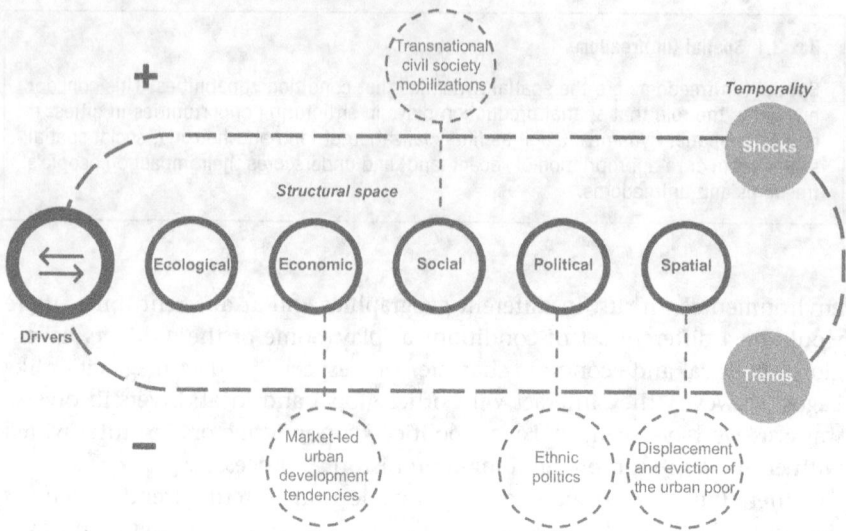

Figure 3.1 Drivers diagram

injustices and open up opportunities for redistribution. For example, the 1970s and 80s model of urban development pushed investment into creating new centres and nodes of activity away from the central area of São Paulo, reinforcing social and spatial segregation (see Chapter 8). However, it also left behind a series of vacant and underutilized buildings in the inner city. These were occupied by urban social movements and became a key resource in struggles for the right to dignified housing (De Carli and Frediani, 2016).

The role of structural drivers in the production of cities has been a key area of work in the critical urban theory literature. Political economy analyses of unequal spatial development demonstrate how the capitalist mode of production generates a process of accumulation and centralization of capital by dispossessing the public of their wealth or land (Harvey, 1973). Others with a different urban political economy perspective have made a conscious effort to address wider inequalities, exploring how structural drivers affect opportunities across social identities (such as race, ethnicity, gender, sexuality) (Connolly and Steil, 2009) and influence the relationship between urban processes, distribution, and mal- or mis-recognition (Young, 1990; Fraser, 1997).

Beyond a political economy debate, it is key to recognize and explore the racialized (see Lokko, 2000; Mele, 2013; Figueiredo et al., 2020) and patriarchal (see Matrix, 1984; Weisman, 1992; Kern, 2020) character of structural drivers of city-making. Many of the material, relational, and subjective dynamics driving city-making have been infused by colonial legacies, deepening entrenched privileges and driving discrimination. Kern (2020) highlights how 'feminist geographers often drew on their own experiences to explore how gender interlocked with other social inequalities and the role that space played in structuring systems of oppression' (Kern, 2020: 16–17). Meanwhile, Lokko (2000) brings together various contributions that reflect how the built environment, as well as the professional and educational sectors associated with it, enforce racial/spatial superiority and cultural hegemony.

It has been argued that the capability approach puts little emphasis on the analysis of the role of structuring processes in the production of freedoms: 'the Capability-Functionings conceptualization serves well to critique conventional welfare economics or the focus on GNP, but appears as an insufficient basis for a whole theory of human development' (Gasper, 2002: 436). Gasper argues that, by perceiving people merely as consumers, investors, and choosers, the capability and human development approaches do not explicitly incorporate the structural conditions shaping people's multiple social roles. In addition, it is argued that Sen does not pay sufficient attention to the structural conditions influencing wellbeing (Stewart and Deneulin, 2002), and does not acknowledge the limitations of market mechanisms in his support for reforms that assure the success of liberalization to tackle poverty and famine (Patnaik, 1998). Sen's concepts can be seen to offer a clear and harmonious route to expand personal freedom by adjusting the lives of individuals to global market competition (Sandbrook, 2000). From this perspective, Sen's concepts would not be changing the market-led development paradigm, but rather serving as conceptual and ethical grounding for the emergence of what Sandbrook calls 'pragmatic neoliberalism' (2000: 1072).

There are similar critiques of the use of Sen's writings by development agencies (such as the United Nations Development Programme) in processes of urban development (Amin, 2013). The focus on human potentials and capabilities is argued to have led to the practice of concessionary urbanism, where one-off concessions in the form of improvements to water or electricity, for example, are provided to avoid future problems such as slum violence, uprisings, or contamination. Concessionary urbanism:

> minimally gestures at the public goods taken for granted in welfare societies, such as access to primary health care or education, basic utilities and services or housing tenure; public goods that ironically turn out to be essential for a capabilities-led approach to development. A concession, almost always rudimentary and sweated for by the poor, arises out of squatters being recognized as needy but illegal subjects rather than as rights-bearing citizens. (Amin, 2013: 484)

Amin argues that the language and concept of capabilities risk putting too much emphasis on the agency of individuals, leaving the conditions shaping the political economy of cities unchallenged. In a similar vein, Harvey (2009) outlines limits to Nussbaum's work, arguing that her capabilities approach does not engage explicitly with the social and spatial factors structuring freedoms in cities. Nussbaum 'neglects to consider how class, ethnic, gender, and other differences become instantiated in socio-spatial structures (such as the ghettos of both rich and poor) that perpetuate differences (some but not all of which are unjust if not down-right objectionable) by way of the geographical structures of segregation in human socialization' (Harvey, 2009: 91).

The implication of these authors is that, when analysing situations like the ones faced by the informal settlement dwellers in Lagos waterfront, the capability approach would generate understandings and responses that emphasize individual freedom and agency; in addressing evictions and housing violations, a capability-oriented response would not necessarily address the conditions affecting the land and housing markets in the city, but rather encourage actions that would make informal dwellers more capable of dealing and coping with such factors.

However, while particular agencies might apply the language of capabilities without critical engagement with structural processes, Sen – and the capability approach more generally – does, in fact, engage in a discussion about the relationship between capabilities and structural processes. This issue has been particularly addressed in the book *Transforming Unjust Structures: the capability approach* edited by Deneulin et al. (2006). The contributors argue that at the core of Sen's work is a preoccupation with eliminating substantial unfreedoms and liberating people from unjust structures.

> The freedom and agency that each individual enjoys is 'inescapably qualified and constrained by the social, political, and economic opportunities that are available to us' (Sen, 1999b: xi–xii). Individual freedoms are inescapably linked to the existence of social arrangements, and 'our opportunities and prospects depend crucially on what institutions exist and how they function' (Sen, 1999b: 142). (Deneulin et al., 2006: 34)

Nevertheless, the capability approach requires 'thickening' with the necessary normative guidelines in order to address unjust structures (Deneulin et al., 2006). A similar argument is that 'the capability approach is, in itself, incomplete as an account of the good since it may have to be supplemented with other values and principles' (Robeyns, 2017: 53). This issue is explored in Chapter 5, in a discussion about aspirations and the interactions between the notion of the good city and the good life.

Sen's work on famine has been 'the first to frame hunger as an issue of structural injustice rather than lack of food availability or a market failure or other natural causes' (Alkire, 2006: 49). It has been a key support in the politicization of famine as an issue of structural injustice, calling for public action and adequate policy response. Alkire (2006) identifies three central aspects of Sen's work in this field. Firstly, in *Poverty and Famines* (1981), Sen argues that famine is not caused by shortfalls in food production or availability, but rather by people's lack of entitlement to food. Secondly, Sen argues that different groups have different powers to command food, and therefore lack of entitlement affects different groups unequally. 'This gave further evidence of injustice: that some weathered the famine intact – or even with economic gain – while others perished' (Alkire, 2006: 49). And thirdly, Alkire points out that Drèze and Sen (1991) highlight the importance and necessity of urgent public action, calling for collective action as well as policy change to address the structural injustices causing famine.

The violations of housing rights experienced by the communities living in the informal waterfront settlements of Lagos can be explored in a similar way. Forced evictions or induced displacement caused by the criminalization of the livelihoods of the urban poor is a process of depriving people of housing entitlements. Following Sen's work, a capability perspective of the situation needs to capture and respond to the economic, political, and social interests associated with the exchange value of land and property in Lagos, which creates the conditions where the legal and political structures are not guaranteeing people's right to live with dignity in healthy and secure environments.

If Sen had been writing about homelessness instead of famine, his analysis would resonate with many of the concerns and analyses developed by critical urban theorists. Adopting Sen's line of argument would move the focus of the debate away from discussion focused purely on housing supply and demand towards examination of the structural injustices shaping people's housing entitlements. Sen's approach suggests calling for the politicization of the housing question and the analysis of its political economy, in much the same way as critical urban theories of housing such as that of Madden and Marcuse.

> Posing the housing question today means uncovering the connections between societal power and the residential experience. It means asking who and what housing is for, who controls it, who it empowers, who it oppresses. It means questioning the function of housing within globalized neoliberal capitalism. (Madden and Marcuse, 2016: 6)

In a more specific way, exploring housing from a capability perspective requires analysis of the hyper-commodification of contemporary housing systems. 'In today's transnational, digitally enhanced market, housing is becoming ever less an infrastructure for living and ever more an instrument for financial accumulation' (Madden and Marcuse, 2016: 26). Harvey's argument about 'accumulation by dispossession' (Harvey, 2003: 144) indicates that the contemporary global economy has as one of its main features a 'new logic of expulsion', as land grabs and evictions have become examples of the development of predatory formations across different geographies (Sassen, 2014). Empirical evidence of the implications of the logic of expulsion can be seen in increased housing insecurity, dispossession, and violent displacements taking place in cities of the global North and South (Brickell et al., 2017). Housing is a global and structural problem (Madden and Marcuse, 2016). UN estimations (UN, 2005) show that, in 2005, the homeless population across the world may be anywhere between 100 million and one billion people (depending on how homelessness is defined). There are indications that 1.8 billion people across the globe lack adequate and affordable housing, and it is estimated that this figure will grow to 3 billion by 2030 (UN, 2019: 44).

The second key element of Sen's work on famine is in relation to the differential power to command food (Alkire, 2006: 49). If applied to the context of housing, a capability approach would recognize the necessity of examining the uneven impact of housing crises on different groups by investigating the relationship between housing opportunities and people's entitlements. This calls for studies to explore, for instance, how gender relations are being shaped by such processes and, especially, unpacking how intersecting social identities (associated with gender, race, age, ability, ethnicity, and class) are being produced by, conditioned by, and affect housing opportunities. Chapter 6 explores the concept of opportunities in the capability approach in more detail and examines its relationship with city-making processes.

Adopted in an urban and housing context, a capability approach would highlight the relationship between structural processes and people's housing aspirations. It is important to critically engage with how processes of hyper-commodification of housing might also permeate the dwelling imaginaries of urban inhabitants, leading to the potential conflation of the ideal of housing security with home ownership (Madden and Marcuse, 2016: 26). In the context of increased vulnerabilities and threats to security of tenure, home ownership is often articulated by politicians and housing programmes (such as the Brazilian My House, My Life programme) as a vehicle for the social transformation of occupants. It is impossible to deny that home ownership is a key achievement for many struggling for housing rights. However, home ownership does not necessarily provide absolute security of tenure as the state can still compulsorily acquire property, and banks can repossess it if mortgage payments are not kept up. Meanwhile, owners need a secure income and access to quality services to allow ownership to be feasible and a worthwhile part of a good life. Furthermore, housing programmes providing incentives for home ownership can become a form of 'unfavourable inclusion' (Sen, 2000: 28),[3] contributing to the commodification of urban space, feeding into processes of speculation, individualizing benefits of housing production, and disrupting opportunities for safeguarding affordable living spaces in the city.

Sen's work has been put into action to address the causes of famine (Alkire, 2006: 50). *Hunger and Public Action* (Drèze and Sen, 1991) calls for various forms of sustained responses to famine, 'such as political protest, journalism and other forms of adversarial as well as cooperative conflicts between the state and participants from the public at large' (Alkire, 2006: 50). In this sense, direct action is a form of democratic practice with the objective of demanding that democratic institutions respond to structural injustices shaping the deprivation of capabilities in societies. Sen argues that self-assertion and solidarity are ways of expanding the 'voice' of collective action against structural injustices shaped by multiple actors and processes that require the coalition and alliance of activists operating at multiple scales with diverse roles in processes of change. Applying these lenses to the context of housing requires recognizing and supporting global efforts led by various local, national, and transnational social movements towards the recognition of housing as a right rather than a commodity.

In this chapter, I have argued that interrogating structural drivers shaping capabilities in cities is key to the application of the capability approach to city-making. Responding to critiques of the capability approach reviewed here, I have argued that Sen and others have, in various places, recognized and developed ways in which structural drivers shape capabilities. Nevertheless, more work needs to be done to engage with the question of how spatial processes influence the distribution and expansion of capabilities in cities.

Notes

1. See photos and videos of the demolition of Otodo Gbame: <https://www.flickr.com/photos/justempower/albums/72157679186063343> [accessed 18 May 2021]
2. One of the most prominent examples of the state using the 'wellbeing of residents' as a cover for a massive land grab was the notorious forced eviction of Maroko in 1990 by the then military government of Lagos led by Colonel Rasaki which rendered over 300,000 people homeless. In 2012, when a Lagos State High Court finally delivered judgement in a case filed in the days before the 1990 eviction, the judge reasoned that, since the Maroko area was flood-prone, 'the government could not be faulted for saving people from drowning.' (JEI: 2017: 3).
3. This process is explored in more detail in Chapter 7.

CHAPTER 4

Practices: Experiences and claims for participation in the Euston area of London, United Kingdom

Abstract

The construction of a new high-speed train line between London and Birmingham meant that Euston Station needed to go through a redevelopment process that would have a profound impact on the surrounding neighbourhood. In the years between 2012 and 2019, local residents tried to influence the process through a variety of participatory practices but had little impact on the overall direction of the development plans for the station and the area. This chapter examines these participatory practices and proposes a shift in the application of the capability approach from a focus on goods and services to a focus on ways of doing things. The focus on practices of city-making relates to social innovation from a capability perspective and contributes to promoting more democratic and equitable ways of making cities.

Keywords: London, participation, practices, choices, social innovation

Introduction

In 2009, the British Labour government established High Speed 2 Limited to research the suitability of a high-speed rail line between London and the West Midlands to be known as HS2. In 2010, Britain's new Conservative and Liberal Democrat coalition government announced its preferred route for Phase 1, connecting Euston Station in central London to Birmingham, with an estimated completion date of 2033. In 2012, the UK government gave the go-ahead to continue development of plans for Phase 1 and announced plans for Phase 2, linking Birmingham to Manchester and Leeds. According to the 2011/2012 Transport Secretary, Justice Greening, the proposed £50 billion rail link would 'provide Britain with the additional train seats, connections and speed to stay ahead of the congestion challenges and help create jobs, growth and prosperity for the entire country' (Railway Technology, 2012). At the heart of the HS2 proposal is the argument that the reduction in train travel times from London to Birmingham (by 41.7 minutes) and to Manchester Airport (by 59 minutes), will have a positive impact on the redistribution of wealth from the south of the UK to the north.

Photo 4.1 Council housing estates around Euston Station (photograph by Laura Hirst)

While there are many contentious issues around the HS2 initiative, my engagement has focused on the participation of local communities in the proposed plans to redevelop Euston Station in order to meet the infrastructural requirements of high-speed trains. A number of community action groups in Camden (the borough in which the station is situated) reacted to the plans with a range of approaches, ranging from outright opposition to attempts to evaluate and mitigate the impacts of HS2 on the area. Between 2014 and 2015, I coordinated three action-learning initiatives through which Masters students from University College London and built-environment professionals explored impacts of HS2 on local residents. These projects aimed to reveal residents' perspectives on how changes to the station could be more responsive to the needs and aspirations of the communities living and working in the Euston area.

This chapter explores the findings of these engagements in relation to the practices of participation that local residents were leading or involved in when trying to influence decision-making processes. I argue that by focusing on practices, rather than on the access to, and use and appropriation of, resources (which is the usual focus of capability approaches), this application has been able to address more explicitly different ways in which cities are made. The recent debates about social innovation in the capability-approach literature are reviewed as productive entry points to discussing practices for capability expansion. The chapter argues that there are diverse sets of city-making practices playing a role in human development in cities and these can include everyday personal, collective, and institutional practices. In this sense, discussing diverse practices of city-making is key when exploring people's real choices in living in and producing cities and how people's choices in terms of different modalities of city-making are key elements shaping their capabilities in cities.

The case of participation processes relating to the redevelopment of Euston Station

The HS2 proposal affects a large area around its terminus at Euston Station. At the time of my research in the area, local residents and business owners were expecting to experience social, environmental, and economic impacts both during and after the lengthy construction phase (expected to last at least 17 years). Key concerns included: the demolition of at least four tower blocks in Camden Council's Regent's Park estate; tunnelling blighting many more homes; the use of Drummond Street – a landmark community location and home to many family-run curry restaurants and sweet and spice shops – as a transport corridor during construction; the loss of several open and green spaces surrounding the station; and delays and disruptions to local movement and travel. There were also expectations of increased air pollution in one of the 10 areas of London with the worst air quality (Carrington, 2017); loss of biodiversity; the excavation of a burial site containing the remains of over 30,000 people; and concerns about noise and accessibility during the construction period.

The Borough of Camden indicated its opposition to the plan, maintaining that the business case was not sufficiently convincing to warrant the significant public expenditure, that the investigation into the impacts of the scheme were inadequate, and that there had been little consideration given to comprehensive mitigation measures for local residents. One of the key points raised by Camden Council was the lack of assessment of consequences for the habitability of houses around the station due to the cumulative effect of different hazards generated by the construction process.

There are a continuing series of government-led participatory practices related to this process. HS2 commissioned several formal consultation exercises during which residents received information and maps through the post and at exhibitions, and were asked to provide feedback on different property compensation and environmental impact plans. According to a study conducted by Asfour et al. (2015), the experience of those taking part in these exercises was of frustration and alienation. Participants argued that information provided was not clear, and that it was highly technical and difficult to comprehend. They also mentioned that consultation officers were unable to answer questions accurately, or respond to issues when residents raised them, because of the long timeframe of the project and uncertainty surrounding it. The consultation processes tended to open up spaces for groups and individuals with experience in participating in such exercises but did not reach out to more marginalized groups and individuals. Finally, the scope of the engagement was also questioned because participants were only asked to comment on details rather than being meaningfully involved in the decision-making process (Asfour et al., 2015). These responses resonate with findings from research by Crompton which revealed those she interviewed shared the view that 'people were being forced into agreement and that the potential to express genuine opinion was hindered by the bounded nature of the formal consultation' (2015: 34).

Another formal government-led participatory space was created in 2016 when the HS2 team formed the Euston Community Representatives Group (ECRG), with the objective of facilitating dialogue between the HS2 developers and community groups. According to the ECRG website (HS2, 2021), the group included representatives from the six adjacent community areas, HS2, Network Rail, and Camden Council, among other stakeholders. An analysis of the minutes of their meetings reveals that community representatives raised several critiques of the ECRG; in particular, that the Community Engagement Framework 'did not reference genuine two-way engagement with the community' (ECRG, 2016: 6). From a meeting I attended in the early stage of this process, it was clear that HS2 officers understood the role of this group as being to communicate HS2 information to the community in order to ensure support for the implementation of plans: the group was not set up to make decisions or provide input into plans and designs. The HS2 representative at that meeting made it clear that the discussions and decisions about plans and designs would be taken by an HS2 team of technical experts, and not by a community engagement group.

Another participatory practice of Euston community groups was the use of petitions to raise their concerns about the redevelopment of the station and there were particular mobilizations around the submission of petitions to the House of Lords select committee considering the HS2 Bill. The HS2 Euston Action Group, which was formed by groups and individuals from Camden trying to coordinate their engagement, developed a comprehensive and detailed document (HS2 Euston Action Group, 2015a) outlining various concerns and impacts which were not being addressed by the HS2 team. While the process of developing this document was very much led by citizens and local groups, and it involved and incorporated a variety of concerns, the scope of petitions was quite constrained. The Lords' select committee addressed only petitions 'arguing for mitigation, compensation and adjustment to meet adverse effects of the bill on particular interests. It was not our role to consider any objections to the principle or policy of the bill' (Select Committee on the High Speed Rail (London–West Midlands) Bill, 2017). Even though Camden Council and community groups tried to build the capacities of local residents to develop petitions that met the technical requirements of the process, this was far from an accessible and inclusive process of engagement.

Beyond these spaces of participation generated by government actors, there were a series of citizen-led practices articulating views on the HS2 proposals in their own terms. Even with the general participation fatigue caused by the various ineffective and inaccessible consultation processes, community groups in Euston demonstrated interest in, and initiative for, processes that were more propositional, fluid, and open ended. Groups such as the Save Drummond Street Group and the HS2 Euston Action Group were formed to increase the visibility of community concerns. Meetings led by tenant associations and interest groups, with the participation of local MPs, discussed potential impacts and explored mechanisms they could use to raise their concerns.

Films made by residents of the area, disseminated through social media, depicted stories of particular people already carrying the burden of the process without appropriate compensation. One of these films (HS2 Euston Action Group, 2015b) tells the story of the traders of Drummond Street who predict that the 17-year construction phase will push them out of business. It is planned that Drummond Street will be a transport corridor providing access to the station's construction site. In addition to the expected reduction in business, traders argue that they will end up having to spend more to manage the hazards generated by the construction process and meet health and safety regulations. They say that HS2 has not paid compensation, and there has been no discussion on alternatives to safeguard their livelihoods. They tell how the traders of Drummond Street have, over the last 30 years, contributed to generating a support system that is especially important for the Bengali Muslim community living in the neighbourhood. They have been key in building bridges between the Bengali community and other groups in Euston, particularly during the 1980s when intergroup tensions were high and there was social conflict in the area. Traders also speak with pride about the investments they made to public spaces around Euston Station in order to improve living conditions. The closing of Drummond Street would be a loss of a key landmark in the city of London, and lead to weakening social cohesion and displacement of communities that have lived and invested in the neighbourhood for many years (Frediani et al., 2014b).

With the objective of addressing these various concerns, local residents and community groups developed an alternative plan for Euston Station. Instead of building tracks on the side of the station, they proposed a 'Double Deck Downwards' scheme, which would avoid the demolition of Regent's Park Estate. HS2 Ltd dismissed the proposal, arguing that it would cost £3 billion more than their scheme (Foot, 2013). However, many community residents argued that the reason HS2 Ltd did not seriously consider their suggestion was that it would reduce the floor space of the station and minimize the potential of revenue generation opportunities from the planned property development on top of the station.

Residents organized several demonstrations and vigils: for example, on 16 May 2017, the third yarn-bombing event took place in Euston Square Gardens. This involved wrapping hand-knitted scarves around trees due to be felled by HS2 (Stop HS2, 2017). The event aimed to raise awareness of both the impact that HS2 would have on green spaces in the area and the contribution trees make to reducing air pollution. HS2 proposals will result in the permanent loss of two-thirds of the local St James' Gardens and half of the open spaces along Hampstead Road. The 2015 version of the plans included replacing these losses with pockets of smaller open spaces scattered across the area. This approach, of replacing lost open spaces with an overall equivalent measured by area rather than by an assessment of their quality, misrecognizes the function of these spaces within the neighbourhood and the city. Residents say that, due to the lack of meaningful participation, the plans do not relate to residents' experience of the place and lead to the loss of key community assets (Frediani et al., 2014b). Events like the yarn-bombing vigil highlight the meanings, values, and functions attached to green spaces, and try to change the HS2 Limited framing of discussions about impact and compensation.

Another participatory practice employed by local community groups has been the development of a Citizens Charter. This initiative was led by Camden Citizens, the Camden branch of Citizens UK, which is a network of Camden-based institutions and groups including churches, mosques, schools, and university departments. In 2014, its members decided to work together to develop a charter that aimed to enhance the negotiating power of community groups and to push for better conditions for local residents and communities to be included in the development plans. After several meetings, listening exercises, participatory workshops, and action-research activities, the charter was drawn up: it outlined 6 principles and 13 commitments that Camden Citizens asked HS2 Limited to agree to. Table 4.1 outlines the content of the charter:

Table 4.1 Citizens Charter for Euston Area (2015)

Principles	Commitments
Good jobs and training	30% of jobs in Euston for local Camden residents during and after construction
	A living-wage zone to be created around Euston during the construction phase
	Employer-led training opportunities for local residents to contribute to Camden Council Knowledge Quarter
Quality affordable housing	The creation of affordable quality homes for local Camden residents
	Evicted residents must be given quality alternative housing in Camden
Proper compensation	Compensation that ensures no one is worse off, including the businesses in Drummond Street
Real engagement	A committed senior member of HS2 Limited to meet regularly with community representatives
	The Charter to be a shared process between local residents, Camden Council and HS2
	A process accessible to all
Protection of health and wellbeing	Historical and cultural sites of significance to be protected and enhanced
	The unique character of open spaces and community facilities to be preserved
A greener safer Camden	Actions taken to ensure Euston is safe and accessible for all
	Camden to be an ultra-low emission zone by 2025

Source: Based on Frediani et al. 2015: 44.

Meetings, films, demonstrations, vigils, and a charter are just some of the citizen-led practices that local residents and groups employed to try to increase their capabilities to influence the developments taking place in the Euston area. Initially, many practices attempted to resist the HS2 process and were often linked to the country-wide network called Stop HS2. As the HS2 project began to appear unavoidable, practices moved from resistance to attempting to influence the process of decision-making and trying to get a better deal for local residents, in some cases using formal channels such as the petitions. Meanwhile, the charter was trying to create another space of negotiation in which civil-society groups could lead dialogue. Unfortunately, so far (2020), it is difficult to see that these practices have had any meaningful impact on HS2 plans and activities.

While citizen-led participatory practices had tactical differences, they all shared a common underpinning concern: they were not against change to the Euston area, but they opposed the content and the process through which change was taking place. In terms of content, citizen-led participatory practices emerged out of discontent with the social and spatial segregation being generated by a redevelopment process that was pushing small-scale businesses and the working-class population to more affordable locations far from the centre of London and with worse access to services and infrastructure. In response to these effects of redevelopment, citizen-led practices attempted not only to contest the proposed plans, but also to indicate alternatives. Engagements focused on presenting alternative regeneration aspirations suggested technical alternatives for the redevelopment of Euston Station that could reduce the impact on the surrounding area (Frediani et al., 2014b; Frediani et al., 2014c).

These practices emerged as a reaction to the formal consultation processes which were seen simply as a way of implementing HS2's predetermined objectives. The formal consultations were questioned in relation to the limited space they created for community inputs meaning important issues went unchallenged and participants were left feeling instrumentalized rather than meaningfully involved. Instead of advancing urban democracy, the formal consultation process increased citizen mistrust of government. Most importantly, this case study is a typical example of how formal consultation processes ignore the various practices that residents employ to express their views and aspirations.

Nevertheless, citizen-led participatory practices were not exempt from their own power imbalances. They have been led and advocated by particular organized groups from Camden, giving more visibility to the needs associated with these groups. For example, little attention was given to the needs and aspirations of more recent migrants or transient populations (such as students) who feel less entitled to claim rights in the face of this long-term development initiative. However, such participatory actions do demonstrate citizens' agency, creativity, and initiative in engaging in the process of city-making. Instead of trying to ignore, delegitimize, or criminalize residents, the basis of creating cities for human development means recognizing and actively supporting these practices so making them more sustainable, inclusive, and resilient spaces for city-making.

Reflections on practices

This case sets up an important debate in relation to the application of the capability approach to processes of city-making: how to shift the application of the capability approach from a focus on access to goods and services to a focus on practices, that is, ways of doing things?

A distinction can be made between 'the means, defined as goods and services, on the one hand and functionings and capabilities on the other hand' (Robeyns, 2005: 98). This distinction has been crucial for the operationalization of the capability approach. Robeyns develops a diagram of the process of transforming goods and services into achieved functionings (2005: 98) which has become a key reference for those interested in using the capability approach for evaluative purposes. The diagram uses the example of a bicycle as a good and explains that 'the bicycle enables the functioning of mobility, to be able to move oneself freely and more rapidly than walking' (2005: 99). This is similar to Sen's argument in *Commodities and Capabilities*:

> bicycling has to be distinguished from possessing a bike. It has to be distinguished also from the happiness generated by the functioning, for example, actually cycling around must not be identified with the pleasure obtained from that act. (Sen, 1999a: 7)

For the operationalization of the capability approach, it becomes crucial not only to understand what the bicycle does to people's lives (what functionings are enabled), but also what other goods and services were available to enable people to move (such as walking, car, bus, etc.). To investigate what goods and services do to people's lives requires engagement with the social, physical, and economic arrangements that condition the transformation of goods and services into functionings (Robeyns, 2005). These arrangements are called conversion factors and are analysed in Chapters 6 and 7.

In this chapter, I argue that the focus on goods and services is a static approach; it focuses on what things are rather than on processes and relations of change. The focus on things (bicycle, house, or water pump) and what they do to people's lives is able to examine the relationship between commodities and their use. But in order to examine processes of city-making and spatial production – the dynamic and relational experiences of producing, using, and appropriating cities – it becomes necessary to examine practices of city-making. Here practices are defined as the modalities of interacting with the city. In the case study presented in this chapter, I focused on the diverse practices of engaging with decision-making processes affecting the changes being proposed to Euston Station and the surrounding environment.

The emphasis on practices, rather than commodities, sheds light on the importance of investigating how social beings interact with and transform the contexts in which they live. For example, Bourdieu's theory of practice (1977) exemplifies the potentialities of focusing on practices in order to examine the relationship between routines, norms, and procedures, and the social structures in which they are situated. Similarly, de Certeau (1984) argues that practices emerge through relationships, rather than as acts of individual behaviour. The analysis of the relationship between ways of operating and people's quality of life moves the lens of the capability approach towards the exploration of systems and processes through which decisions are made and activities carried out. Therefore, I would argue, this way of interrogating practices would allow the capability approach to focus on governance arrangements and the regimes that shape processes of change. As illustrated in Figure 4.1, a set of diverse types of available or desirable practices are produced through particular governance arrangements. The range of practices showing how people can access a particular service or good in the city composes the practice possibilities space.

The response to HS2 plans to redesign Euston Station reveals the different participatory options available, claimed, or produced by local residents and business owners in order to influence the process. Writing petitions, an option created by the state to allow the public to react to particular bills, had a predefined scope, norms, and regulations also created by the state. Meanwhile, the consultation activities were participatory options created by a private company, HS2 Limited, funded by the government and responsible for developing and promoting the high-speed rail network in the UK.

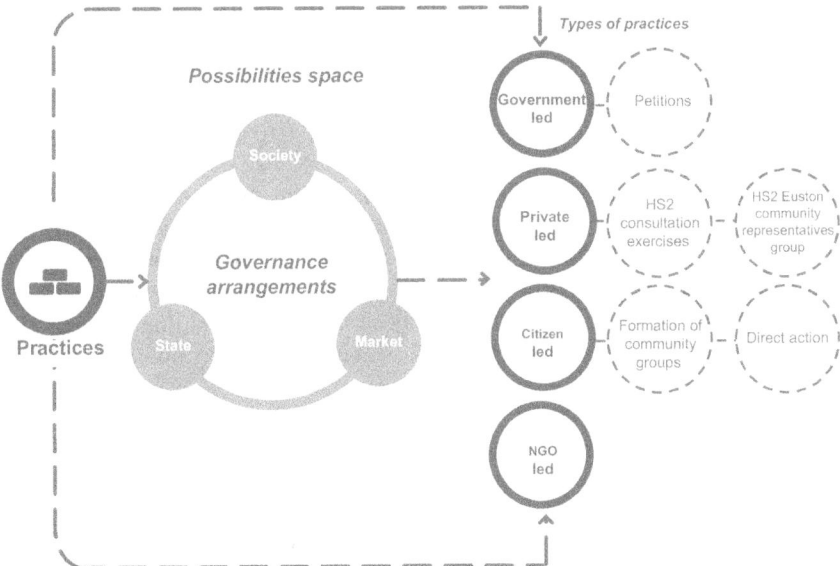

Figure 4.1 Practices diagram

Citizens also created their own participatory practices: they formed local groups, developed an alternative plan for the station, and carried out direct actions. The focus on practices allows for the interrogation of these different ways of participating in the process of decision-making, and of the extent to which these options provide meaningful choices for the public to influence the plans associated with the redevelopment of Euston Station.

An important special issue of the *Journal of Human Development and Capabilities* devoted to social innovations examined how particular ways of doing things are shaped by and shape capabilities (Chiappero-Martinetti et al., 2017). Instead of using the capability approach purely as an evaluative framework to explore the outcomes of social innovation, many of the contributions to this issue help to redefine the notion and practice of social innovation through a capability lens and point to the need for social innovation to recognize the practices, agency, and voices of marginalized groups. These articles also highlight the importance of setting up mechanisms for institutionalizing social innovation in ways that 'liberate reflection and imagination from narrowly economic and political perspectives and from cognitive and institutional pressures to "fit" people into prevailing structures with the attendant risk of merely reproducing ways of doing and being' (Chiappero-Martinetti et al., 2017: 144).

In this special issue, there is a particularly relevant discussion of the various grassroots practices associated with food cooperatives in the city of Valencia (Pellicer-Sifres et al., 2017). This study focuses on organic food-buying groups and goes into detail of how the groups organize themselves, make decisions, respond to challenges, and relate to wider human development issues associated with the agro-food system. The authors propose a framework for examining grassroots social innovation for human development which focuses on the dimensions of agents, purposes, drivers, and processes of practices. This is an extremely useful approach to recognizing and promoting practices of innovation by marginalized groups that build pathways for human development.

Meanwhile, debates in the planning discipline about what constitutes planning practice have examined the various ways within which cities are being made. Instead of understanding planning practice purely as an activity carried out by built-environment professionals and formal institutions, various authors have emphasized the importance of the different ways through which the norms and procedures of producing cities are enacted. For example, planning is:

> not a singular, specific thing: it is a plurality of practices constructed and enacted by people in social and material contexts. When the subjects of planning advocate for changes to the form of the city, when they directly intervene in the built environment in ways that challenge, confirm or re-interpret official plans, and when they report, ignore or actively conceal violations to planning rules and policies, they participate directly and often materially in the practice of planning. (Thorpe, 2017: 577)

The debate about what constitutes planning practice is at the heart of current contestations of the dominant and exclusionary framings of planning. Many authors have argued that dominant planning approaches do not speak to the experiences of contesting and making cities located outside the formal planning system. While relevant in the global North, this debate has been particularly taken forward by those arguing that traditional planning is unable to capture the mechanisms and procedures shaping city-making in the global South. Various practices of city-making have been associated with notions of insurgency (Miraftab, 2009), co-production (Watson, 2014), 'Southerness' (Bhan, 2019), or agonism (Gualini, 2015). Such calls have been motivated by the wider objectives of democratizing planning debates by questioning planning's Western and technical lens; and highlighting under-recognized and under-valued forms of producing cities, from autonomous self-help processes embedded in everyday practices of city-making to large-scale partnerships led by civic entities in collaboration with private and public institutions.

For example, in the context of debates about service delivery in informal settlements, the different ways water is supplied are associated with different practices shaped by different governance arrangements.

> The peri-urban poor gain access to water and sanitation services through a broad range of practices and arrangements. Some of these are formal, 'policy-driven' mechanisms explicitly supported by the state, such as private tankers licensed to sell water. There is also a wide array of arrangements operating on the basis of solidarity, reciprocity or need, such as the provision of water as a gift among community members, as well as cases of water-pushcart vendors who might access water through different means and sell it to members of their own community. These mechanisms might be characterized as being 'needs-driven' and are rarely supported by the state. (Allen et al., 2006: 338)

Butcher's research into access to water in informal settlements in Nepal develops the idea of a water portfolio in order to study:

> the ways in which residents draw upon different sources to fulfil varied water needs, from drinking to cooking, to washing. This challenged simple conceptions of 'access', building the case for a deeper examination of the reasons why residents choose different sources over others – which is often based on embodied, emotional or social reasons. (Butcher, 2019: 253)

Like the concept of a water-supply wheel (Allen et al., 2006), Butcher's portfolio model recognizes the heterogeneity and socially embedded nature of water access and management.

Similar directions have been followed in the field of housing: for instance, in a study of the practices associated with civic-led processes of occupation and rehabilitation of vacant buildings in inner-city São Paulo (De Carli and Frediani, 2016) (see Chapter 8); and a study of home-making practices in informal settlements in Viña Del Mar in Chile which examines how gender relations are negotiated through the process of designing, building, and maintaining houses (Ossul Vermehren, 2019). Such studies respond to the call for a 'vocabulary of urban practices rooted in the traditions of Southern inquiry' (Bhan, 2019: 13). Drawing on practices of squatting, repair, and consolidation in Indian cities, Bhan argues that Southern urban practices are incremental, uncertain, temporally fluid, speculative, transversal, and rooted.

Approaching practices of city-making from a socially embedded perspective highlights how practices are not purely technical or managerial arrangements. Practices of city-making are sites of micro-politics; they are both products and shapers of gender, class, and other power relations in the city. Feminist readings of urban political ecology have similarly examined the relationship between physical infrastructure, identity, and subjectivity (see, for example, Datta, 2016; Doshi, 2017; Heynen, 2017). These works are important because they explore 'how processes of ecological change and spatial distribution intersect with ideological constructions of gender – raising the importance of examining symbolic narratives for how they may generate or reproduce inequalities as attached to material practices' (Butcher, 2019: 35). Feminist approaches have also explored how a system of practices can together generate ecologies of care in the city.

> When thinking through embodied ecologies we must take care to not slip into naturalizations and eschew political agency (Simonsen, 2013). Differentiated embodied experiences result in a range of claim-making practices including collective demands for land, resources, dignity, health and safety. Alternative arrangements of (non-)human natures – urban school and community gardens, alternative food and non-violence movements (Hayes-Conroy and Hayes-Conroy, 2013; Moore et al., 2015) – produce ecologies of care that challenge neoliberal modalities of engaging with self and others. (Doshi, 2017: 127)

These calls to engage with the complexities of practices of city-making are key lessons from feminist readings of urban ecology. The focus on bodies moves away from dualistic and reductionist understandings of city-making practices by providing a lens through which to engage with the contradictory and potentially regressive logics of the process (Doshi, 2017). For example, 'in Mumbai, women slum residents have pursued elite-biased redevelopment in the aspiration of attaining better living conditions through resettlement, sometimes at the expense of other embodied needs and more marginalized urban residents' (Doshi, 2017: 127).

A capability perspective on city-making requires the recognition that cities are produced through a variety of practices that have different organizational arrangements as well as spatial and governance typologies. Some of them are embedded in formal planning systems and established professional practice, but others might be obscured by the blind spots in planning discussions associated with people's everyday practices of spatial production and resistance.

> **Box 4.1 Portfolio of options**
>
> The concept of a portfolio of options draws on Hamdi's notion of an 'architecture of opportunity' (2010: 61) and it has been used during Architecture Sans Frontières – UK (ASF-UK) workshops focused on participatory design and planning (Frediani, 2016). It relates to a range of practices associated with the delivery of particular services or goods in the city. The concept aims to recognize and interrogate existing and diverse ways of making the city, while also capturing other speculative and potential practices. Within the ASF-UK work, the term 'portfolio of options' has referred to a range of practices associated with specific aspects of city-making including land tenure (options such as individual titles, collective ownership, community land trusts) and housing construction arrangements (individual self-help, collective self-help, building cooperative, small-scale contractors, or large-scale contractors, among others). Through participatory engagements, these options are collectively analysed in terms of trade-offs related to, for example, time, cost, technology, political viability, and capacities (Hamdi, 2010: 67).

Being able to illustrate and document these everyday practices is a starting point from which to examine people's real choices and freedoms. As is argued in Chapter 9, a capability perspective on city-making can reveal, deepen, and extend the portfolio of options (see definition in Box 4.1) available to people to transform, use, and appropriate cities in ways that expand human development.

This involves recognition without romanticism, revealing and questioning power relations that are being contested as well as those being reproduced through such processes. A capability inquiry asks not only 'What practices?', but also 'Whose practices?'. It aims to reveal the burdens and benefits of these various ways of making the city. By doing this, a capability perspective is able to interrogate the possibilities and constraints present in the various sites of city-making – those within official planning systems as well as those outside the purview of the state – in practices led by the state as well as by individuals, and civic and/or private entities. In this sense, the focus on freedom and agency does not assess particular types of practices as better or worse in relation to a list of properties or characteristics. The discussion of the participatory practices enacted in Euston illustrates that spaces of participation created by the state can be emancipatory, expanding the capabilities of marginalized groups to influence decision-making meaningfully, but others can be as disempowering as the consultative engagements pursued by HS2. At the same time, practices of participation shaped by insurgent and civic-led processes can open up spaces to inform a more equitable creation of cities, but such processes can also reproduce relations that continue the marginalization of particular groups. It is not practice itself that is or is not capability enhancing but, rather, what it does in people's lives. What the capability approach re-emphasizes is the importance of recognizing and documenting the variety of practices of city-making, calling for wider and inclusive understandings of the various ways in which cities are produced.

Additionally, a capability perspective is inevitably concerned with asking: 'Practices for what?'. What are the relationships between people's aspirations and practices of city-making? Practice 'must be freed from being seen only as a necessity' (Bhan, 2019: 652). Practices are motivated by values and aspirations. But they are also agents in the production of people's imaginaries of the good city and the good life. The link between practice and aspirations is elaborated in the next chapter.

CHAPTER 5
Aspirations: Re-imagining urban regeneration in Woodstock, Cape Town, South Africa

Abstract

The process of urban regeneration in the inner-city Cape Town neighbourhood of Woodstock is threatening to reinforce the city's social and spatial inequalities. In response, local NGOs and community groups have been promoting another way of imagining the future of the neighbourhood, calling for more inclusive and redistributive values to guide the regeneration process. This chapter draws on their experiences to examine how the notion of aspirations has been addressed in the urban development and capability literature. The chapter calls for democratic processes of city-making to instigate public deliberations on the nature and connections between the ideas of the good city and the good life.

Keywords: Cape Town, regeneration, aspirations, functionings, adaptive preferences

Introduction

Woodstock, a neighbourhood of Cape Town located next to the city centre, is going through a rapid process of transformation. Historically, Woodstock has been a place where a variety of low-income groups have been able to access affordable housing in close proximity to transport connections and economic opportunities. These conditions are particularly significant in a city that is characterized by a deep social and spatial inequality shaped by apartheid urban planning through government legislation such as the Group Areas Act (1950). The 'coloured', Indian and black populations were evicted from inner-city neighbourhoods and relocated to segregated areas in peripheral parts of the city. But Woodstock was one of only two areas in wider central Cape Town that was not affected by the Act, thus allowing it to retain its diverse population.

Since the early 2000s, Woodstock has been affected by an intensification of property development, generating a sharp increase in property prices and attracting investment by small, medium, and large-scale developers. As a result, lower-income groups are being displaced because they cannot afford

Photo 5.1 Resident of Woodstock involved in the Re-imagining Woodstock campaign (photograph by Development Action Group)

the increased costs of living in Woodstock or because they are forcibly evicted from informally inhabited houses or plots of land. The transformations taking place have triggered social mobilizations calling for a more democratic and inclusive form of urban regeneration. Through everyday practices of community forums, organized demonstrations, and informally inhabiting unused spaces, the imagination of the future in Woodstock is being contested.

My engagement with Woodstock took place between 2015 and 2018 through a collaboration with the Cape Town–based NGO, Development Action Group (DAG). Through a city-wide campaign, driven mostly by groups of back-yarders, DAG facilitated a series of conversations and public forums to 're-imagine Cape Town'. As a result, an advocacy strategy was formulated. This targeted strategic areas of the city and called for a model of urban development that could address existing spatial and social inequalities. Woodstock was one of the prioritized locations. In partnership with local groups and organizations, DAG started to conduct research on the processes of change in the area and to reveal the aspirations of residents for the future of the neighbourhood. DAG's Re-imagining Woodstock campaign recognized and gave visibility to the perspectives of marginalized and vulnerable groups living locally, as well as those in other parts of the city, on the future of Woodstock.

This chapter draws on information collected during the 2015 Architecture Sans Frontières – UK (ASF-UK) workshop which aimed to support DAG in its campaign. The workshop employed a series of design-based participatory methodologies to reveal urban regeneration aspirations for Woodstock. Based on this case study, the chapter discusses the role of aspirations and imaginaries in the process of city-making.

The case of the Re-imagining Woodstock campaign

The history of Woodstock illustrates how social, political, economic, and spatial changes have affected the values and imaginaries that people attach to this place. In the pre-colonial period, the area that is now known as Woodstock was settled by indigenous hunter gatherers of the Khoisan tribes. From the 18th century, the lower slopes of Devils Peak were inhabited by Dutch agrarians. By the beginning of the 19th century, numerous farms and estates had sprung up. The slave trade was central to the economy of the time and, under a milkwood tree on a property by the sea, slaves were sold, and convicts and slaves were hanged. However, in the late 19th century, Woodstock was known as a fashionable seaside suburb, especially after 1862 when the railway connection to Cape Town was completed and its beach became a popular destination. The new transport link led to major changes to the suburb: farms were subdivided for housing developments and its population increased rapidly. In the early 20th century, Woodstock was again transformed as factories were established in the area. The population increased in size and diversity, as workers came looking for livelihood opportunities mainly in the manufacture of glass, leather, and textiles. This wave of transformation was consolidated in the mid-20th century when land reclamation replaced Woodstock beach with space for further transport and industrial developments.

During this industrial period, Woodstock was also particularly affected by planning regulations. While Woodstock residents did not face forced removals under apartheid, the 1950 Group Areas Act led to a series of restrictions. Some parts were zoned as 'white' and later rezoned as 'coloured'. Other areas remained unassigned to a specific racial group, therefore allowing 'coloured' people to rent or buy property in Woodstock (Garside, 1993; Urson, 2019). Meanwhile, 60,000 people – mainly 'coloured' families – were forcibly removed from the neighbouring District Six which had been categorized as a 'white' area. This had wider effects as many of those working in Woodstock lived or had tight social networks with people in District Six. Therefore, Woodstock workers and residents experienced loss of housing opportunities and weakening of their social support system. By the 1990s, the opening up of South African markets to the global economy led to the closing down of many of the textile factories which could not compete with imports from Asian countries.

Post-apartheid Woodstock was marked by an influx of artists, architectural businesses, and small advertising enterprises attracted by the neighbourhood's proximity to the central business district, its remaining Victorian architecture, and its mix of residential and commercial use. This transformation 'was not triggered by any top-down political intervention but was based on the individual location decisions of artists and cultural practitioners'

(Wenz, 2012: 23). This early influx was not linked to any attempt to create an economic cluster or large property development (Wenz, 2012). Nevertheless, the scenario gradually changed when developers and investors started to realize the economic potential of such a central but derelict area. This resulted in creative-industry-led urban regeneration that pushed property and rental prices up. Sale prices for apartments and houses in Woodstock have at least tripled since 2004 as a result of property speculation. In areas where large-scale developments are being constructed, this increase is even sharper: for instance, prior to 2004, property prices on Bromwell Street did not exceed R135,000, but in 2015, when large-scale redevelopment had taken place, a Bromwell Street property sold for R5.9 million (Pillay, 2016).

Development increased sharply after 2007 when the government designated Woodstock as an urban development zone (UDZ): UDZs were part of a National Treasury programme providing tax breaks for investors to encourage commercial and residential developments. This, combined with the dismantling of rent controls in 2003, meant that low-income tenants became particularly vulnerable to the market forces operating in Woodstock. As well as large companies responsible for expensive developments such as the rehabilitation of the Old Biscuit Mill as retail, studio, and office space, middle-scale property developers have also found investment opportunities. Houses have been bought up, subdivided, and rented, especially to migrants from other African countries looking for accommodation close to livelihood opportunities.

The outcomes of this process are still in the making, with various intended and unintended consequences. But it is unquestionable that recent developments in Woodstock have caused market-led displacement of those who can no longer afford to live in the area, as well as forced evictions of 'irregular' occupiers of property and land. While there is as yet (2021) no evidence of the total number of people displaced from Woodstock, researchers and the media (Pillay, 2016) have documented cases of whole streets being evicted (Pillay et al., 2017) and relocated to 'temporary relocation areas' such as Blikkiesdorp, in the outskirts of the city 25 km from Woodstock. These tin settlements do not meet minimum living conditions and reproduce social and spatial isolation, exclusion, and marginalization. Instead of being temporary solutions, these areas become the only housing option available for evictees. As a result of these experiences, there is a general feeling that the government has enabled market forces to do to Woodstock what the Group Areas Act did not manage to do during the apartheid period. (For more on how local residents have experienced these processes in Woodstock, see Orderson, 2018.)

In response, in 2015, DAG launched a campaign called Re-imagining Woodstock, aimed at articulating a more equitable and just vision of change. ASF-UK conducted a workshop using its Change by Design methodology (Frediani, 2016) to support this campaign and reveal the diverse needs and aspirations associated with the area. The workshop facilitated a series of participatory design-based activities with local residents, key government and civil-society stakeholders, and representatives of low-income groups from other areas of the city. A number of working groups approached the visions for Woodstock from different entry points. Three groups focused on different scales (dwelling, community, and city) and one group focused on the cross-cutting theme of policy and planning. The information so generated was systematized by identifying underlying principles for the urban regeneration of the area. These were then presented and worked on in an action-planning workshop involving representatives from government, civil society, and residents to advance a more socially just urban regeneration agenda.

The findings of the workshop revealed the diverse set of aspirations associated with a more inclusive process of regenerating Woodstock and were compiled as a report (Bainbridge et al., 2015). In relation to housing, residents of the Pine Road 'Wendy houses' (small prefabricated wooden houses located on land owned by the City of Cape Town), emphasized the need for **truly affordable** housing options. At the time of the workshop, the government had plans for a social housing project in Pine Road that they believed would benefit the street's Wendy-house dwellers. However, local residents feared they would not be able to meet the minimum monthly income requirements (between R3,200 and R6,400), as some were unemployed and others, working in the informal sector, were unable to generate the income proofs required by social housing institutions.

People who occupied 19 stables in Bromwell Street had similar concerns. The residents of the stables were a mixed group, most of whom were struggling with prolonged hardship and living in extreme poverty. Many of them had grown up in Woodstock as part of tight social networks with neighbours who supported them to meet daily needs. Most had been occupying this site for around three years; however, its longest-standing resident had been there for 15 years. The prospect of relocation was yet another strain on people who feared isolation and losing their support structures and livelihoods. Even if precarious, their current jobs (such as guarding and washing cars, or sex work) were all dependent on relationships established in Woodstock. Instead of being subjected to more threats and strains, residents of the Bromwell Street stables expressed the view that regeneration should also be about providing **care and support** for extremely vulnerable populations. Simply being relocated to a flat or house would be of limited benefit to them. They argued that regeneration was needed to sustain and enhance the social support systems of vulnerable groups, otherwise many would end up back in informal and precarious living conditions.

The report also recorded the example of Gympie Street which has been notoriously associated with extreme drug-related violence. This stigma has overshadowed a more complex history of diverse life trajectories. There are long-term residents who have seen many friends and relatives move out of Gympie Street and Woodstock after selling to property developers or not being able to afford the increasing rents. Property developers with limited recognition of or respect for tenants' rights have been buying and subdividing houses to rent at exorbitant rates to a recent influx of migrants from other African countries. Residents pointed out that many of their neighbours had been unlawfully and unfairly evicted as a result of the large-scale property developments in and around the area. Therefore, people from Gympie Street raised the need for regeneration to foster **diverse, as well as secure, forms of tenure**.

Residents of Springfield Terrace housing estate also increasingly felt the threat of being pushed out of the area. The housing estate was initiated in the early 1990s as a public–private partnership pilot project to demonstrate the viability of medium-density housing in a well-located area of Cape Town. During the DAG workshop, residents shared their experience of facing sharp increases in charges, mostly due to changes to water-supply rates. One of the residents reported that from one month to another in 2015, levies increased from R383 to R618 a month. Due to the nature of ownership, through sectional title, flat owners can be evicted if they fail to pay these charges. Many owners felt they might not be able to cope with further increases, but at the same time, they would not be able to sell property at a price that would allow them to purchase another place in Woodstock. They would have to move to cheaper and more peripheral locations in Cape Town losing their support networks and easy access to jobs and services. For a regeneration process to be inclusive, it has to be able to secure **reliable and affordable access to services**.

In addition to exploring these perspectives on the relationships between regeneration processes and dwelling practices, the workshop facilitated conversations on regeneration aspirations associated with public spaces. A group of workshop participants focused on Trafalgar Park, a public space whose planning and management has been increasingly influenced by private-sector interests. The city government's lack of investment and its reliance on private funds for public-space improvements has led to the threat of public needs and aspirations being undermined by business interests. However, park users and passers-by particularly stressed that, for regeneration to be inclusive, **public spaces need to remain a common asset** that foster connections among people from different social groups and are developed and managed through inclusive and participatory decision-making processes.

The workshop also engaged residents from four other low-income localities in Cape Town under pressure from the transformations taking place in the city: Freedom Park Tafelsig, Michells Plain; Factreton, Kensington; South Road, Wynberg and Plumstead; and Egoli, Philippi Horticultural Area. These areas are also characterized by strong community mobilization and involved in DAG's Re-imagining Cape Town campaign. Representatives of community-based organizations from these four localities argued that for regeneration to be inclusive, it needed to be based on **meaningful participation**: building and supporting existing community structures and, in particular, reaching out to the most vulnerable and marginalized residents. Among other aspirations, they also argued that opportunities generated by regeneration should be distributed fairly across the city, with the objective of **addressing the social and spatial segregation** of Cape Town, rather than reinforcing it.

The case of Woodstock reveals the intersections between aspirations for physical, social, and economic wellbeing and imaginaries of inclusive processes of city-making. The workshop conversations about dream homes, neighbourhoods, and cities addressed people's imaginaries of the fundamental connections between the good life and the good city. They also revealed multiple life-style options and aspirations, as well as diverse experiences of the city. Nevertheless, aspirations and imaginaries can also be conflictive, as practices of city-making can also be means to contest particular city visions. In the case of Woodstock, this was manifested most strikingly in Bromwell Street, where the Old Biscuit Mill development is located next to the stables occupied by an extremely vulnerable population, representing two of many different visions of what Woodstock is and for whom it exists.

Reflections on aspirations

This chapter brings to the forefront the need to problematize the intersections between the notions of the good city and the good life. Lefebvre (1991b) articulates the importance of thinking about space in contesting the reproduction of the contemporary city, where market-driven hegemonic structures have conditioned all areas of social life, including the ability to envision alternative futures. Thus, a key form of contestation in urban areas has been conflicts over differing spatial imaginaries in the city, and calls for imaginaries to be driven by the vision of 'cities for people, and not for profit' (Brenner et al., 2012: 2).

Friedmann's seminal works on planning (1987; 2000; 2013) provide a particularly productive entry point for the exploration of links between critical urban theory and the capability approach. In 1987, Friedmann defined radical planners as those supporting emancipatory struggles for freedom from oppression. After many years focusing on different forms of resistance to oppression, his later work proposes a positive vision for the notion of the good city. And at the heart of his vision is the recognition of the right to human flourishing. He argues that to strive for to the good city requires the encouragement of utopian thinking:

> the capacity to imagine a future that departs significantly from what we know to be a general condition in the present. It is a way of breaking through the barriers of convention into a sphere of the imagination where many things beyond our everyday experience become feasible. All of us have this ability, which is inherent in human nature, because human beings are insufficiently programmed for the future. We need a constructive imagination that we can variously use for creating fictive worlds. (Friedmann, 2000: 463)

Similarly, in her book *Justice and Politics of Difference* (1990), Young proposes a series of virtues of city life that strive towards the good city: 1) *social differentiation without exclusion* – making reference to the importance of open and fluid spaces; 2) *variety* – city life providing and supporting diverse activities; 3) *eroticism* – focusing on the attraction and pleasure of encounters with the novel, strange, and surprising, as well as different and unfamiliar subjectivities and meanings; and 4) *publicity* – which refers to the need for accessible spaces in the city that allow people to express themselves, hear others, and decide on how institutions and social relations should be organized. These four virtues are 'unrealized possibilities of the actual', but 'a normative ideal of city life must begin with our given experience of cities, and look there for the virtues of this form of social relations' (Young, 1990: 265).

The most explicit articulation of ideas of the good city and the good life from a capability perspective is put forward by Fainstein (2000; 2009; 2011) who argues that Sen's work is useful for urban institutions and programmes because it urges monitoring and evaluation systems to focus on the enhancement of the capabilities of the relatively disadvantaged, rather than on cost–benefit analysis.

> In Sen's attack on utilitarianism, he argues against the analysis typically employed by cost–benefit accounting as it is used to justify urban capital programmes in most cities. These analyses tend to exaggerate benefits and underestimate costs, rely on aggregates, and ignore distributional outcomes. A more sensitive form of analysis asks the questions: Who benefits and who assess what outputs each group in the population receives? (Fainstein, 2011: 56–57)

In the same work, she also argues that Nussbaum's list can be useful for encouraging urban policy and planning to engage with the various dimensions of the good life without having to sacrifice one dimension over another. She proposes a set of policy directives in furtherance of equity, diversity, and democracy. However, while these directives outline extremely relevant and practical guidelines for urban policy and planning, they lack a deeper articulation of the conflictive imaginaries and subjectivities embedded in urban experience. In contrast to these lists of capabilities as policy elements, my work (Frediani, 2015; 2019a) has applied Sen's capability approach in a way which implies understanding the interactions between the notions of the good city and the good life as a set of values, aspirations, and imaginaries that are discussed, elaborated, and reflected through people's experiences of places where they dwell. I argue that the capability-approach literature has engaged in a series of debates about aspirations and values that goes beyond Fainstein's application of Nussbaum's work in ways that can inform these ongoing discussions in the critical urban theory literature.

At the core of the capability approach is a preoccupation with quality of life as people's freedom to pursue the things they value and have reason to value. These doings and beings that people have reason to value are called 'functionings', and they refer to issues such as being well-nourished, being part of a supportive social network, having decent sources of livelihood, and participating meaningfully in decision-making processes affecting their lives. However, this raises a series of questions: are functionings real achievements or doings and ways of being that people have the potential to achieve if they wish? Who defines these values? Why focus on the values that people have reason to value? And how do these values relate to the notion of aspirations? There has been an extensive exploration in the human development and capability literature of these issues, which are relevant to reflections on the meaning of good in discussions of the good city/good life.

In the capability approach, the term 'functioning' has been used in slightly different ways. In his earlier work, Sen (1985) makes reference to *potential functionings*, which refer to the dimensions of wellbeing that are within people's reach if they wish to achieve them, while *achieved functionings* are the doings and beings that people have actually achieved. In Sen's later work, a person's potential functionings are also called a person's capability set. More generally, then, the term 'functioning' has been used to refer to achieved functionings and 'capability' as the potential functionings in one's capability set. As Sen explains:

> The capability set would consist of the alternative functioning vectors that she can choose from. While the combination of a person's functionings reflects her actual achievements, the capability set reflects the freedom to achieve: the alternative functioning combinations from which this person can choose. (Sen, 1999b: 75)

But who defines these doings and beings that people have reason to value? Sen has highlighted the importance of guaranteeing the various processes that enable open discussions, debates, criticism, and dissent, acknowledging them as key to 'generating informed and considered choices' and 'crucial to the formation of values and priorities ... we cannot, in general, take preferences as given independently of public discussion' (Sen, 1999b: 253). There are at least seven different methods used in the capability-approach literature to identify dimensions of poverty and wellbeing, prioritized in relation to the purpose and scope of different engagements (see Table 5.1 and also Alkire, 2002; Clark, 2014; Qizilbash, 1996). Such articulation is useful because it helps the discussion to move away from the binary 'list or no-list' debate which has created a false dichotomy between universalism (associated with Nussbaum's work) and extreme particularism (associated with Sen's work). The focus on various different methods of identifying dimensions of wellbeing calls for further debate on the implications of using a variety of methodologies and methods to ground, compare, complement, and triangulate a process of recognizing dimensions of the good life.

In the context of urban development, these discussions raise some important issues. Could a set of values be defined in relation to the visions of the future of a place, producing values that integrate notions of the good life as well as the good city? I understand such values as principles for urban development based on people's aspirations for the future. I have approached

Table 5.1 Capability-approach methods for identifying dimensions of poverty and wellbeing

Method	Based on ...
1. Existing data	... availability of data with suitable characteristics for measurement purposes – for example, the Human Development Index.
2. Normative assumptions	... informed guesses of researchers or transparent and justified use of normative assumptions – for example, Maslow's Hierarchy of Needs (1943) or Nussbaum's list of central human capabilities (2000).
3. Public 'consensus'	... a legitimate consensus-building process which may (or may not) directly involve the general public – for example, the Universal Declaration of Human Rights (drafted by the UN and endorsed by governments through democratic processes); or the Sustainable Development Goals (SDGs), the formulation of which included a direct appeal to global publics with an internet connection to help select relevant dimensions through the My World survey.
4. Ongoing deliberative participatory processes	... group discussion and participatory forms of analysis in which people identify, reflect on, and justify the capabilities they have reason to value – for example, Biggeri et al.'s work on children's capabilities (2011), Frediani's research on housing (2019a), and participatory poverty studies that seek to identify dimensions of ill-being.
5. Inference from anecdotal evidence	... expert analysis of existing evidence that has *indirect* relevance for identifying valuable dimensions of life – for example, relevant capabilities might be inferred from: a) case studies or life histories of poverty; b) surveys of consumer preferences or behaviour; or c) happiness and subjective wellbeing surveys (such as the World Values surveys' insights into cultural differences in values).
6. Studies of human values and aspirations involving open-ended interviews or surveys	... studies specifically designed to uncover human values and aspirations in an effort to identify important capabilities from the bottom up – for example, Clark (2002), Biggeri et al. (2006), Clark and Qizilbash (2008), Ibrahim (2008), and Hodgett and Clark (2011).
7. Mixed methods including various forms of 'empirical philosophy'	... approaches for selecting dimensions that draw on more than one method – for example, Clark calls for a form of empirical philosophy that involves confronting normative assumptions with human values (2002: 5); and Robeyns (2003) has proposed criteria for selecting capabilities, sparking a lively debate on the respective roles of philosophy and democracy (see Byskov, 2017); while Biggeri and Libanora (2011) have proposed a practical procedure for identifying people's capabilities.

Source: Frediani et al., 2019a: 13–14

my work (Frediani, 2015; 2019a) using aspirations as an overarching concept and one that is more easily understandable than functionings; aspirations are similar to achieved functionings in that they include the things that people aspire to and are being pursued or enabled; but they also include the things that people aspire to that are within their reach if they wish to pursue them (potential functionings); and the things that people aspire to but are not able to pursue because they lack the capabilities to do so (which I term *unattainable functionings*). Figure 5.1 outlines these components and characteristics of aspirations. The rights and principles space depicts the range of aspirations that are identified through the dialogue between policy obligations and commitments, as well as urban inhabitants' values associated with just and sustainable city-making.

People's aspirations for changing the city in ways that bring about human development are constituted by these types of functionings. For example, in Cape Town, the aspiration of being cared for and supported was a key motivation for informal dwellers to live in Woodstock. While this aspiration was not articulated as an achieved functioning – there was a lot of room for improvement – the participatory engagement revealed both the importance of recognizing this aspiration in the regeneration process and also, to some extent, the existing ways through which vulnerable groups have been able to build support networks in the area. Participants also highlighted the

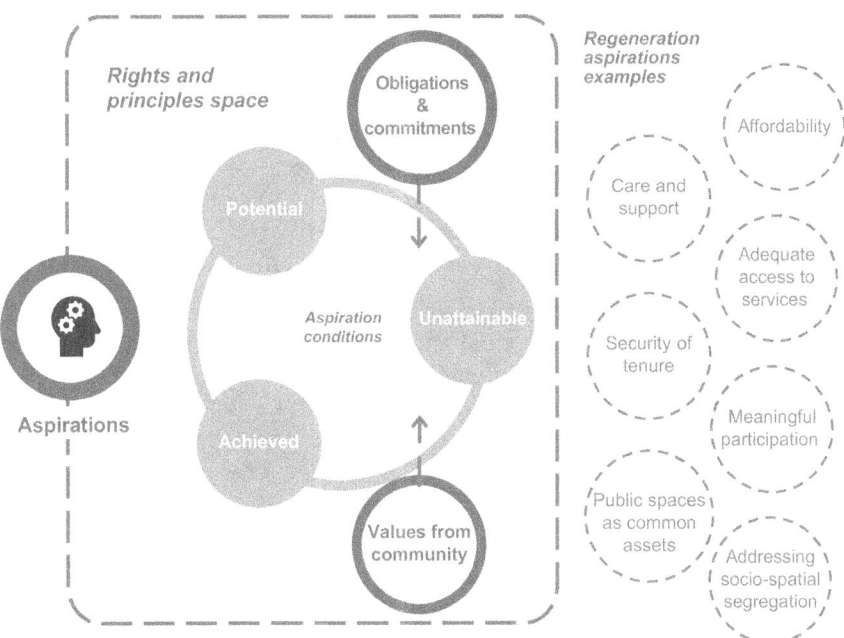

Figure 5.1 Aspirations diagram

importance of retaining public spaces as a common asset which was valued as a potential functioning. The workshop participants stressed the significance of opportunities to continue using and appropriating public spaces in inclusive ways, enabling encounters between different people. The implication for regeneration is the need to consider the policies and planning processes that would allow public spaces to be managed and appropriated as commons rather than privatized or designed and managed in a way that reproduces segregation and differential access. Finally, the engagement revealed valued unattainable functionings – the aspirations of Woodstock residents to have diverse and secure forms of tenure recognized and promoted. The participants argued that the current available tenure options did not meet their needs because there are no government or non-government initiatives creating realistically affordable and accessible housing options. In addition, the informal dwellers were in constant threat of forced evictions and market-led displacement, creating uncertainty and affecting their capabilities to advance wellbeing.

In relation to the methodologies available to reveal such aspirations, in my work I have applied mixed methods centred on participatory processes. However, I have but connected and compared people's aspirations with policy commitments and obligations to strengthen the links between the capability approach and rights-based approaches to development. For example, in the case of the regeneration aspirations for Woodstock, the expression of the aspiration for having diverse and secure forms of tenure recognized and promoted emerged through a series of participatory activities correlating these aspirations with issues recognized in national policy in South Africa, and in international obligations and commitments, as well as being informed by previous research investigating tenure conditions in inner-city areas of Cape Town. Such a process of triangulation is meaningful because, on the one hand, it makes the research more robust, and on the other hand, it also creates a mechanism for holding policies and procedures to account, thus making links between research and practice. For example, the aspiration to promote diverse and secure forms of tenure is recognized in Article 35 of the UN's New Urban Agenda, endorsed by the South African government:

> We commit ourselves to promoting, at the appropriate level of government, including subnational and local government, increased security of tenure for all, recognizing the plurality of tenure types, and to developing fit-for-purpose and age-, gender- and environment-responsive solutions within the continuum of land and property rights, with particular attention to security of land tenure for women as key to their empowerment, including through effective administrative systems. (UN, 2017: 13)

On a similar note, Article 2.26 of the Constitution of South Africa states that: '1) Everyone has the right to have access to adequate housing; 2) The state must take reasonable legislative and other measures, within its available resources, to achieve the progressive realization of this right'. Adequacy is defined by seven criteria, one of them being tenure security. However, neither the various infrastructure development initiatives led by the Cape Town city council, nor the planning and zoning instruments used to accelerate investments in the area, recognize the need to engage with the security of tenure issues of the diverse population of Woodstock. Furthermore, a series of existing studies have documented how some of these ongoing processes are sources of insecurity for tenants living in the area (Watson, 2009; Scheba and Turok, 2020) and have led to the displacement of the most vulnerable residents of Woodstock (Fleming, 2011; Wenz, 2012). This participatory research has, therefore, shown that an aspiration valued by local residents and recognized in national and international policy has not been secured or promoted by urban policy and planning processes.

These reflections on the engagement in Cape Town illustrate that the 'voicing of aspirations [is] an excellent tool to decide which dimensions of wellbeing to target in a human development intervention' (Conradie and Robeyns, 2013: 565). In this sense, looking retrospectively at the work that I have been doing in the field of urban planning and design, the concept of aspirations has provided a method to identify and pursue future values, allowing collective reflections to focus on the things people want to see changed, improved, deepened, secured, and/or sustained. Applying the concept of functionings in the context of an evaluative framework is more static and focused on present circumstances than applying that of aspirations which opens up the possibility of talking about the future in ways that are more dynamic and embedded in socially constructed contexts.

Three key issues can be identified in relation to aspirations:

> First, aspirations can be expressed individually or collectively ... Second, aspirations are not properties of persons simply waiting to be uncovered; rather, aspirations are formed at the moment we start to contemplate them ... A process of becoming aware of one's aspirations, in which people are in a reflexive way invited to reflect on and express the aspirations they have, reconsider them, and possibly revise them, may both lead to the birth of new aspirations or to the discovery of latent aspirations ... Third, aspirations are dynamic. One of the contextual elements that influence aspirations is the experiences that one has had. (Conradie and Robeyns, 2013: 561–562)

Aspirations are socially constructed and it is important to consider the potential threats to what people value: in adverse circumstances, aspirations could be limited in ways that lead to resignation and acceptance of particular violations or deprivation of opportunities. In the capability literature, such limited aspirations are referred to as 'adaptive preferences', and the term has been related to preferences that might be adapted to avoid disappointment in the face of harsh realities, preferences shaped by social conditioning, or preferences distorted by persistent forms of exploitation and injustice (Sen, 1987; 1992).

While Sen raises this issue of adaptation as a potential challenge to revealing what oppressed people need and value about the advancement of human development, he also highlights that public deliberations are fundamental to ensuring that preferences and values are scrutinized: 'We cannot, in general, take preferences as given independently of public discussion, that is, irrespective of whether open debates and interchanges are permitted or not' (Sen 1999b: 153).

Various mechanisms to address the potential risks of adaptation have been proposed (Frediani et al., 2019a). For example, a procedure might attempt to encourage participants to detach themselves from their particular realities by facilitating processes that make them look at their experiences as a 'quasi-impartial spectator' (Biggeri and Libanora, 2011: 83). Drawing on data generated through survey activities with children, Biggeri and Libanora argue that instead of asking a child about the opportunities he or she would like, asking about opportunities any child should have enables a wider and richer discussion about different dimensions of wellbeing. This draws on Sen's suggestion for overcoming adaptive preferences which itself draws on Adam Smith's theory of moral reasoning:

> We can never survey our own sentiments and motives, we can never form any judgement concerning them; unless we remove ourselves, as it were, from our own natural situation, and endeavour to view them as at a certain distance from us. (Smith, 1759: 110)

In my own work, I have found this procedure extremely effective. It meant framing questions in a way that allowed participants to both talk about their own experiences of the city and discuss the opportunities people of diverse social identities should have. This encouraged participants to reflect on aspirations and urban experiences from the perspective of social diversity, while also enabling them to look at themselves and others from a slightly externalized perspective. It has been really useful to then build on these narratives by developing personas around different ways of experiencing the city highlighting diverse sets of aspirations for city-making and using them to facilitate participatory workshops. These personas were produced to reflect the different experiences of the city interconnecting with aspects of social identities (gender, age, abilities, ethnicity, class). In the Cape Town action-research, we anonymized some of the life stories shared by residents of Woodstock and used them in a final action-planning workshop with residents, built-environment practitioners, academics, and government officials. The use

---

Box 5.1 Adaptive preferences

Adaptive preference is a concept used within the capability-approach literature to describe a process through which people's ability to aspire and make choices is compromised by their adverse living conditions. For example, Sen argues that preferences 'can be moulded by social conditioning and a resigned acceptance of misfortune' (1990: 133). Thus, adaptive preference is a concept that brings to the forefront the role that structures of inequalities and discrimination can play in value formation and shaping mindsets.

of personas helped to facilitate a deeper engagement with the diverse realities in the neighbourhood, recognizing disparate needs and aspirations for the future of the neighbourhood.

In relation to the concept of adaptive preference, a distinction is often made between what one values and what one has reason to value (Khader and Kosko, 2019). The focus on what one has reason to value can be seen as a fundamental entry point to unpack the importance of public reasoning and deliberation in addressing adaptive preferences. One of the main strengths of the capability approach is that 'it does not take people's preferences at face value' but promotes a critical engagement with how people's aspirations are produced, articulated, and communicated (Khader and Kosko, 2019: 196). In this way, collective processes of decision-making are crucial for recognizing aspirations and deepening the process of value formation. However, these processes would need to be informed by existing commitments to some valuable functionings, in order to avoid the risk of deliberation leading to the acceptance of oppressive and harmful functionings (Khader and Kosko, 2019: 197). Recognizing the need to negotiate between normative and embedded ideals of change, and to consider context-specific processes of value formation and identification, is a central component of, as well as a challenge to, the application of the capability approach.

Debates about aspirations and city-making processes highlight the role of discussing people's experiences of spaces and their future visions for them in the formation of their aspirations. Generating collective imaginaries about particular areas of the city, and debating the diverse aspirations associated with such imaginaries, helps people to encounter, recognize, and negotiate difference; it can reveal the diverse possibilities of future trajectories of city-making, and encourage critical thinking about one's own aspirations, as well as considering whose aspirations are prioritized in processes of urban change. At the same time, it is crucial to link these processes to wider nationally and internationally recognized commitments and recognized obligations. The growing interest of governments in developing national urban policies can be extremely useful as a means to operationalize the aspirations recognized in the UN's New Urban Agenda and SDG 11.

Talking about aspirations can enhance people's capacity to bring about change by generating alternative visions for city-making (Conradie and Robeyns, 2013). Deliberations about people's aspirations for city-making can enhance 'informed critical agency' – the 'freedom to question established values and traditional priorities' (Drèze and Sen, 2013: 232). Finally, I would argue that exploring alternative visions can also create opportunities to advocate a more socially and environmentally just process of city-making by connecting people's experiences and values to policy and planning frameworks, showing synergies, contradictions, and violations. Therefore, it is precisely in the collective imagination of the interface between the nature of the good life and the good city that there is an entry point to approach city-making as means of expanding human development.

CHAPTER 6
Abilities: Housing (un)freedoms in Nova Primavera estate, Salvador da Bahia, Brazil

Abstract

The relocation of stilt dwellers into the Nova Primavera housing estate in Salvador da Bahia, Brazil has generated uneven effects on the capabilities of local residents. While an improvement on the housing conditions in the stilt settlement, the layout and quality of the houses on the estate have compromised various capabilities residents have to pursue their housing aspirations. This chapter examines how spatial arrangements affect urban dwellers' capabilities in relation to housing. By bringing together debates on access to assets with the capability approach, I argue that configurations and appropriations of space play a key role in shaping people's capabilities in cities.

Keywords: Salvador da Bahia, abilities, assets, place, conversion factors

Introduction

In the early 2000s, the state government of Bahia in Brazil implemented a housing programme, called Ribeira Azul, in the areas of Alagados and Novos Alagados in Salvador da Bahia. The programme aimed to eradicate the stilt settlements of these neighbourhoods by relocating residents to nearby housing estates; it was funded by the World Bank and implemented in collaboration with Cities Alliance, an international partnership hosted by the UN Office of Project and Services. While these international agencies have often referred to the Ribeira Azul programme as an example of best-practice slum upgrading, local residents and organizations have highlighted various limitations of the programme, and the negative impact it had on residents' capabilities to pursue their housing aspirations.

This chapter draws on evidence collected for my PhD research (Frediani, 2007), which analysed the resettlement process in the Nova Primavera housing estate, built as part of one of the stages of the Ribeira Azul programme. The research explored how residents' housing capabilities were affected by the project and the resettlement process. The programme generated benefits such as the improvement of environmental conditions in the area and services and physical housing more robust than those of the stilt houses. But there were also limitations due to poor and inappropriate housing design combined with the

Photo 6.1 Residents of Novos Alagados in the Nova Primavera housing estate (photograph by author)

lack of meaningful participation by local residents, groups, and organizations in the relocation process. As a result, the spatial arrangements of the housing estate did not meet local housing needs and aspirations, compromising key capabilities and pushing many vulnerable residents to sell their property informally and move out of the estate. Given the difficulties of finding affordable accommodation in the area, these residents had few alternatives other than moving to more peripheral neighbourhoods or returning to the houses of other family members, so creating overcrowding.

This chapter draws material from a series of participatory research activities conducted between 2001 and 2007 in close partnership with the Novos Alagados neighbourhood association Sociedade Primeiro de Maio (Frediani, 2019a). Dimensions of housing were identified and examined through semi-structured interviews and a focus group facilitated with an interactive card game (Frediani, 2019a: 279). As a way of making the evidence more accessible and meaningful to local residents and organizations, filmmaker and photographer Gabriel Boieras and I produced a documentary entitled *Ferida Aberta* (*Open Wound*) that outlines the main findings of the research (Frediani and Boieras, 2007).

The research highlights the importance of spatial arrangements in enabling or disabling access to resources in the city. Drawing on this case, the chapter relates discussions of urban access and control over assets to the concepts of abilities and capacities. In particular, the chapter articulates the role of spatial arrangements (i.e. housing typology, water and sanitation system, design of squares, streets and footpaths, etc.) in shaping residents' access and control over assets (i.e. access to social capital, services, livelihood opportunities etc.).

The effects of the Ribeira Azul programme

During the colonial period (1500–1815), the dense and high Atlantic forest surrounding Tanheiros and Cabrito Cove in Salvador attracted many slaves escaping from sugar-cane plantations in the region. Runaway slaves of different West African origins got together in the forest to form communities of resistance, called *quilombos*. There is limited research on these insurgent settlements, and it is hard to know their numbers and sizes. However, it is known that they were not just temporary communities but developed deep and long-term connections with the local territory. In the area of Alagados and Novos Alagados, the *quilombo* of Urubu was the most famous. It was formed in 1826 and soon became a symbol of resistance in the area due to its organization and leadership. It had a *terreiro de candomblé* (place for the practice of religious activity of African origin) and was a space where the social identities of African migrants could be expressed and constructed. Its first and most famous leader was an African woman, Zeferina, who is still a symbol of liberty, strength, and resistance for the residents of Novos Alagados.

The first informal stilt houses (known locally as simply stilts) in Tanheiros Cove were recorded in 1946 and the area soon became known as Alagados (from the Portuguese for flooded). The residents of Alagados came mainly from the surrounding areas and Salvador's inner city looking for alternatives to rented or guest accommodation. A study in 1973 shows that 79.3 per cent of the families in Alagados came from Salvador (Carvalho, 2002). The wooden houses were rapidly constructed by collective effort, built on stilts over the swamp and the sea with no water or electricity connections. The main reason for building over water and not on land was because the Navy had control of the water and was perceived to be less vigorous in its control than the local police and military on land.

Nevertheless, despite the water-based location of the settlement, the local police made their first brutal attempt to eradicate the stilt housing in December 1949. They were stopped by the strength of media reaction and the organization of the occupiers. At that time, there were already 2,000 houses in the settlement and, by the 1960s, the process of densification had increased. In 1967, the annual growth rate was 27 per cent and 64,5000 people lived in the area (Carvalho, 2002). In the 1970s, the population growth stabilized at around 3 per cent, matching the annual growth rate of the city of Salvador. The main reason for this stabilization was the natural constraint of the depth of the water: the stilt house settlement had expanded further out into the sea and arrived at depths at which further construction had become impractical.

Infrastructural investments in the 1970s generated a new wave of growth, resulting in the expansion of stilt houses into Cabrito Cove, which became known as Novos (New) Alagados. In 1971, Suburbana Avenue, a road connecting the inner-city area of Salvador to surrounding cities, was built. Later in the 70s, two industrial centres were built in neighbouring municipalities and Suburbana Avenue became the main route between the industrial centres and the city. The first settlers of Novos Alagados were families evicted for the construction of the motorway who did not receive sufficient compensation to allow them to buy houses in the area. They were followed by other new residents looking for cheap accommodation between the city centre and the industrial areas. By 1984, there were 1500 households living in stilt housing in the Cabrito Cove area (Carvalho, 2002).

The residents of the stilt houses of Alagados and Novos Alagados did not perceive their stilt houses as temporary accommodation, but as a means to acquire permanent houses by gradually improving and transforming them into solid, safe, and stable homes. The process of construction of the houses and occupation and improvement to the area involved three stages (Carvalho, 2002). First, houses varying in size from 16 square metres to 100 square metres were constructed on piles about seven metres tall set into the sea floor. From the beginning houses were built in rows, leaving enough space between them so that in the future, once land had been reclaimed, there would be enough space for paved streets. In this first stage, access was created by bridges made of wood discarded from construction sites. The second stage started with gradually filling in the sea with rubbish provided by the municipal government. The infill was then improved by adding sand and other materials to make it more solid. In the final stage of consolidation, the streets were paved, and houses were improved and connected to electricity and water. Wood was replaced by brick, and in some cases, houses can now securely have up to three floors.

This self-help and incremental process of city-making illustrates a typical approach by the state when dealing with informal settlements – apparently ambivalent but actually exploitative. On one hand, the Brazilian state criminalized stilt settlements, while on the other, it recognized and supported their gradual improvement by using the poor as agents of waste disposal. While these conditions produced insecurity for stilt residents, by not guaranteeing secure tenure, and reinforced a city-wide unjust distribution of environmental hazards, the poor did use the state's attitude, and the waste, as opportunities to provide housing for thousands of families in the area through a bottom-up and collective process of city-making.

The first state intervention to improve the quality of living for the residents of Alagados drew on existing collective abilities of city-making. The 1973 Alagados upgrading project was an *in situ* physical improvement initiative drawing inspiration from John Turner's writings on self-help housing (Turner, 1972). The intervention aimed to improve the quality of the built environment through land reclamation and contracting residents to upgrade houses and connect them to infrastructure services such as water and electricity. Local contractors were supervised by engineers and architects hired by the government, and the process and product of intervention were seen by the occupiers as a victory. The land reclamation was questioned in terms of its environmental sustainability, but Carvalho (2002) argues that, at the time, this intervention represented an innovative and participatory model of urban development.

Following the growth of stilt housing over Tanheiros Cove and its expansion into Cabrito Cove in the 1970s and 80s, the government launched a new upgrading programme targeting Novos Alagados and Alagados in 1998 – Ribeira Azul. The initiative was mostly funded by a World Bank loan and a grant from the Italian government, implemented through a partnership between the state government of Bahia and the Italian NGO, the Italian Association of Volunteers in Active Service, and supervised by the Cities Alliance. The objective of the US$80 million programme was to improve the physical aspects and environmental conditions of the neighbourhood and strengthen local social assets. Through its nominally participatory strategy, Ribeira Azul aimed to eradicate the stilts and to alleviate poverty. My PhD focused on the relocation of residents from Cabrito Cove to the nearby housing estate of Nova Primavera. The estate was built in the second stage of the programme and finalized in 2004.

The Nova Primavera estate covered four hectares with housing for 312 households who had been previously living on stilts over the River Cobre at Cabrito Cove or were resettled due to demolitions related to the implementation of the project. Each housing unit is around 44 square metres and the design of the housing estate resembles a village, with many open spaces and courtyards, which aim to encourage sociability.

My research focused on the identification of the housing aspirations of residents targeted by the programme, and explored the effect of the relocation on residents' capabilities to achieve these aspirations. Through focus-group activities and semi-structured interviews with local residents, five key housing aspirations were identified (see Table 6.1). These housing aspirations are associated with the everyday housing practices of local residents and reveal the underlying intentions and values embedded in the way local residents interact with their dwelling spaces.

Having identified these dimensions of housing, the research explored the impacts of the upgrading programme on residents' freedom to achieve their housing aspirations. Here, I focus on the findings related to how the typology of the housing estate and the process of designing it influenced residents' ability to pursue their housing aspirations.

As explained earlier, the self-help process of gradually improving the stilts enabled residents to feel a strong sense of ownership of their space, as they were actively engaged in the process of developing their dwelling and environment. This collective and incremental form of city-making represents a particular model of urbanization that draws on and supports social assets among family members and neighbours, such as relationships of collaboration and solidarity (Carvalho, 2002). In Nova Primavera, local residents stressed the importance of making extensions to their houses in order to maintain tight family support

Table 6.1 Dimensions of housing

Housing aspirations	Definitions
Individualize and expand	Freedom to interact with one's environment in a way reflecting one's culture, social, economic, and political interests. This dimension was articulated as investing in one's property as a mechanism of social mobility.
Maintain social networks	Freedom to maintain and expand the bonds of relationships that are valued as a positive for the housing process. Such networks were articulated as crucial elements in fostering a sense of belonging and enhancing support systems in neighbourhoods.
Healthy environment	Freedom to have security of tenure, sustainable access to infrastructure and services, resilience against environmental threats, access to health care and education, and safety.
Participate in decision-making	Freedom to participate in decision-making in communities and in the city. This aspect was raised as an important issue not only in the implementation of upgrading projects, but more widely as a goal of democratization in the city.
Affordable living costs	Freedom to afford the costs of living. This dimension was particularly emphasized due to the fear that upgrading programmes would generate costs that households could not afford and therefore might push the most vulnerable groups to move to distant peripheral, but more affordable, areas.

Source: Compiled from Frediani, 2007.

systems, especially in a locality where there is a substantial number of single mothers working long hours, and where family members and neighbours provide crucial care for, and contribute to the upbringing of, children.

Residents also described how the physical characteristics of stilt settlements also enhanced a sense of safety and communal living. The process of incremental and collective construction and maintenance of the settlement combined with physical proximity between houses to generate strong social ties between households as they supported each other through everyday hardships and against violence from police or criminal organizations.

In contrast, residents were told that they were not permitted to expand and individualize their living environment in Nova Primavera. Technical officers from the local government stated that the main reason was that extensions lacking solid foundations would lead to walls becoming cracked and weakened, affecting the structural stability of the houses. While compromising the potentials of home-making practices to nurture relationships of solidarity and care, this disruption from familiar processes of incremental improvement also led residents to feel a general detachment from their dwelling spaces. Residents argued that they did not have a sense of ownership of their houses and felt as though they were only ever temporary occupants.

Meanwhile, those who did extend their houses have experienced unanticipated physical and social consequences. As a result of ground-floor extensions, many walls did indeed start to crack. The extensions of the residents of the ground floor of two-storey flats generated conflictual claims over the slab of the extension. As residents of the ground floor extended their units laterally at the ground level, the roof potentially provided an opportunity for further extension for residents on both floors. The ground-floor household argued that the roof of the extension was their space for future growth, while the upper-floor household claimed that it was now a terrace for their future extension. The design of water and sanitation systems also added further tensions between upper- and ground-floor neighbours. The water tank for a ground-floor household was placed in a space in the upper flat and, similarly, to reduce costs of installation, sanitation was an interconnected system, meaning that if there were blockages in, or damage to, the pipes in one of the flats, both flats would experience disruptions. All these factors combined meant a profound change in social relations, turning bonds of solidarity into competition and conflict, leading to community fragmentation.

In the Ribeira Azul programme, the freedom to participate in decision-making processes was one of the most controversial issues of the programme. Government officials indicated that, due to pressure from the World Bank, the participation of local residents was a high priority. The programme set up a committee of elected street leaders to meet regularly with technical officers, NGOs, and government officials. Government officials argued that this was necessary because the community-based organization, Sociedade Primeiro de Maio, was influenced by the opposition party and it did not represent most of the dwellers from the area.

Criticisms of Ribeira Azul's participatory strategy came from residents, community leaders, scholars, and local councillors. They argued that the committee of street leaders had a consultative role and no decision-making power. The illusive form of participation weakened social and political assets in the community, as the creation of new representative structures threatened existing forms of mobilization such as Sociedade Primeiro de Maio. Furthermore, residents elected to the project's committee found that local people were turning against them because the community's ideas and concerns were not having any effect on project design and implementation. According to local councillor Emiliano José da Silva Filho, 'Novos Alagados fought for a worthy housing project, not for propaganda and bureaucracy, not for this project about which the population has not been asked its opinion and which it does not accept' (da Silva Filho, 2001, cited in Frediani, 2007: 149).

This case study highlights the importance of the relationship between city-making practices and residents' abilities to achieve their valued aspirations. Spatial productions that fail to recognize this relationship can potentially create new obstacles and reproduce cycles of marginalization. In the case of Nova Primavera, it resulted in the most vulnerable households selling the flats acquired through the upgrading programme on the informal market, and settling in even more peripheral locations of the city (Soares and Espinheira, 2006).

Reflections on abilities

This discussion of the role of city-making on people's abilities and capacities to pursue their aspirations aims to make a useful contribution to debates about the application of the capability approach. The case study of Novos Alagados illustrates quite clearly that the spatial configuration of places matters and shapes people's freedoms in cities. While the relationship between spaces and access to assets has been the subject of extensive consideration in urban geography, planning, and design, the actual interface between space and abilities has not been explored in much depth in the capability and human development literature. I argue that space – its design, production, and appropriation – is an inherent aspect of people's imaginaries and aspirations, and how they access and control the resources around them. The concept of place-based assets is of particular importance in understanding how processes of city-making shape people's capabilities. In this sense, place-based assets are a key component of the conversion factors affecting the way people translate practices into achieved dimensions of wellbeing.

The concept of access to assets is central to debates about how urban planning and design interventions could alleviate poverty by building on existing place-based potentials and pathways. Moser (1998; 2006) has been fundamental in elaborating an asset-based approach that defines assets as tangible and intangible resources that can be 'acquired, developed, improved and transferred across generations' (Ford Foundation, 2004). Initially, these resources were defined in terms of physical, financial, human, social, and natural assets. Other dimensions were later proposed, such as aspirational (Appadurai, 2004), physiological (Alsop et al., 2006), productive (Moser and Felton, 2007), and political assets (Ferguson et al., 2007), and similar approaches have been applied to the examination of urban livelihoods (Rakodi and Lloyd-Jones, 2002). They have all emphasized the importance of exploring not only the availability of particular resources in places, but also people's actual access shaped by power relations embedded in the design, use, and appropriation of places. This highlights the difference between availability of, and access to, resources. For example, the existence of water taps in a particular informal settlement does not guarantee that all residents can actually access water, nor does it guarantee its quality and reliability. Often, water taps are controlled by local landlords who lock them and then charge for their use. At the same time, safe access to taps, water quality, and supply reliability varies: access to taps is conditioned by social dynamics within communities, and the potential risks of water contamination and leaks depends on the nature of the relationship with water providers. While community-led water services can play a crucial role in fostering human development in cities, it is important to highlight that it is not possible to equate simple availability with access to secure and good-quality services.

These assets-based frameworks can help to illustrate the diverse inputs and relationships that shape people's capabilities. Kleine (2010; 2013) establishes this connection between assets and capabilities by identifying nine different types of resource that shape a person's access to a portfolio of resources. These include material, financial, natural, geographical, human, psychological, information, cultural, and social resources (2010: 681). In a similarly way, I have found it useful to draw on asset-based frameworks to specify how people's diverse abilities shape their capabilities. Figure 6.1 illustrates how the asset framework can be applied to examine people's abilities and it refers to examples from the case of Nova Primavera. The assets space represents the quality of people's access to and control of different assets, constituting their abilities to pursue their valued city-making aspirations.

The capability approach helps to reinforce the importance of focusing not only on the availability of resources, but also on actual freedom to access and use them. This debate in the capability-approach literature is particularly addressed through the notion of conversion factors (see Box 6.1).

Robeyns' definition of conversion factors (see Box 6.1) makes reference to two key aspects of place-based assets shaping people's capabilities: firstly, the actual configuration of physical space, associated with the quality of the built environment (by referring to the lack of paved roads); and secondly, the importance of access to such assets, which is shaped by societal norms (such as women not being allowed to cycle without being accompanied by a male family member).

Territorial conversion factors are key in transforming local endowments of resources (endogenous and exogenous) into capabilities: 'conversion factors are interrelated with the territorial setting where agents are embedded, and thus influence their behaviour in the process of choice' (Biggeri and Ferrannini, 2014: 42). In Biggeri and Ferrannini (2014) and Biggeri et al. (2018), the authors

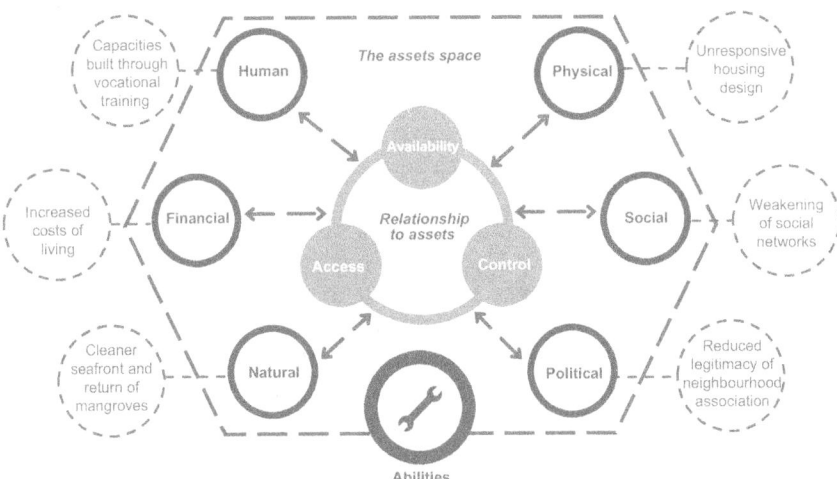

Figure 6.1 Abilities diagram

> **Box 6.1 Conversion factors**
>
> Conversion factors are defined by Robeyns as the personal, social, and environmental conditions that influence the freedom people have to convert resources into a functioning. Personal conversion factors relate to the personal abilities, capacities, and skills people have when using a particular resource. For example, 'If a person is disabled, or in a bad physical condition, or has never learned to cycle, then the bicycle will be of limited help to enable the functioning of mobility' (2005: 99). Social conversion factors relate to policies, social norms, and power relations, while environmental conversion factors relate to issues around climate and geographical location which play a role in transforming goods into functionings. Drawing on the bicycle example, Robeyns explains: 'if there are no paved roads or if a government or the dominant societal culture imposes a social or legal norm that women are not allowed to cycle without being accompanied by a male family member, then it becomes much more difficult or even impossible to use the good to enable the functioning' (2005: 99).

highlight that place-based assets are crucially important in the expansion of capabilities because: 1) the human rights and capabilities people have reason to value are also – but not exclusively – place-dependent; 2) participation and agency freedoms are mostly locally experienced; and 3) people's capabilities and agency are embedded in and conditioned by territories as 'the changing properties of the immediate settings in which people live and in which their personal and societal development interact (...) shape the exercising of human rights and capability space' (Biggeri et al., 2018: 129; see also Biggeri and Ferrannini, 2014).

In applying the capability approach more directly to inform planning debates, Basta (2016) makes a similar point, arguing that planning should not be concerned only with the production of spatial goods that meet different needs and aspirations, but should also be concerned with enhancing the abilities of people to access them in ways that augment their capabilities:

> Spatial goods, by their very nature, are not always adaptable to the different capabilities of individuals. In the example of the elderlies incapable of reaching the green area by themselves, no matter how nearby the area is, the green area cannot be thoroughly 'adapted'. And even where it can, this may result in the discrimination of others (e.g. children). What can be – and according to my interpretation of Sen, shall be – adapted is extending the reach of the planning intervention from the good to the capabilities of those who can enhance their functionings through it. This would imply, for example, ensuring that sufficient social assistance is provided to the elderly so that they can enjoy the green as much as others. The general implication of this 'extension' of planning interventions is that the latter do not 'end' with the provision and maintenance of the good; they 'end' with enhancing the 'intrinsic' capabilities of the individuals for which the 'extrinsic' nature of the good is meant for. (Basta, 2016: 203–204)

Beyond a spatial planning discussion, the case of Nova Primavera also highlights that the process and features of housing design play a key role in shaping capabilities. This relationship between design and the capability approach has been approached by various authors in the human development and capability network, but mostly from the entry point of product, technology, and service design. Nevertheless, the work of Dong (2008) and Oosterlaken (2009) are particularly relevant to the debate on spatial design and capabilities. Dong tackles the process of design from a justice perspective and argues that design policy should be focused on expanding citizens' 'capability to design' (2008:82). His work makes a meaningful contribution to the debates on participatory design and co-design by addressing the conditions shaping the participation of citizens in design processes. Meanwhile, Oosterlaken focuses on the actual design product, and she articulates the impact of the design features of artefacts on people's capabilities. Oosterlaken links the capability approach with debates from the field of philosophy and sociology of technology to elaborate the idea of 'capability sensitive design' (2009: 97). The notion of conversion factors helps both Dong and Oosterlaken shed light on the human, social, physical, and political assets that need to be in place to enable design processes and products to advance capabilities. (For more on the implication of this debate to participatory design in the context of urban development, see Frediani and Boano, 2012.)

The role of place-based assets in expanding human development was explored by various authors in the 2018 special issue of the *Journal of Human Development and Capabilities* on Communities and Capabilities. In the editorial, Tonon emphasizes the role of social assets in expanding wellbeing, arguing that social interactions and ties can 'become instrumental in securing local democracy as well as vitality within the community, since they promote social equality among its members by generating habits of public association, while offering social support both to individuals and to the communities as a whole' (2018: 122). Biggeri et al.'s 2018 examination of a community-based rehabilitation (CBR) programme implemented in Mandya and Ramanagaram Districts (Kanataka State, India) reveals the various place-based assets that such community infrastructure can provide to improve the capabilities of persons with disabilities living in marginalized territories. Their study shows, for example, how the CBR programme has been able to increase access for persons with disabilities to pensions, health services, mobility aid, and income-generating activities. They also argue that the self-help groups set up by the CBR programme have been able to address stigma and support the participation of persons with disabilities in their family and community life. Overall, they show that 'programmes such as CBR that rely on collective action and community rehabilitation as levers of change can produce high effects, thanks to the synergies with the community itself, by making the socio-institutional context more sensitive and prone to adapt norms, policies and services to different needs' (Biggeri et al., 2018: 140).

These existing capability studies acknowledge the role of place-based assets in responding to the deprivation of capabilities but they do not necessarily engage explicitly with spatial arrangements and spatial production.

One exception is the work of Kleine (2010), which recognizes norms on usage of space as a structural factor shaping people's access to resources and agency. Kleine approaches space (material or digital) as a means to reveal how formal and informal regulations shape people's agency. Thus, the work does not address the relationship between capabilities and the physical properties of space or its mode of production in a more substantial manner.

While not engaged in the debates and literature of the capability approach, Wallman (2011) draws on the work of eighteenth-century landscape designer, Lancelot 'Capability' Brown to explore the capability of places; that is, to show how places enable encounters with and expressions of diversity. Places, and the system that produces them, have particular properties that affect social relations. This interesting repositioning of the language of capability from people to systems opens up a series of insights into the role that the capability approach could have in interrogating the relationships between places and social relations that shape people's access to assets.

Along similar lines, various studies in urban design, planning, and geography have been exploring the role of spatial arrangements and characteristics in enabling human flourishing. Lefebvre's work has been particularly relevant in emphasizing the importance of investigating people's everyday lives to interrogate the relationship between physical/morphological characteristics of the environment and social relations. For example, women have more restricted experiences of and access to public urban space due to the sense of insecurity generated by characteristics of urban physical and social environments (Kallus, 2001). Women's sense of security can be influenced by lighting, trees and vegetation, types of activities, forms of surveillance, and land use, as well as by women's role in a particular society and their access to information about violence. From a capability perspective, it is possible to argue that this shows quite convincingly how a particular dimension of women's wellbeing (security) is influenced and shaped by women's access to physical assets (i.e. public urban space), and conditioned by spatial characteristics (i.e. lighting, vegetation) as well as social relations (i.e. gender roles).

My work focusing on city-making from a capability perspective has attempted to bring together these different approaches to place-based assets and their implications for wellbeing. Instead of focusing merely on spatial goods, I argue that practices of city-making influence how resources are distributed, accessed, and appropriated in the city. In the case study described in this chapter, it is possible to analyse the extent to which the particular upgrading programme implemented in Salvador had an effect on the distribution of assets for its intended beneficiaries. Furthermore, the approach implemented in the Ribeira Azul programme did not recognize or support existing ongoing practices of city-making, which limited the project's responsiveness to the diverse needs and aspirations of the residents.

Similarly, research conducted with my colleagues Jean François Trani and Julian Walker on the wellbeing of children with disabilities in informal settlements in Mumbai observed how relocation of households from informal settlements to high-rise buildings led to the weakening of social networks among neighbours and exacerbated their sense of insecurity. As widely acknowledged in the literature in this field, low-rise housing with more direct connection between houses, and streets, pathways, and public spaces can play an important role in enabling low-income households to sustain livelihood activities while undertaking household and communal care responsibilities. Our interviews demonstrated that the move to high-rise buildings particularly affected girls with mental impairments, who were locked alone in their apartments during the day because their families feared they could be sexually assaulted while other household members were at work (Walker et al., 2013).

In both these cases, I have observed that urban development projects that intend to upgrade informal settlements are shaped by predefined ideals of urban modernity, where good liveable environments are associated with values of individual freedom and there are no external encroachments or threats. Such a lens considers the fuzzy boundary between what is public and what is private in informal settlements to be a threat to healthy and liveable environments. As a consequence, the aesthetics and spatial configurations of upgrading projects have tended to prioritize clear distinctions between private and public spaces. However, the mixed uses of private and public spaces in informal settlements plays a fundamental role in local processes of place-making: 'During the day the small streets become the continuation of the houses, semi-private spaces, while the majority of the houses with their open doors also become semi-public spaces. The idea of the *favela* as a big collective house is common among residents' (Jacques, 2001). As I have argued elsewhere (Frediani, 2009), upgrading projects have often aimed to split and separate private spaces from public areas by defining clear spatial and legal boundaries between the two forms of space. This has led to the replacement of flexible and dynamic spatial arrangements with a spatial rigidity that compromises social ties and limits access to spaces in which to perform productive and reproductive activities. A capability perspective on these issues calls for recognition of existing processes of city-making, approaching them not only in terms of 'freedom from' (threats, restrictions), but also on how spatial arrangements and processes play a role in the positive aspects of freedom – 'freedom to'. In interrogating the fuzzy relationship between public and private uses of space, the capability approach allows an examination that reveals not just the potential encroachments on freedoms, but also possibilities for the enhancement of capabilities, and for whom.

Unfortunately, policy makers have often overlooked the potential role of informal settlements in reducing poverty and enabling human flourishing. Visagie and Turok highlight the potential of the high-density characteristics of informal settlements, and argue that 'observers focus on static assessments of economic and social problems [of informal settlements], rather than household trajectories or emerging capabilities over a period of time' (2020: 357). They focus particularly on the economic potential of informal settlements and argue that informal settlements often function as 'low-cost gateways to economic opportunities' and may operate as 'incubators of productive enterprises' (2020: 357).

Therefore, the recognition of place-based assets in the production and expansion of capabilities in cities is important, not only in equitably enhancing opportunities, but also in questioning dominant, oppressive, and exclusionary understandings of city-making. Capturing, interrogating, and supporting place-based assets is fundamentally about taking on board ideals of cosmopolitan planning (Sandercock, 1998), by questioning Enlightenment positivist concepts of cities that develop dualistic interpretations of urban processes (such as formal and informal; modern and non-modern; inclusion and exclusion), and linear ideals of urban progress. Sandercock proposes a perception of cities based on freedoms, interactions, movements, multiplicity, and diversity: 'a shift from linear time and physically inert space to new ways of conceiving of space and time, dialectically, socially, and historically' (1998: 29).

In relation to the example of the Nova Primavera estate, this discussion brings to the forefront the necessity of recognizing that, in the relationship between spatial production and capabilities, struggles for freedom have historical legacies. Racist colonial legacies are still present in urban planning and development trajectories in Salvador, reinforcing urban segregation as well as symbolic, material, and relational forms of discrimination (Figueiredo et al., 2020). In the colonial period, *quilombos* were, like informal settlements in current liberal democratic societies, territorial formations that questioned predefined and dominant notions of spatial production. In the search for freedom, dwellers in *quilombos* and informal settlements found a means to produce places they could call home, addressing unfreedoms, and building relationships and capabilities. Within these territories, inevitably, dwellers reproduce elements of dominant structures as often as they create innovations, sustain misrecognitions and exploitative relationships as often as they foster emancipation and liberation. The connection between place-based assets from a capability perspective helps to interrogate these intricacies and complexities, contradictions and nuances. But most of all, they can promote ways of approaching and understanding city-making that are situated and grounded in people's everyday experiences of places.

CHAPTER 7
Opportunities: Democratizing urban governance through neighbourhood planning associations in Kisumu, Kenya

Abstract

The Kisumu Water and Sewerage Company Limited (KIWASCO), in partnership with local neighbourhood planning associations, has implemented a series of community-led water delivery initiatives in Kisumu's informal settlements. While the initiatives have improved informal settlement dwellers' access to water, it has had uneven effects on the opportunities for residents to influence decision-making in the city. This chapter examines the experience of the informal settlement of Manyatta B and discusses the contributions that a focus on opportunities can make to the understanding of city-making from a capability perspective.

Keywords: Kisumu, water, governance, delegated management model, conversion factors, unfavourable inclusion

Introduction

Kisumu is the third largest city in Kenya, with a growing population of approximately 500,000 people. The city is strategically located near Lake Victoria, close to the borders with Uganda and Tanzania. The formally planned area of the city is surrounded by a series of self-built settlements which constitute 60 per cent of the city's land area. Even though landowners have formal titles to these areas, they are often referred to as informal settlements, as their residents, who are mostly tenants, lack adequate access to housing, water, sanitation, sewerage, and social services. From early 2000s, they have been experiencing sharp increases in rental costs, created by the pressures of urban development fuelling demands for land and housing close to Kisumu's inner-city area. These urban conditions are some of the reasons why nearly half of Kisumu's population lives below the poverty line.

Since 2008, the international NGO Practical Action has been working with neighbourhood planning associations in the informal settlements surrounding inner-city Kisumu, with the objectives of strengthening the organizational capacities of these associations and improving wellbeing of residents by supporting the implementation of community-managed water and sanitation initiatives. This engagement has led to experimentation with

Photo 7.1 Water kiosk in Kisumu's informal settlement (photograph by author)

various mechanisms and partnerships aiming to enable local residents and groups to install and manage such facilities. One of these mechanisms has been the delegated management model (DMM) for water delivery, which entails the formation of community groups to manage the connections between community water facilities and the main pipes owned by Kisumu water and sewerage suppliers (in this case, Kisumu Water and Sewerage Company Limited (KIWASCO)). The community groups are responsible for the distribution, maintenance, and day-to-day management of water connections within a neighbourhood, while the city's water company provides the main water connection and supply at a subsidized rate.

My engagement with this process took place between 2012 and 2015, when I coordinated a partnership between Practical Action and the Masters Programme in Social Development Practice at the Bartlett Development Planning Unit (DPU), University College London, focused on activities associated with an annual two-week long field trip in Kisumu. Students from each annual cohort spent four months working on this research, including three months of preparatory activities, two weeks of field work, and two weeks back in London producing reports outlining main findings of their studies. The field trip activities were planned and implemented in close partnership with the neighbourhood associations as well as supporting NGOs, such as Practical Action and the Kisumu Urban Apostolate Programme.[1] During field work, students used a variety of qualitative research methodologies including semi-structured interviews, focus-group discussions, and participatory photography (Frediani and Hirst, 2016). The field trip engagement was supported by the research activities of a PhD student I was supervising at the time, Stephanie Butcher, who investigated the everyday water practices in informal settlements in Kisumu. The students' reports[2] and Butcher's research output (Butcher, 2016) provide a good insight into some of the impacts of the work of neighbourhood planning associations aiming to improve the wellbeing of Kisumu's urban poor.

This chapter focuses on the findings from this work in the neighbourhood of Manyatta B, particularly exploring how the DMM initiative shaped the opportunities for local residents to expand their capabilities. The case study shows that projects can develop the abilities of the urban poor by expanding their access to assets without necessarily addressing the lack of opportunities for more inclusive processes of city-making. Thus, the concept of opportunities is analysed in this chapter by exploring the role that policy and planning processes play in shaping capabilities in an urban context. I interrogate opportunities for city-making by tracing the links between the notion of conversion factors and the debates in urban theory on how to understand the uneven distribution of opportunities in cities and the reproduction of urban poverty; and shed particular light on how relationships, norms, and procedures produced through city-making shape people's capabilities.

The case of the delegated management model in Manyatta B, Kisumu

In 2013, Manyatta B contained a population of nearly 30,000 people, with a high-density mix of building owners and rental tenants. Over 65 per cent of residents had access to water through communal standpipes, while some also accessed water through individual household connections, tanks, or boreholes. These forms of water supply are at great risk of contamination, due to the high water table in the area combined with inadequate sanitation provision, poorly sited pit latrines, and frequent flooding. These factors have a direct effect on the health of local residents, causing frequent incidences of waterborne diseases such as typhoid and dysentery (Martínez Cure et al., 2013).

With the objective of generating a more effective and efficient water supply and drainage system, the 2002 Kenya Water Act encouraged a move from state-led provision of water to a privately run system, managed and maintained by water service providers (WSPs). In Kisumu, the managing WSP is KIWASCO. The Act also opened up the possibility for community-based and small-scale operators to provide water services in informal settlements. Drawing on initiatives in other African contexts (in, for example, Mozambique, Ghana, and Uganda), the DMM was put forward by Kenyan government water regulatory entities to facilitate the provision of water in informal urban settlements. The model requires the utility company to sell bulk water to an agent based in the informal settlement who has been contracted, through a competitive and transparent selection process, to operate and manage the neighbourhood section of the water network. The selected master of operators then manages their customers at the neighbourhood level, billing for services in a way that allows them to repay the utility company and to capture profits that can be used for maintenance or other activities. Apart from aiming to increase the quality and quantity of water services, DMM initiatives sought to open new arenas of decision-making to local residents. It is in this regard that the DMM has the potential to operate as more than a model of effective service delivery by also allowing citizens greater control over their urban environment and deepening democratic practices.

In Manyatta B, the Manyatta Neighbourhood Development Group (MANEDEG) has been selected as the local operator. Their customers are individuals and groups managing water distribution points. From MANEDEG's perspective, DMM was seen as a mechanism to enable access to affordable water, while simultaneously generating livelihood opportunities for local residents and strengthening community capacity to participate in matters related to urban governance. From KIWASCO's perspective, on the other hand, this model aimed to reduce leakage, vandalism, and illegal connections to combat a reported 66 per cent loss of water in the Manyatta area, representing a financial burden to the company and reduced service to consumers (KIWASCO, 2007). By using a DMM in informal settlements, the utility companies expect that difficult to manage 'spaghetti networks' would be replaced by a more structured, ordered network for each neighbourhood.

The Masters students' research in Manyatta B focused on the DMM initiatives implemented as part of a wider participatory planning project led by Practical Action, called People's Plans into Practice. The project was implemented between 2008 and 2013 with the objective of strengthening the capacity of residents of informal settlements in Kisumu and Kitale to participate in decision-making processes in the city. The students' report (Martínez Cure et al., 2013) revealed that the DMM initiative in Manyatta B increased access to water and brought about a series of wellbeing benefits. Based on analysis of water policy documents in Kenya, the students identified six relevant dimensions of wellbeing that had been improved by the DMM method of water delivery: security of livelihoods, bodily health, water security, safety, empowerment, and community cohesion. The evidence of their research is that new water kiosks installed in the neighbourhood, through this model have generated many positive impacts on the wellbeing of local residents along each of these dimensions (see Table 7.1).

However, at the same time, the students' research indicated that the DMM reproduced a market logic for service delivery, transferring new burdens and responsibilities to local groups who did not have the necessary conditions or resources to cope with them sustainably and equitably. This logic of commodification of water services is possibly viable in contexts where local groups are resourced and well-organized, but can introduce new burdens on more vulnerable residents and localities. For example, decisions about where master meters will be installed are based on feasibility studies driven by criteria of economic viability and potentials for cost-recovery. As a result, residents in lower-income areas of the informal settlements in Kisumu, located away from

Table 7.1 Effects of the DMM on wellbeing

Dimensions	Findings
Security of livelihoods	The DMM offered increased opportunities for income generation through the running of water kiosks and water delivery points, while also reducing water prices (20 Ksh for a 20-litre jerrycan from water vendors reduced to 3 Ksh from kiosks and water points).
Bodily health	The DMM facilitated a reduction in the physical effort required by water fetchers (primarily women and children) and increased consumption of clean water through improved proximity to water points and better affordability.
Water security	Residents felt they could rely on the quantity and quality of water provided through the DMM.
Safety	Personal safety for water operators and consumers is perceived to have improved, particularly for women.
Empowerment	The DMM project has opened new spaces for dialogue between community residents, KIWASCO, and the government.
Community cohesion	Residents thought that DMM activities facilitated new spaces of interaction, improving local networks, and forging bonds of solidarity among residents.

Source: Compiled from Martínez Cure et al., 2013.

main streets, are less likely to be considered for DMM services. Similarly, most water and sanitation facilities are more likely to be located in areas that are more densely populated, wealthier, and beside a road. The costs and risks of installing and maintaining lengthy pipelines makes it unviable for households in more deprived areas of informal settlements to benefit from such models of service delivery (Butcher, 2016; Schwartz and Sanga, 2010).

Thus, the logic of commodification of water services embedded in the DMM resulted in the increased devolution of risks and responsibilities to local communities. From KIWASCO's perspective, a key motivation for the implementation of the DMM was to reduce the costs of water lost from burst pipes or vandalism. However, 'what is made less evident is that this risk does not simply disappear but is rather absorbed by the managing operators, who are responsible for paying back the bulk water fees, regardless of how this is distributed (or not) throughout the neighbourhood' (Butcher, 2016: 15). Community groups find it challenging to keep records of their accounts and to cope with maintenance costs due to, for instance, the theft of the master meter, leakages, bursts, or illegal connections. Furthermore, while the intention of increased privatization was to allow water-users to regulate WSPs, in reality, community groups are unable to exert much influence on KIWASCO practices, and the government authorities do not mediate this relationship. Local communities' lack of bargaining capacity results in the devolution of risks to community groups without the compensatory provision of resources or support, and thus assures great potential benefits for KIWASCO, which is able to tap into a vast informal market with little investment or responsibility.

Community groups have not been passive objects of this commoditization of water services and devolution of risks and responsibilities (Butcher, 2016). Instead, they work to appropriate such processes and establish more empowering sets of relationships. For example, in the informal settlement of Kondele, the tender for the master of operators was awarded to the local neighbourhood planning association, Manyatta Residents Association (MRA). This strategic link between MRA and the DMM resulted in a greater emphasis on equitable distribution of resources than on cost-efficiency and cost-recovery. In addition, as Butcher (2016) has argued, the communities' increased responsibilities for maintenance of water pipes was used by some groups to simultaneously conduct mapping and documentation activities in the settlement. The information collected enhanced the capacity of groups to negotiate further benefits with KIWASCO and other stakeholders.

Although the DMM has the potential to enhance local residents' access to and control of their water services, the lack of management support, unequal distribution of risks, and limited government mediation compromises the effect this model of service delivery could potentially have on the relations governing the distribution of resources in the city. Therefore, the studies by Martínez Cure et al. (2013) and Butcher (2016) argue that this form of public–private partnership promotes a mode of production in the city that commodifies the delivery of, and access to, resources in ways that tend to reproduce inequalities and still leaves the most vulnerable behind. Despite improvements in specific dimensions of wellbeing related to better access to water, 'the model as it currently exists serves as a mechanism to cope with the current system of entitlements, rather than working to contest the unequal distribution of resources and recognition' (Martínez Cure et al., 2013: 34).

Reflections on opportunities

As outlined in the introductory chapter of this book, the distinction between capacities and capabilities is fundamental for the understanding of the capability approach. If we understand capacities as a set of abilities people have to pursue their aspirations (as defined in the previous chapter), the key added value of the capability notion is the incorporation of the conditioning environment shaping these capacities. The conditioning environment is the set of norms, regulations, and processes that enable, expand, or constrain people's capacities to pursue the aspirations they have reason to value. Therefore, capabilities are shaped not just by abilities but also by people's real opportunities to put their capacities to actual use.

These discussions on abilities and opportunities are at the core of Robeyns' definition of conversion factors that 'influence how a person can be or is free to convert the characteristics of the resources into a functioning' (2005: 46). Issues related to social norms and policies are aspects of social conversion factors that stem 'from the society in which one lives, such as public policies, social norms, practices that unfairly discriminate, societal hierarchies, or power relations related to class, gender, race, or caste' (Robeyns 2005:46). However, instead of approaching these issues as simply part of social conversion factors, I argue that it is useful to highlight the importance of opportunities shaping and shaped by people's access to different types of assets. In this sense, the interrogation of opportunities (as norms, procedures, and relationships) is given more visibility and prominence in this application of the capability approach, as it influences the various conversion factors as well as people's aspirations (see Box 6.1 in the previous chapter for a definition of conversion factors).

Furthermore, the research of the DMM in Kisumu highlights that opportunities are shaping conversion factors at different scales: micro, meso, and macro. In the context of this engagement, the micro scale relates to the norms, procedures, and relationships established around the water taps. Some water taps are collectively managed, others are managed by individuals. Some are located next to the main street bordering the settlement, others are within housing compounds and managed by local landlords. These characteristics of location and organizational arrangement shape opportunities by producing particular sets of norms and relationships. At the meso level, there is the network of water pipes and the neighbourhood dynamics affecting the maintenance and operations of the water system. The way that DMM is managed locally has a direct impact on the distribution of opportunities within the settlement, as it affects the distribution of risks, burdens, benefits, and responsibilities. Finally, at the macro level, opportunities relate to the interactions between the system of water delivery at neighbourhood and wider city stakeholders. It highlights the importance of exploring the power dynamics between KIWASCO, local authorities, and neighbourhood associations involved in this process. Figure 7.1 illustrates key components and characteristics of opportunities, as well as examples from reflections about the DMM in Kisumu. The institutional space represents the field of action where opportunities are generated and/or constrained. This space is constituted by the relations of power produced by actors and institutions, policies, and norms as well as processes and procedures.

Much work in critical urban theory unpacks the various ways in which norms, procedures, and processes create differential access to opportunities in the city. The capability approach has a lot to gain from these debates, as they can refine and deepen the way in which the notion of conversion factors can be applied in the interrogation of processes of city-making. In this chapter, I employ four epistemic lenses to provide insights into how the field of critical urban theory has approached the uneven distribution of opportunities in cities (Yap and McFarlane, 2020); these are: urban political economy, urban political ecology, feminist urban theory, and postcolonial urban theory.

An *urban political economy* approach mostly focuses on how norms and procedures of 'an' economy's mode of production, exchange, and capital flows contribute to urban inequalities. This approach, inspired by the various

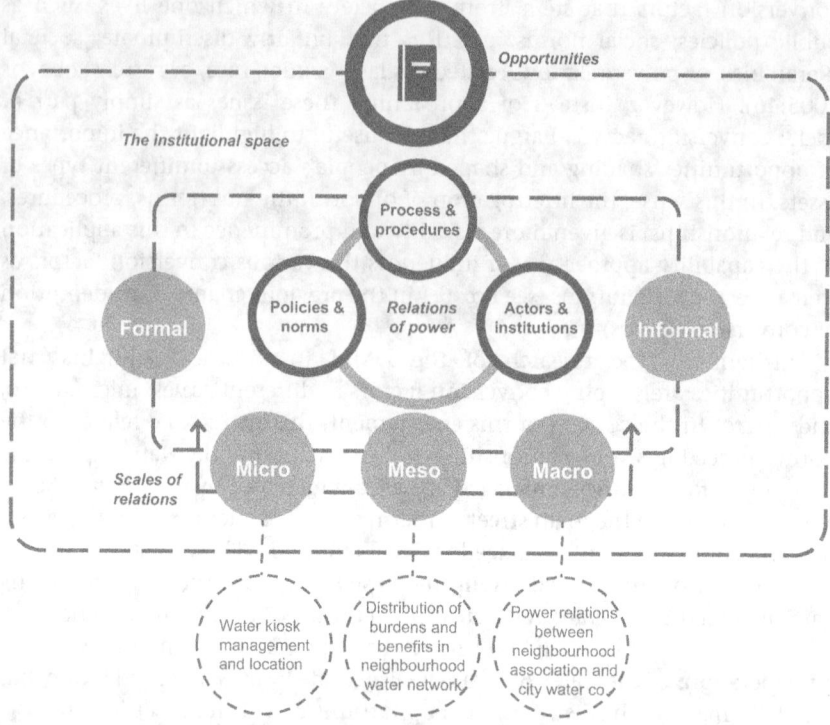

Figure 7.1 Opportunities diagram

works of Harvey (1973; 2008; 2009), is particularly useful for understanding how the operations of capitalist urbanization creates unequal distributions of opportunities in the city. Urban interventions shaped by market-driven ideologies tend to emphasize the expansion of individualistic responses by the poor, leaving wider forces of privatization and speculation unchallenged.

In the field of development planning, there have been useful readings of urban development policy paradigms highlighting the historical tendencies of macro political economy processes to condition urban governance. For example, there are numerous studies investigating the economic, social, and political norms shaping and influencing the urban sector in the global South (e.g. Burgess et al., 1997; Davis, 2006; Jenkins et al., 2007; Zetter and White, 2002; Hamza and Zetter, 2004). These studies have brought to the forefront the role of market enablement in urban governance: shaping policies that increase processes of privatization and investments to attract foreign direct investments, reducing public expenditure on basic services, and limiting universal access to infrastructure. Such an urban political economy perspective explores how multi-scalar processes of capital circulation affect power relations between specific socio-spatial units of governance that result in differential opportunities in cities (Schiller and Çağlar, 2011).

The logic of market enablement has infiltrated the discourse and practice of participation, by approaching it as a means to reduce costs and improve the efficiency of urban services. Participation in urban service delivery has been used as a mechanism to legitimate the rollback of the state (Burgess et al.,1997; Allen, 2013), leading to the 'perverse confluence' of citizen participation and neoliberal governance (Dagnino, 2007). In this context, efforts to improve living conditions in informal settlements through spatially targeted welfare programmes have often led to a series of adverse inclusions. Sen (2000) calls this process 'unfavourable inclusion', and explains:

> Indeed, many problems of deprivation arise from unfavourable terms of inclusion and adverse participation, rather than what can be sensibly seen primarily as a case of exclusion as such. For example, when there are reasons to complain about 'exploitative' conditions of employment, or of deeply 'unequal' terms of social participation, the immediate focus is not on exclusion at all, but on the unfavourable nature of the inclusions involved. (Sen, 2000: 28–29)

An analysis of the types of opportunities generated by the DMM in Kisumu through the lens of political economy highlights some of the risks of these unfavourable inclusions. The DMM practices draw on a series of synergies with the Water Act of 2002, which set the framework for the privatization and decentralization of water services in Kenya. In particular, it resonates with the pro-poor focus added in 2007, outlined in guidelines for the Pro-Poor Implementation for Water Supply and Sanitation. Together with the Urban Areas and City Act (Republic of Kenya, 2011) and the County Government Act (Republic of Kenya, 2012), this created a policy environment that set the tone for the implementation of private–public partnerships, intended to make services delivery in informal settlements cost-efficient. In practice, this led to increased responsibilities for community groups with little devolution of the power to affect decision-making processes. An urban political economy lens would also interrogate the potential risk of increased land prices, stimulated by the investments in infrastructure in the area, resulting in higher rents that push the poorest population out to more marginalized locations, making them more vulnerable to socio-environmental risks.

Box 7.1 Unfavourable inclusion

The notion of unfavourable inclusion has been used by Sen (2000) to explain the perpetuation of injustices that takes place through a process of inclusion in exploitative systems of relations. In the urban development literature, this notion is connected to the debates about the effectiveness of individual titling in advancing security of tenure of informal settlement dwellers. Tenure regularization can take informal settlement dwellers into a property market system that is unfavourable to their security of tenure. This process of unfavourable inclusion can lead to market-driven displacement, caused by gentrification and increased costs of services and taxes that disproportionately affect low-income tenants (Durand-Lasserve, 2006; Payne et al., 2009).

In relation to conversion factors, an urban political economy perspective would highlight two important issues. Firstly, that city-making practices are not isolated from the particular contexts in which they are situated. To understand the kind of opportunities enabled by practices of city-making, the capability approach needs to pay more attention to political economy by exploring more explicitly how socio-institutional and environmental conversion factors are forged locally (Biggeri and Ferrannini, 2014: 45). Not only is it crucial to understand how such logics shape social relations, but also to reflect on the roles that particular city-making practices play in such relations. How are city-making practices contesting or reproducing these logics of the political economy? In the case of Kisumu, what are the implications of the incentives given by the DMM and wider policy environment to enhance the commodification of social relationships, prioritizing financial exchanges over other forms of social or political values?

Urban political ecology is the second epistemic lens to be considered here, and it is 'primarily concerned with the urbanization of capital and nature, and how the entanglements between the two transform relations among bodies, materials, ecologies, economics and politics' (Yap and McFarlane, 2020: 263–264). From this perspective, studies have focused on processes of urbanization by tracing the metabolic circulatory flows of water, waste, energy, bodies, and other processes (Swyngedouw and Heynen, 2003). The norms, procedures, and processes shaping opportunities in the city are revealed through the interrogation of flows and relationships. Urban political ecology brings together analyses from political economy perspectives and the recognition that these are negotiated and shaped by the characteristics of particular ecosystems and materials.

> [C]ities are dense networks of interwoven socio-spatial processes that are simultaneously local and global, human and physical, cultural and organic. The myriad transformations and metabolisms that support and maintain urban life – such as, for example, water, food, computers, or movies – always combine physical and social processes as infinitely interconnected. (Swyngedouw and Heynen, 2003: 899)

This brings up a second key contribution of the urban political ecology perspective, which is its emphasis on the importance of the politics of scale, highlighting how such 'dense networks of interwoven socio-spatial processes' (Swyngedouw and Heynen, 2003: 899) are produced through the interactions of actors, norms, procedures, instruments, and flows operating within and across different scales, from the local to the global. Urban political ecology reminds the capability approach about the importance of interrogating the relationship between nature and society, suggesting that freedom in the city is shaped by the interactions taking place between social and environmental systems that benefit some social groups while generating burdens for others.

In the light of this interest in flows and materialities, urban political ecology approaches have been used to research water practices. Swyngedouw's study of the 'urbanization of water' in Guayaquil has been important, arguing that 'the water problem is not just merely a question of management and technology, but rather, and perhaps in the first instance, a question of social power' (2004: 175). It is fundamentally important to address de-politicized readings of access to water and shift focus to the flows of power embedded in, and reproduced through, water systems.

The case of Kisumu similarly demonstrates that analysing the policies, roles, responsibilities, relationships, and technologies in which the DMM water system is located, reveals the specific power imbalances and spaces of contestation related to it. Complementing an urban political economy perspective, urban political ecology recognizes that power is not only shaped by market relations, but also through interaction with the natural and social environments within which it is located. The notion of conversion factors needs to recognize these particular connections. Urban political ecology would emphasize that the conditioning environment affecting the ways people use particular resources to achieve the aspirations they have reason to value is produced, not by different types of conversion factors (i.e. environmental, political, economic, or social), but by the relationships between them, and the power imbalances produced in such encounters.

In examining forms of power imbalance, *feminist urban theory* illustrates how particular groups of social identities are disproportionately vulnerable to becoming trapped in conditions of poverty, violence, and discrimination in the city (Falú, 2009; Nieves Rico and Segovia, 2017). Feminist urban theory reveals how the various ways urban spaces are conceived, perceived, and lived produce gendered norms and relationships (Matrix, 1984; Weisman, 1992; Massey, 1994; Kern, 2020). This approach has been particularly important in pointing to how productive and reproductive gender roles are replicated through everyday practices in the city, and in urban policy and planning frameworks (e.g. Moser, 1993; McDowell, 1999). The spatiality of gendered norms and relationships has become a focus of research and theory, not only in reference to gender issues but also in relation to understanding norms produced at intersections of different social identities (Beebeejaun, 2017). Such relationships create mal- and misrecognitions in the city, but they can also be powerful sites reconfiguring relationships in more insurgent and emancipatory forms. It is important for the capability perspective to interrogate the uneven distribution of opportunities in the city through the lens of politics of difference (Young, 1990).

In the case of the DMM in Kisumu, a feminist and politics of difference approach can reveal who is bearing the costs and risks of this form of water management, and how that relates to existing inequalities in the city. The DMM works with a differential model of access to water services and most vulnerable groups, and particular marginalized social identities, continue to be excluded from the benefits of this initiative (Butcher, 2016). The model in itself does not challenge gender norms associated with access to and control over services (Butcher, 2016). While the perception of women as household managers allowed them to engage in extra income-generation activities associated with services related to reproductive and community roles (such as operating a water kiosk), this was not translated into wider recognition or power to engage more meaningfully in economically productive or political roles. Butcher draws on an interview with 'Dora', a resident of an informal settlement in Kisumu, to elaborate this point:

> As interpreted by Dora, women's work was legitimated and accepted where tied with reproductive concerns related to the household or community care, while publicly obscured or devalued where related to productive or political roles. She cited, for instance, the fact that even while they are considered 'household managers,' decisions still primarily had to be channelled through the male head of house rather than approaching landlords or other authorities directly (though this process might be made simpler in cases where the landowner was a woman). Reflecting on this, another woman shared her experience on queues at her nearby kiosk, where she perceived men – when they collected water – received preferential treatment on busy mornings. She attributed this to the widespread recognition – espoused by both female and male kiosk operators – that men might be pressed for time before the working day. Querying this logic, she turned to the rest of the group: 'But don't I have jobs to do too?' (2016: 18)

In relation to the concept of conversion factors, feminist urban theory firstly emphasizes the importance of investigating and revealing the types of relationships being produced and incentivized through particular practices of city-making. Secondly, it draws attention to the fact that these relationships are constructed by the ways social identities are perceived, manifested, and lived in particular places. A feminist urban theory perspective would highlight that it is not only access to and control over resources that are conditioned by such social relations but also people's value systems and ideals. The implication for city-making practices interested in advancing human development is that they need to explore how the process of converting practices into achieved functionings addresses roles associated with both particular and intersecting social identities. This form of exploration would help to foster city-making practices that contest discrimination, oppressions, and exclusions, while encouraging more emancipatory relations based on values of recognition, reciprocity, and solidarity.

Finally, *postcolonial urban theory* indicates how colonial legacies infiltrate the norms at work in the production of cities and how these are understood by urban theorists. Neo-colonial urban relations have been reproduced through the hegemonic visions of the relationship between modernity and the city (Roy and Ong, 2011). This is expressed, for example, in the increased commodification and financialization of spatial production, and the dissemination of a particular aesthetic of high-rise modernity in the fantasies of international built-environment consultants invested in notions of smart cities or eco-cities (Watson, 2013). Hegemonic visions of the relationship between modernity and city-making can also be reproduced through efforts of international development initiatives in urban contexts. Robinson explains:

> By urban modernity I mean the cultural experience of contemporary city life, and the associated cultural valorization and celebration of innovation and novelty. And by development, I mean the ambition to improve life in cities, especially for the poorest, along certain policy-informed paths. A political investment in development, and the institutional promotion of development as a way of improving life in poor countries, following Escobar (1995), we can call, 'developmentalism'. These two concepts are closely entwined. Together they work to limit both cultural imaginations of city life and the practices of city planning. For without a strong sense of the creativity of cities, of their 'modernity', the potential for imagining city futures is truncated. (Robinson, 2006: 4)

The lens of postcolonial urban theory has also been used to question the ways that city-making has been understood and represented by urban theorists and practitioners (Yap and McFarlane, 2020; see also Holston, 2008; Chattopadhyay, 2012; Mbembe and Nuttall, 2004; Yiftachel, 2009; Roy, 2009; Roy and Ong, 2011). Similarly, much work in postcolonial theory has crucially highlighted the contestation of hegemonic identities and ideals of modernity through everyday practices of subaltern urbanism (see, for example, Simone, 2004). These studies show that cities are normally conceived, researched, and represented in ways that reinforce a Western and Northern epistemology, compromising recognition of the complex and multifaceted practices through which city-making is taking place. In response to this, *Southern urban theory* questions the ways in which knowledge about cities is being produced and circulated. The postcolonial project in urban studies is about recognizing subaltern knowledges of city-making, produced in geographies with different trajectories of modernization and revealing diverse visions of modernity.

These debates in postcolonial urban theory highlight the importance of interrogating the quality and types of relationships that are reproduced through particular processes of converting practices and resources into achieved functionings. Even if a functioning is being realized, it can, at the same time, feed into power imbalances and narrow hegemonic and exclusionary visions of modernity. In the case of Kisumu, examining the operations of the DMM highlighted how practices can reproduce exclusionary hegemonic identities, but also showed how institutional spaces were opened up for them to be reconfigured. On the one hand, the DMM fed into the ongoing process of commodification of water resources, in which NGOs created a system of subsidization and incentives for setting up new enterprises and so contribute to the privatization of water services. On the other hand, these enterprises have created and deepened relationships among local groups and with government authorities that generated greater recognition of the capacity of informal settlement dwellers to be active partners in processes of planning and management.

This review of different urban theory approaches to exploring understandings of the uneven distribution of opportunities in cities and the reproduction of urban poverty develops the notion of conversion factors in various ways. An urban political economy lens pushes the study of conversion factors to address more explicitly the macro-economic and political tendencies shaping opportunities locally and how local practices respond to them. An urban political ecology perspective provides conceptual and explanatory tools through which to interrogate the interactions between different types of conversion factors, such as personal, social, and environmental factors. Feminist urban theory reminds us that how people experience conversion factors is shaped by socially produced diverse and intersecting identities. And finally, postcolonial urban theory examines conversion factors in the light of the type of city-making opportunities being produced in dominant discourses and in everyday practices. The lens of urban decoloniality calls for the problematization of the underpinning hegemonies and epistemologies being promoted in prevailing practices of city-making.

To conclude: abilities and opportunities together constitute the factors shaping people's capabilities to convert city-making practices into particular human development outcomes. While the concept of abilities addresses people's access to and control over particular assets, that of opportunities highlights the importance of the set of relations embedded in the institutional landscape shaping city-making. The focus on opportunities helps recognize that, under certain conditions, collective and situated practices are capable of contributing to democratizing city-making and enhancing human development values and aspirations. This chapter calls for a rethink of the notion of conversion factors, moving away from positivistic understandings based on the logics of input/output and, instead, approaching these factors as constructivist and relational phenomena that capture complex, historical, and political nuances. In the next chapter I explore the notion of agency and how it helps to navigate and produce opportunities for more capability-centred processes of city-making.

Notes

1. To read more about this engagement with and reflection on the types of partnership established for this field trip, see Boni and Frediani (2020).
2. To access the reports, see the programme website: <https://www.ucl.ac.uk/bartlett/development/programmes/postgraduate/msc-social-development-practice/sdp-overseas-practice-engagement> [accessed 19 May 2021].

CHAPTER 8
Agency: Claiming rights through the occupation of vacant buildings in inner São Paulo, Brazil

Abstract

Ocupação Marconi is an informal occupation of a vacant building in inner-city São Paulo. Local residents have exercised collective action to increase their capacity to shape and influence processes of city-making. The experience of social mobilization and spatial production of this building highlights the role of collective forms of city-making in enabling critical awareness and advancing rights to the city. This chapter examines the experience of Ocupação Marconi in order to interrogate the relationship between city-making and agency. It brings together the capability approach to notions of agency with debates in urban studies and planning on everyday and collective practices of city-making.

Keywords: São Paulo, occupation, agency, conscientization, social production of habitat

Introduction

Across Brazil, despite apparently supportive legislative frameworks (for example, the 2011 city statute) and programmes (such as the national housing programme, Minha Casa Minha Vida), housing for low-income groups is still in short supply and, critically, continues to be characterized by highly skewed social and spatial distribution (Ferreira, 2012; Cardoso, 2013). The peripheralization of the poor in many Brazilian cities remains a well-entrenched phenomenon and is exacerbated by processes of inner-city renewal. São Paulo is no exception. In a context marked by a lack of affordable housing, the number of low-income populations located in peripheral informal settlements and dormitory municipalities has increased disproportionately over the past two decades, accentuating socio-spatial inequalities across the urban region (Kowarick and Marques, 2011; Kohara, 2013). Successive attempts to regenerate declining inner-city districts through a variety of public and privately led initiatives have reinforced this pattern. Such attempts to reclaim the city centre seems to bring São Paulo's experience in line with prevailing international patterns, where urban regeneration reinforces socio-spatial segregation.

Photo 8.1 Residents of Ocupação Marconi in their flat (photograph by Gabriel Boieras)

Since the 1990s, the city centre of São Paulo has been the scene of informal occupations in response to these processes, led by local housing movements. These occupations are understood by their proponents to be means to simultaneously draw attention to, and to question, the logic of commodification of the city, and to affirm the right of the urban poor to remain in well-located areas (Tatagiba et al., 2012; De Carli et al., 2015; Earle, 2017). The São Manoel building, located on Marconi Street in the city centre, is one of several vacant buildings occupied by social movements. The building was occupied in 2012 and has become one of a number of occupations operating under the umbrella of the housing movement called Movimento da Moradia para Todos (MMPT).

The case study in this chapter examines the practices of occupation of vacant buildings in inner-city São Paulo, based on an action-research initiative I was part of in 2014. Through the study of this particular occupation, known as Ocupação Marconi, this case illustrates how residents have enacted and expanded their agency through everyday practices of managing services, engaging in social mobilizations and demonstrations, and attending the civic education activities coordinated in the building. The case explores the potential of occupations to expand capabilities, but also the limitations created by the physical and legal risks experienced by residents.

The concept of agency adopted in the capability approach is explored in relation to its role in deepening democratic practice and in the expansion of personal and collective capabilities. Agency is defined as the ability to reflect critically on one's situation and to act on it; thus, agency has a personal as well as a collective character. Debates about agency in urban studies will be related to a discussion of the role of spatial production and the expansion of agency, and also pay attention to how city-making can play a role in processes of alienation or emancipation.

The case of Ocupação Marconi in São Paulo

The central districts of São Paulo have been sites of contestation between different actors and interests since at least the beginning of the 20th century. In the early 1900s, elite and lower-income groups coexisted in the central area where large-scale infrastructure and office buildings were interspersed with high-density rental units known as *cortiços*. By the 1950s, rapid population growth, inner-city congestion, and car-based urban development pushed real-estate investments towards non-central locations creating new nodes of activity. The emergence of these new centralities reduced the desirability of the inner city for the middle classes, sparking a process of abandonment and deterioration that still continues. Even when real-estate values fell, property owners retained vacant and underutilized buildings in expectation of future redevelopment and increased revenue. In the meantime, several owners also defaulted on property taxes, which triggered a series of legal irregularities and wrangles over ownership. In 2010, 90,000 residential properties were reported empty across municipal São Paulo (Earle, 2012); approximately 40,000 of these were located in the central district (Kohara, 2013). Throughout this process of de-investment, the city centre remained an attractive location for the urban poor due to important advantages in terms of access to public transport, informal and formal livelihood opportunities, cultural activities, and public health and education facilities.

Since the late 1990s, social movements have seen this scenario as an opportunity to advocate for affordable housing options for the urban poor in well-located areas of the city. In São Paulo city centre, there are numerous active social movements including MMPT; Movimento Sem-Teto do Centro (MSTC); and Movimento dos Trabalhadores Sem-Teto (MTST). At times, some of these movements operate in coalitions such as the União dos Movimentos de Moradia de São Paulo (UMM) and the Frente da Luta para Moradia (FLM). These movements use occupations as a means to simultaneously provide housing for low-income people in well-serviced urban areas, point to the contrast with market-led development policies in São Paulo, and contribute to wider struggles for urban reform across Brazil.

Designed as a thirteen-storey office building in the 1930s, and situated in an area well supplied with infrastructure, services, and amenities, Edificio São Manoel had been emptying out since the 1980s; in 2012, the only spaces in use were the shops and bar on the ground floor. Since September 2012, the building has been squatted by MMPT. In 2014, there were about 130 households, totalling approximately 450 people, occupying the building.

Each of the thirteen floors is divided into units of 25 to 30 square metres and almost all services – including toilet facilities – are shared. In addition to the residential spaces, Ocupação Marconi has dedicated common spaces that bring the residents together in different ways. Key among these is Salão Marighella (Marighella Hall), a large meeting room used by the MMPT leadership to hold weekly residents' meetings and internal events, as well as for events open to others. Some of these events are related to the occupation's connections to a larger and complex network of social movements under the auspices of the housing branch of the national social movement network called Central de Movimentos Populares (CMP) which is linked to a range of civil-society and technical support organizations. Salão Marighella is the space for hosting interactions with this extensive network. Residents also collectively run a common kitchen and nursery. There are a number of less organized spaces for encounter, including a laundry room, the building's courtyard, and the stairway. On each floor, the corridors and shared facilities are obvious spaces of interaction and manifestations of the building's collective management.

This chapter draws on previous publications about Ocupação Marconi (De Carli and Frediani, 2016; Frediani et al., 2018a) to outline stories of three residents that illustrate different ways in which everyday practices of using and appropriating the building have had a role in the expansion of their agency. The residents are anonymized and referred to here as Emmanuel, Francisco, and Raquel.

Emmanuel's story mirrors many of the dynamics taking place in inner-city São Paulo. He is a Haitian migrant in his early thirties who lives in the building with his partner and child: at the time of our interview, he had been living in the building for over a year. He left Haiti following the devastating earthquake that hit the island in 2010 and arrived in Brazil after a perilous journey across Central and South America in search of better life opportunities. He is one of thousands of undocumented Haitians who, every year, make the journey to Brazil through the 'jungle route' across Central America, Venezuela, and Peru, entering the country in Acre in the Amazon region. They are able to remain in Brazil on humanitarian visas. During our interview, Emmanuel provided many details about his journey across the continent and the country.

Like many others, Emmanuel did not become involved with the occupation on the grounds of his political views, but rather because of his present needs and aspirations for the future. Since 2013, living in the building has allowed him to have a place to stay in the city; to create new livelihood opportunities, thanks to the proximity to the city's central districts; and to raise his daughter in a safe environment. When talking about the occupation, Emmanuel's sentiments echoed those expressed by many other dwellers during our conversations: the building is a landing place – a place of arrival or an entrance to the city – as well as a platform for creating the social and material conditions for a better future. Emmanuel expressed the hope that he would eventually be able to move out of the building and find a place for himself and his family. But at the same time, he commented on the support and sense of stability that the participating in the occupation generates:

> When one needs anything, people help. A foreigner, when he arrives without work ... if you know how to behave, the occupation is good. If you are quiet, no one will be able to help. But if you say: 'I need a job, if you know people who are looking for workers, let me know,' you will find people here who will say, 'There is a vacancy, if you want to go, I'll give you the address.' And if you have no job, no money, you end up one or two months without paying [the monthly allowance to MMPT], but when you work, you pay. It's like, I tell you, the occupation is like a support.

The various life trajectories of the residents of Ocupação Marconi intersect with each other through the day-to-day maintenance of the material and immaterial infrastructure of the building. Life in Ocupação Marconi is structured with set rules, norms, procedures, and a strict bureaucracy often resembling that of many cohousing communities. As Francisco, one of the coordinators of the occupation, explained during a transect-walk across the building, Ocupação Marconi is entirely managed by its residents, who meet regularly and do most of the work required to maintain the building. Collective tasks focus on door-keeping and security; the routine maintenance of common areas, including waste removal and the cleaning of shared spaces such as hallways, corridors, stairs, and bathroom facilities; the shared management of the communal kitchen and the building's nursery; and routine repairs to all hydraulic and electrical installations. In the first year of the occupation, the building's elected leadership also organized a series of seminars on citizenship education, aimed at developing residents' capacity to navigate their rights and responsibilities, particularly in relation to questions of human rights, housing, and the legal frameworks governing urban development and management in Brazil.

Francisco emphasized that the management of communal spaces and activities is based on principles of communal interest and collective self-governance. Residents are organized in floor-based groups with each floor administered as a semi-independent unit and coordinated by a floor representative like himself. This enables detailed management of the communal toilets and other self-organized services such as garbage collection and cleaning. Francisco pointed out the dedicated notice boards on each floor – with notices often translated into several languages – which provide a means of communication among residents and with the floor representative.

This floor-based system is networked through weekly assemblies of all residents and is coordinated by a building representative who is, in turn, the interface between the building's occupants and MMPT leadership. The relations between Ocupação Marconi and other housing movements in São Paulo are also governed and mediated through a similar structure of nested forms of representation.

It is important to highlight that, notwithstanding the open and communal nature of decision-making in Ocupação Marconi, its representative system has limitations and faces threats. The leadership structure is centralized, hierarchical, and based on a number of vertical control mechanisms that aim to ensure safety and security in the building by compelling observance of the rules of cohabitation and by centrally coordinating action against external threats such as evictions, invasions, and criminal infiltrations. In interviews, some of the residents emphasized the challenges of living within this strict framework of shared norms that govern many aspects of personal everyday life. Francisco, while recognizing the challenges, also argued that the norms are 'necessary for the common good'. For instance, they guarantee safety by prohibiting the consumption of alcohol and drugs in the building; and they distribute costs and burdens more equally by establishing that everyone needs to contribute financially to the maintenance of the communal infrastructure.

> Here, as anywhere, there are rules. Our own statute describes them. Once there are rules, we need to accept them for the common good of all. Imagine if, in an occupation like this, we allowed people inside who are high or drunk, or people who disrespect their families: this place would turn into chaos ... Here we try to get people to understand that we depend on each other. Here it is not possible for people to only focus on their self-interest, because it will not work. So there is no point for people to be isolated and try to solve their problems by themselves, we need to solve them together.

One of the initiators of the occupation and a former building coordinator, Raquel, emphasized two key roles that Ocupação Marconi plays in challenging and reshaping the relationship between housing movements and external actors. In her view, firstly, occupations like Marconi challenge the ongoing stigmatization and criminalization of social movements. The criminalization of social protest, and of building and land occupations specifically, is one of the main priorities for change by social movements at the city-wide level, because it hinders their capacity to mobilize participation and solidarity across the city, and limits their room for manoeuvre in negotiations with both state actors and the private sector. Secondly, occupations demonstrate the disjuncture between, on the one hand, existing progressive policies and planning frameworks that seek to further the right to the city and the social function of property and, on the other, São Paulo's low-income housing deficit and the presence of vacant buildings in the city. By squatting underused and unused buildings, MMPT highlights this disjuncture and illustrates the possibility of creating affordable housing for vulnerable groups in the city's central areas.

Raquel described in detail the building's leadership's numerous initiatives to change public perception of the occupation. One example is the efforts undertaken by residents to contest an eviction lawsuit started by the building's owner a few months after the building was first occupied. On this occasion, residents took pictures of all households living in the building, each in their own home space. Photographs were included as supporting evidence in the submission to the court, in order to make judges aware of the profile of residents and to highlight the vulnerability of occupant households and the role of the occupation in providing shelter for elderly people, single mothers, and children. On a later occasion, the building's leadership organized a collective Sunday breakfast in the street in front of the building, with the objective of introducing residents to their neighbours and to passers-by. The event was filmed by a supporting collective of designers and filmmakers, and the output of this collaboration was made publicly available on a video-sharing website later in the year (MUDA_coletivo, 2013). Similarly, in 2014, the occupation was listed on the website of international couch-surfing network couchsurfing.com under the slogan: 'We offer more than a sofa: a room and a life experience!' These narratives were carefully curated by the leadership and featured by a number of newspapers and websites, allowing residents to reframe their presence in the city as a driver of sustainability and social innovation.

Raquel emphasized that, instead of focusing on antagonistic relations with the state, Ocupação Marconi, MMPT, and CMP together strategically appropriate and re-interpret the formal frameworks of urban rights in Brazil in order to challenge exclusionary patterns of urban development. When we interviewed Raquel and other key MMPT actors, their attention was focused on operationalizing the social function of property as defined by the 2011 city statute, and on the production of alternative modes of housing in inner São Paulo. During a housing demonstration in São Paulo, Raquel elaborated the strategic role that social movements have in setting an agenda and influencing policy and planning:

> This demonstration today was organized by social movements that are active in the inner-city area of São Paulo... Today we intend to walk to the door of the courthouse, and our idea is to ask for a hearing to present the agenda of social movements. What we see are judges who think we are criminals. But no, we want to remind them that we are low-income working families, and we are fighting for a constitutional right. We intend to go to the doors of the town hall as well, because we want the buildings pledged by the government to be finally expropriated and used for social interest. Our concern now is that our achievements in the city centre might end up in the hands of the middle classes that can afford them, and this is what the government has told us. But no, we want housing in the city centre to be intended for social interest. When people go to the street, we show these institutions that our issues are pressing. A family today has to choose: either pay rent, or eat. We will show the government and the judiciary powers that our families need homes now, temporarily in an occupation or as permanent housing. The important issue is that families should live with dignity ... The people

have to mobilize to make the government govern for all, and not only for a minority.

Reflections on agency

These stories of three residents of Ocupação Marconi highlight two main issues relevant to the interrogation of city-making from a capability perspective: firstly, that the process of occupying, managing, and living in Ocupação Marconi has a direct impact on residents' agency; and secondly, the various tensions, synergies, and trade-offs between the expansion of agency and wellbeing residents experience in their everyday life.

For Sen, agency is a fundamental concept that helps to interrogate and expand human freedoms. For development processes to bring about meaningful change, 'the people have to be seen ... as being actively involved – given the opportunity – in shaping their own destiny, and not just as passive recipients of the fruits of cunning development programmes' (Sen, 1999b). In his writings, agency refers to 'what a person can do in line with his or her conception of the good' (Sen, 1985). This places emphasis on the need to not only explore freedom in relation to the opportunities available to people, but also recognize their abilities to make choices and act on them. Agency is closely related to notions of power and control: it is an important lens through which to understand people's power to bring about change and the extent to which they can control the procedures by which choices are made (Alkire, 2013). Agency also relates to

> the ability to define one's goals and act upon them ... it refers to people's capacity to define their own life-choices and to pursue their own goals, even in the face of opposition from others ...While agency tends to be operationalized as 'decision-making' in the social science literature, it can take a number of other forms. It can take the form of bargaining and negotiation, deception and manipulation, subversion and resistance as well as more intangible, cognitive processes of reflection and analysis'. (Kabeer, 1999: 438)

In my work, the expansion of agency is closely associated with a Freirian concept of critical consciousness (or conscientization); that is, becoming aware of the conditions shaping injustices and enhancing people's abilities to respond or address them. Freire argues that a process of conscientization takes place when people recognize that they are not just living *in* the world – their lives are not shaped purely by their contexts – but that consciousness is produced through people understanding that they are living *with* the world, questioning and reconfiguring their relationships with the world. '*Consciousness of* and *action upon* reality are, therefore, inseparable constituents of transforming act by which men become beings of relation' (Freire 1970: 52). Furthermore, Freire highlights the importance of projective thinking – developing alternative

AGENCY: CLAIMING RIGHTS IN SÃO PAULO   113

imaginaries of the future – as a crucial element in disrupting cultures of silence and fostering critical consciousness.

Crocker's work on the capability approach brings these different aspects of agency together, outlining an approach to questions of agency that addresses people's ability to act and critically reflect on their conditions. 'Person[s] are agents to the extent that they are able to scrutinize critically their options, themselves decide (rather than have the decision made by someone else or some external or internal force), act to realize their purposes, and have an impact on the world' (2008: 219–220). Figure 8.1 outlines these main components of agency, referring to reflections from the case of Ocupação Marconi. The facets of agency include collective and personal critical awareness, and the ability to act as well as the action itself.

However, agency does not necessarily relate to the ability to act towards a more equitable, sustainable, or just society. 'Agency can also be exercised

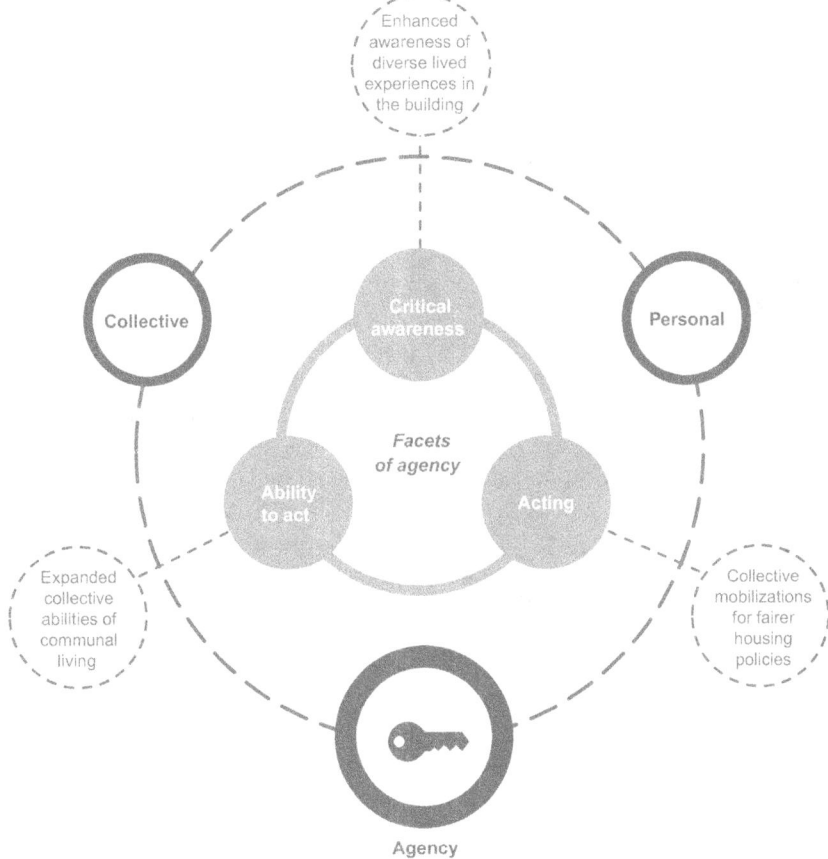

Figure 8.1 Agency diagram

in the more negative sense of "power over", in other words, the capacity of an actor or category of actors to over-ride the agency of others, for instance, through the use of violence, coercion and threat' (Kabeer, 1999: 438). Agency always needs to be interrogated in relation to values associated with the good life and this is the sense in which Sen's work explores the relationship between wellbeing and agency, arguing that freedom and achievements are made of both wellbeing and agency components. People act on the basis of their aspirations for wellbeing, but their actions can also be based on values and commitments that might be counterproductive to the expansion of their wellbeing. 'Sen's empirical concept of agency enables him to claim that people *can* and often *do* act to realize other-regarding goals, even when to do so is disadvantageous to themselves' (Crocker, 2008: 161).

Bayat's critical urban theory perspective has been crucial to the debate about the relationship between agency and everyday practices of city-making. He draws on his experience in Iranian cities to depict everyday forms of urban resistance as 'the quiet encroachment of the ordinary'. Experiences of informal use and appropriation of urban spaces (like Ocupação Marconi) tend to involve collective action by people seeking to make 'steady and significant changes in their own lives' (Bayat, 1997: 56). These silent and patient acts of the urban disenfranchised are mechanisms of redistributing social goods and opportunities in the city. Given the exclusionary aspects of formal procedures and regulations, quiet encroachment of the ordinary also seeks to expand autonomy in ways that make governing arrangements more responsive to urban dwellers' needs and aspirations. The 'street politics' described by Bayat highlights tactics of the urban poor to enhance their ability to affect change through processes of city-making.

As another form of agency, the practices of collective occupation of vacant buildings in inner-city areas of São Paulo can be seen as a 'pedagogy of confrontation' (Barbosa, 2014: 104; see also Freire, 1970). The process of collectively appropriating vacant buildings is a pedagogical experience: the practices of mobilization and direct action generate collective learning and, from this, the possibility of creating new political subjects and alternative imaginaries for urban development. Acts of resistance and confrontation can deepen awareness of the possibilities for resisting injustices in the city, and potentials for bringing about change (Barbosa, 2014). 'The "pedagogy of confrontation" highlights such conflicts as opportunities for the construction of personal as well as collective knowledge, and as a transformative process in which dwellers become subjects of their own knowledge and of political action' (Frediani et al., 2018a: 262). Collective and conflictive practices of city-making expand agency by deepening critical awareness about current living conditions and the possibilities of bringing about transformative change in urban contexts (Barbosa, 2014).

This connection between Freire's pedagogy of the oppressed (1968) and practices of inhabiting the city has also been at the core of the articulation of the notion of the social production of habitat, promoted by members of the civil-society network, Habitat International Coalition. This concept, mostly grounded in Latin American self-help and self-managed housing practices, emphasizes the emancipatory potentials of a collective process of planning, designing, building, and managing housing and habitat.

> Social production of habitat, especially that supported by collective self-managed processes incorporating training, participative responsibility, organization, and active solidarity among the inhabitants, contributes to strengthen community practices, direct democratic exercise, participants' self-esteem, and more vigorous social coexistence. The growth of organized inhabitants' management capacity and their control over habitat production processes; the channelling of resources from savings, credit, and subsidies within the communities in which the actions unfold, and the subsequent strengthening of popular market circuits, contribute in turn to strengthen the economies of individual participants, the neighbourhood community in which they are located, and the popular sectors as a whole. Placing the – collective and individual – human being at the centre of their strategies, work methods, and actions, puts innovative processes in march with profound content and impact toward transformation of reality. (Ortiz, 2003: 40–41)

More recently, feminist approaches to the social production of habitat have highlighted its potential to address gender inequalities in cities. By incorporating notions, discussions, and practices of care within the construction of collective housing processes, many experiences in Latin America have demonstrated how these processes can promote the recognition of social diversity and address gender disparities. The notion of the social production of habitat approaches the design, planning, building, and managing of habitat as sites where social relations are discussed, negotiated, contested, and/or reconfigured, opening up possibilities to expand agency in various ways.

Therefore, this exploration of the relationship between city-making and agency highlights that spatial production has agency, as it has the potential to affect structures shaping human development in cities. Awan et al. make this point by developing the concept of 'spatial agency'. Their work, and the various cases they document, demonstrate how the 'continuous cycle of spatial production' and 'all the people and processes that go into it' can play a role in transforming physical and social structures and bring about empowerment. They argue that spatial agency makes a crucial contribution to the field of architecture: the 'consequences of architecture are of much more significance than the objects of architecture' (2011: 33). Furthermore, the authors recognize those involved in spatial production as spatial agents, and they argue that for them to promote spatial agency, they need to carry out spatial judgements (by empowering social relationships), recognize mutual knowledge (by sharing knowledge and respecting the knowledge of others), and enable critical awareness (by being self-critical and avoiding impositions) (2011: 33).

I would like to conclude this chapter by going back to the stories of Emanuel, Francisco, and Raquel (drawing on the text of De Carli and Frediani, 2016) to outline different ways in which city-making processes can shape people's agency. The story of Emanuel reveals that Ocupação Marconi, like other occupations in the city centre, contains heterogeneous realities where diverse stories and experiences of exclusion and marginalization coexist and interweave. It is these encounters of difference and coexistence that directly affect residents' agency by deepening critical awareness of diverse experiences and struggles for more socially just forms of inhabiting the city. The communal nature of life in the building embodies a 'coexisting heterogeneity' (Massey, 2005: 9). It provides a space for contingent encounters, acting both as an open ground where residents' personal life spheres intersect and influence one another, and as a strict cohabitation framework marked by everyday difficulties generated by the overall state of precarity, the scarcity of resources, the conflictive proximity to neighbours, and the rigid norms governing communal life. Long- and short-term residents portray Ocupação Marconi as both a place of forced coexistence and a shared home; this mix of positive and negative associations generates a form of belonging and, eventually, the emergence of a sense of commonality.

As Emmanuel explained:

> Everyone in the occupation is looking for a future. Even if I do not know very well all the rules, I'm here, too, looking for a future with them, and when we have to go out to the streets [making reference to demonstrations or carrying out other occupations], I go along with them, to participate in all activities.

By participating in the occupation, personal life stories gain presence and meaning in relation to each other, allowing residents to acknowledge similarities and interdependencies. This simultaneity of vulnerabilities and aspirations, now put in relation to one another, becomes visible to both the building's residents and other social actors in the city, and eventually facilitates the emergence of new collective meanings and moments of political becoming.

The story of Francisco highlights how agency is shaped through the collectively produced norms of use and appropriation of space. Across the building, practices of belonging and cooperation are continuously re-invented through the definition of these norms and the negotiation of daily interactions – be it through the sharing of cooking facilities or childcare responsibilities, or the participation in housing rights demonstrations, or engagement with the judicial system to avoid eviction. Despite the obvious difficulties of nurturing principles of horizontality and self-governance under the circumstances of extreme vulnerability that mark the occupation, throughout our interviews, residents mostly acknowledged the necessity and significance of these norms and interactions for the construction of a collective sphere within the building. It is through these activities, and participation in the building's assembly, that residents establish links beyond their personal preoccupations and eventually generate novel forms of political membership and solidarity. This collective process of making norms for the use and appropriation of the building enables the expansion of residents' agency by shaping practices of communal living while directly and indirectly challenging the structures of power that engender exclusion in São Paulo.

And finally, the story of Raquel illustrates how participation in collective forms of production of the city can enhance people's agency by expanding their ability to influence and change policy and planning frameworks. Through a realistic, detailed understanding of the wider legal and policy environment within which they operate, housing movements aim to reveal leaving buildings vacant to be an unlawful practice and a transgression of the city statute (Earle, 2012) while also producing models of housing that better respond to the existing formal definition of citizens' rights and responsibilities. Over the past few years, this process has led to a series of overtures from public authorities, which in some cases have recognized occupations and their residents as key agents in debates on affordable housing in São Paulo. To provide an example of this involvement, representatives from housing movements have been important actors in the Conselho da Cidade – a working group on issues of urban development involving civil-society and state actors. Their engagement has resulted in the introduction of important elements to the strategic plan of the city, including the designation of five occupied buildings as areas for *habitação de interesse social* or housing for public interest. Such recognition of the need for social housing in well-located sites represents significant success: however, the advances do not necessarily recognize the model of housing production underpinning the movements' practices.

Drawing on the case of Ocupação Marconi, this chapter has outlined how personal and collective practices of city-making expand people's agency in three ways: these practices can deepen critical awareness of the conditions and diverse experiences of injustice in cities while, at the same time, fostering imaginaries for more just urban development; they can nurture collective abilities and foster people's capacities to act and shape their lives in the city; and they can strengthen collective bargaining power to influence policy and planning processes.

By bringing together this ecology of spatial practices, it is possible to see Ocupação Marconi as a system of relationships that re-imagined the way spaces are produced in inner-city São Paulo. In the form it took at the time of my study, Ocupação Marconi was not only unlocking agency through spatial practices but was also setting an important precedent by providing an example of a more caring and social economy. Instead of being driven by monetary exchange value, this constellation of spatial practices was driven by need, solidarity, and the desire to make cities more inclusive and democratic. Approaching collective forms of spatial production as a form of resistance and an alternative to market-led economic models has been a key debate in the literature about urban commons (Stavrides, 2016) and commonning (Iaione, 2016; Petrescu, 2017; Petrescu and Gibson, 2017; Petrescu et al., 2020). Further work is needed to bring together and explore the connections between these debates and the capability approach. Conversation between the literature on urban commonning and the capability approach can provide a fertile and complementary contribution to the articulation of more humane and sustainable urban economies.

CHAPTER 9
Trajectories: Pursuing buen vivir through participatory neighbourhood planning in Quito, Ecuador

Abstract

After more than 10 years of social mobilization, the community of Los Pinos living on the outskirts of Quito managed to secure their right to settle in the area and, in so doing, set a precedent for how participatory processes can help to localize the implementation of the Ecuadorian buen vivir (good living) agenda. This chapter deploys the analytical elements introduced in previous chapters to explore the trajectory of the Los Pinos community in achieving security of tenure. This trajectory highlights the role that participatory planning and design methodology can play in enhancing collective agency and promoting capabilities through processes of city-making. Using Sen's concept of cooperative conflict helps to examine capability trajectories in cities and, at the same time, bridge debates between capabilities and planning disciplines.

Keywords: Quito, participatory planning and design, trajectory, cooperative conflict

Introduction

This chapter explores the case study of the Los Pinos neighbourhood, located on the outskirts of Quito, Ecuador. Los Pinos is a peri-urban site on agricultural land owned by the Ministry of Agriculture (MAGAP) in the municipality of Mejia, on the southern edge of Quito. The site is an area of approximately 13 hectares and was previously considered unsuitable for urban use. It was occupied by an 'invasion' in 2006 when over 300 families settled on the plot of unused public land. Instead of building shacks straight away, residents decided to plan the process of occupation. A community development committee, called Comité de Desarrollo Comunitario 'Los Pinos', was set up and representatives were elected to it every two years. A partnership between the community development committee, academics from Universidad Politécnica Salesiana Ecuador, and Architecture Sans Frontières – UK (ASF-UK), produced a set of principles and guidelines for the development of Los Pinos in 2013. The process of developing these principles and guidelines followed ASF-UK's Change by Design (CbD) methodology (Frediani, 2016), which facilitated participatory spatial engagements through different scales

Photo 9.1 Los Pinos resident (photograph by author)

(dwelling, community, city) and stages (diagnosis, dreaming, developing, and defining) of community action-planning. The participatory planning process aimed to help the Los Pinos development committee coordinate the development of the settlement and to provide an instrument to argue for security of tenure and other social and physical benefits to be provided by the state and other potential partners.

As a result of the long-term mobilization of the community, and the socio-technical support they received, local residents gained the right to settle in the area. The experience of Los Pinos represents the trajectory of a very diverse community which managed to build alliances and partnerships that led to the securing of tenure and an international award for innovative practices for the social production of habitat. In addition, it sets a precedent for how to democratize the production of spaces in Quito, and how to support the implementation of national and local development agendas.

This chapter examines this case, and the participatory planning and design process that was implemented, using the analytical components articulated in the previous chapters. While the concept of trajectories has not yet been explicitly addressed by the capability approach, it is a useful notion for exploring the connections between the different analytical elements presented in this book. The concept also supports more explicit engagement with the role of time in the negotiation of capabilities. In this chapter, the case study and academic debates are drawn on to identify capability trajectories in cities, and the role that participatory spatial methodologies can have in revealing and supporting them. Through the concept of capability trajectories,

I utilize the notions of the capability approach articulated previously in this book to engage in projective thinking and planning. I argue that the notion of cooperative conflict, developed by Sen to describe power relations within households, is key to unlocking the potential of the capability approach to influence planning practice.

The case of the trajectory of Los Pinos for securing tenure

The use of the ASF-UK CbD process in Los Pinos was underpinned by a desire to interrogate spatial processes and imaginaries while acknowledging three main concerns: 1) the diversity of interests and identities of local communities; 2) the asymmetries of power between stakeholders in the process of consolidating the settlement; 3) and the need to unpack issues associated with the different scales of urban development. To address such concerns, the participatory planning and design workshop was developed in partnership with the Los Pinos development committee and lecturers from Universidad Politécnica Salesiana who provided socio-technical support to the local community. The workshop focused on the urban experience, identifying links between local processes and wider issues associated with urban trends. Activities during the workshop included a series of participatory spatial action-research and visioning exercises as well as design charrettes involving workshop participants, local residents, and key informants. This chapter draws on findings from this workshop (outlined in Frediani et al., 2013).

Throughout the activities and discussions of the workshop, diagnoses were aimed at moving from merely describing the manifestation of injustices towards reflections that addressed trends and processes driving current living conditions. The workshop documented key **structural drivers** that affected the urban trajectory of the Los Pinos community, and highlighted that struggles for housing rights in Ecuadorian cities are part of a crucial wider concern to address human development in the country. In 2012, it was estimated that 36 per cent of Ecuadorian households were living in physically inadequate housing, and more than half of the country's households lacked adequate access to water, sewage, and electricity (Alova and Burgess, 2017). These inadequate conditions are particularly concentrated in urban areas: nearly 70 per cent of the national population lives in cities, and 35 per cent of the Ecuadorian urban population lives in informal settlements (UN, 2015).

In the case of Quito, urbanization has meant not only the arrival of a new urban population from rural areas, but also the displacement of the poor from central areas of the city to the outskirts and surrounding municipalities. This process of peripheralization has been led by a system of urban governance that has privileged capital accumulation over following an agenda of urban equality and distribution of opportunities in the city. At the time of the ASF-UK workshop (2013), the Municipality of Quito was promoting large-scale infrastructure projects (such as a new airport and underground) which have enabled land speculation that has contributed to inner-city Quito becoming unaffordable for low-income groups and deepened the city's socio-spatial segregation. This market-led approach to municipal governance meant that Quito's municipality preferred to push the low-income groups from central areas of the city towards neighbouring municipalities, rather than deal with the need to provide them with access to services. As a result, between 1994 and 2012, the historical city centre of Quito lost 41 per cent of its population, and these residents had to settle in areas with poorer access to collective infrastructure and facilities (Carrión and Erazo Espinosa, 2012).

This context has been a major structural driver shaping the trajectories of the Los Pinos community. Of the 300 families involved in the initial occupation of the site in 2006, 62 were living in the area in 2013 and 178 were associated with the Los Pinos development committee. These families came from inner-city areas of Quito, as well as several other provinces of the country. As a result, the Los Pinos community was quite ethnically diverse. A study of the initial 300 families shows that 81.6 per cent self-identified as *mestizo* (mixed), 12.6 per cent as indigenous, 3.5 per cent as of African descent, and 2.3 per cent as *montubio* (from the countryside of coastal Ecuador) (Chicaiza, 2016). Los Pinos was a refuge for those who could not afford to live in Quito and also a site of arrival for newcomers from other provinces. The housing trajectory of those coming from Quito confirmed a wider pattern of peripheralization. Many of those taking part in the participatory planning and design workshop declared that they had moved to Los Pinos in search of 'improved overall "life stability" and security of tenure; decreased living costs and the possibility to invest their income in different ways other than rental payments [US$40–120 per household]; and healthier living conditions' (Frediani et al., 2013: 70).

This process of urbanization has also affected environmental sustainability in the surrounding Pichincha province. Los Pinos is situated near the Pichincha and Atacazo volcanoes. These hills cut through Quito, stretching into municipalities on its northern and southern borders. The consolidation of settlements in hills located in the inner city, combined with the intensification of urbanization on the hillsides in the northern and southern parts of the city, has meant that many natural creeks have been polluted or closed down. This has generated a series of environmental risks, such as the loss of biodiversity and increased risk of flooding and landslides. Los Pinos is particularly exposed to environmental threats from current urbanization trends since it is located at the foot of the Pichincha hills.

But Ecuador's Good Living National Plan (Plan Nacional para el Buen Vivir) 2009–2013 (SENPLADES, 2013) had advocated a very different model of governance and development. Drawing on notions and aspirations that emerged within indigenous social movements, the national development plan was based on the 2008 Constitution (República del Ecuador, 2008), which set seven key objectives:

> improvement in the quality of life; a just, democratic, productive and solidarity-based economic system with equal distribution of development benefits and dignified and stable work; the promotion

of participation and social control including equitable representation of diverse identities in all areas of public power; the recuperation and conservation of nature and the maintenance of a sane and sustainable environment guaranteeing equal access; the guarantee of national sovereignty and Latin American integration; the promotion of an equitable, balanced, and articulated territorial ordering; and the protection and promotion of cultural diversity, social memory, and cultural patrimony. (Walsh, 2010: 19)

While the plan opened up substantial scope to redirect development away from a preoccupation with economic growth per se, and towards a more socially and environmentally just pathway, 'there remain serious shortcomings in term of its impact at the local level' (Prada-Trigo, 2017). The Los Pinos workshop revealed that this process produced by the tension between a dominant market approach to urban governance and a national plan focused on ideals of *buen vivir*, and underpinned by uneven distribution of environmental risks – has been a key structural driver shaping the trajectory of the Los Pinos community.

After this initial diagnosis, activities focused on the production of design principles based on the **aspirations** of local residents. In this 'dreaming stage' of the ASF-UK CbD methodology, it is important to position the debate about aspirations in the context of critical engagement with current conditions and urban trends. The search for spatial principles aims to establish a bridge between the wider processes of urban change and the everyday manifestations of, and meanings expressed in and by, the production of space. In Quito, the articulation of spatial imaginaries for the site of Los Pinos emerged out of the values associated with different scales (dwelling, community, and city) and policy and planning processes. Local residents and activists were interested in linking localized spatial imaginaries to the broad development agenda of *buen vivir*. Thus, activities aimed to capture and reveal principles associated with the spaces of *buen vivir* in the city. Table 9.1 shows the integrated principles and how they relate to the principles emerging from consideration of each scale.

Some important reflections on the relationship between aspirations and space arose from the workshop in Los Pinos.

First, it is interesting to note that, while activities were focused on the spatial imaginaries of the territory of Los Pinos, issues discussed were not associated with that space only but concerned with the broader municipality/region in which the community is located, and with wider processes of urbanization. The focus on aspirations opened up the possibility of a dialogue that engaged with multiple scales. This was particularly relevant in the discussions of responsible management of natural resources, for example, which involved wider consideration of the management of watersheds and creeks, and preservation of the Pichincha ecosystem.

Secondly, the activities generated a set of contextualized aspirations which were in line with the broad visions of *buen vivir* and other relevant policies.

Table 9.1 Planning and design principles

Integrated principles	Dwelling	Community	City	Policy and planning
Promote socially inclusive processes			Participation in the improvement of environmental conditions	Adaptable processes and products
Articulate relations with external actors			Reinforce existing knowledge networks; increase relations among neighbourhoods	Reinforce existing networks
Strengthen community organization				Strengthen the organizational structures of the community
Inclusive design of the built environment	Respond to cultural diversity through multiple housing typologies	Accessible design of the neighbourhood	Integrate urban and rural agendas	Equitable spatial opportunities
Right of permanence	Provide the freedom to expand and adapt according to changing needs	Ability to maintain proximity to family and social networks	Short- and long-term stability in space	Security of tenure
Respond to generational changes			Intergenerational solidarity	Intergenerational equity
Economic security	Housing affordability in the short and long term	Creation of economic opportunities in community spaces	Increase income-generating opportunities	Integrated development; secure and sustainable provision of services
Live according to one's possibilities		Utilize available resources to their full potential		
Basic qualities for dignified housing	Allow the opportunity for independent housing environments; provide quality and comfort for a dignified way of life	Adequate response to the conditions of the locality; ability to maintain proximity to family and social networks		Strengthen the community's capacity to resist shocks, stresses, and exclusionary trends
Access to dignified public services			Equitable access to the city	Dignified quality of spaces and services
Adequate balance between rural and urban lifestyles	Provide an appropriate balance between urban and rural conditions	Appropriate balance between urban and rural conditions	Live in an urban–rural area	
Responsible management of natural resources		Sustainable design of infrastructure and neighbourhood; equal access to resources in the community	Inhabiting a healthy environment enabling healthy lifestyles	

Source: Adapted from Frediani et al., 2013: 88–89.

For example, in the Good Living National Plan (2013–2017), Objective 1 is to 'consolidate democratic governance and construct the people's power'. The plan states that to achieving this objective requires the country to 'consolidate democratic, effective institutions, lend vitality to citizen mobilization, stimulate to social organization, and keep the constitutional power alive, which is the basis of the people's sovereignty' (SENPLADES, 2013). The aspirations of the residents of Los Pinos are precisely to act on such an objective by promoting socially inclusive processes and strengthening community organization focused on territorial development. A second key overlap between the national plan and the aspirations of the members of the Los Pinos community is a preoccupation with the connections between urban and rural lifestyles. The national development plan aims to guarantee *buen vivir* and 'overcome social and territorial inequalities, with harmony between rural and urban settings' (SENPLADES, 2013: 56). Los Pinos residents saw it as important to address this issue by securing adequate balance between rural and urban lifestyles, precisely because of their diverse lifestyles and aspirations. The participatory process was a fundamental support for the community's recognition of such differences in lifestyles, allowing them to generate a shared commitment to foster norms and practices responding to multiple aspirations.

After the stages of diagnosis and dreaming, the ASF-UK CbD methodology enters a 'developing stage' which documents and co-designs a set of **city-making practices**. Unlike many other informal settlement dwellers, Los Pinos community members initially took a strong position against densification as they did not want to duplicate inadequate living conditions. New houses were built gradually, alongside the slow upgrading of services, and this opened up possibilities for deeper and wider conversations about different choices for the future of the site. During the CbD workshop, options identified and discussed were associated with several issues, such as housing typologies, land tenure, services, and connections to the surrounding neighbourhoods and Quito. Many social diversity issues started to become apparent from the way people were currently building their dwellings on the site as well as from their future aspirations. For example, some residents highlighted the importance of having an outside kitchen and sufficient land for cultivation and livestock. Other residents articulated an aspiration for a more densified settlement composed of detached houses with foundations sufficient to allow adding upper storeys in future (which would enable commercial use of the ground-floor level). The process also revealed diverse sets of current and potential forms of land ownership and management, including different levels and combinations associated with individual and collective forms of ownership and management. These underpinning differences in lifestyles led to a series of internal tensions, which manifested in disputes over the leadership of the Los Pinos development committee.

> Most participants portrayed their 'dream' Los Pinos as an urban neighbourhood characterized by a large amount of green space for

> leisure, gardening and family agriculture. Yet a key topic of dispute concerned the presence of livestock, cattle, sheep, and particularly pigs, revealing a key cultural contrast within the neighbourhood. The presence of the animals is perceived as a resource by some, and as a potential source of disease and aesthetic of rural poverty by others. As a consequence, residents who opposed the presence of livestock concluded that these particular activities should not be left to individual initiative, but rather regulated by the community as a whole. (Frediani et al., 2013: 78)

A further series of options for communal spaces were discussed including, for example, the improvement of the football pitch, neighbourhood community centre, and sites for urban agriculture.

At the city scale, residents suggested practices to improve links and connections between Los Pinos and surrounding communities. They suggested small physical interventions, such as the introduction of smoother road surfaces, as well as more strategic projects to open and share vital community spaces (such as the football pitch). Residents also suggested some key recreational spaces that could be located outside Los Pinos' boundaries. The city-scale exercises generated demands for interventions that went beyond the scope of the settlement and its surrounding communities and required improving access to infrastructure and services and environmental management at a metropolitan level. For example, residents articulated the need for an integrated and affordable system of transport between Quito and its surrounding municipalities. And discussions on environmental management focused on the need to approach the preservation of creeks as part of a wider network of green corridors across the foothills of the Pichincha and Atacazo volcanoes. (For more on the city scale of the ASF-UK CbD methodology, see De Carli and Frediani, 2021.)

With ASF-UK CbD methodology, these sets of city-making practices are brought together in a community action-planning exercise – a portfolio of options – in which options are discussed and negotiated in relation to aspirations collectively developed during the diagnosis and dreaming stages. Through debates elicited by negotiations over specific design and planning options, this exercise is approached not as mediation or resolution of conflicts but rather as a mechanism to discuss trade-offs, priorities, differences, and values. As Till (2005) also argues, the focus on options enables design to move away from a problem-solving approach towards one that addresses the process of making sense of realities: 'If form-giving is understood more deeply as an activity of making sense together, designing may then be situated in a social world where meaning, though often multiple, ambiguous and conflicting, is nevertheless a perpetual practical accomplishment' (Forester, 1985: 14).

The portfolio of options exercise has the fundamental objective of revealing and discussing the conditions that would enable or disable city-making practices to fulfil valued aspirations. In other words, the developing stage of the methodology requires an engagement with the **abilities** and **opportunities** people have to pursue their valued aspirations.

In the context of Los Pinos, the policy and planning analysis revealed an opportunity space shaped by openings and challenges. Through the use of the 'web of institutionalization' analysis tool (Levy, 1996), interviews with community members and representatives, and key stakeholder informants led to the identification of opportunities and the abilities needed to leverage these opportunities. One of these findings related to the process of securing tenure and illustrated the connections between opportunities and abilities shaping the community's freedom to achieve their valued aspirations. During the workshop, MAGAP, as landowners, committed to providing residents with security of tenure on the condition that a land-management plan was developed. This was seen by the community as an opportunity to produce a development plan in a participatory manner and to advocate a more responsive and collective form of housing production. In the long term, if achieved, this could be an important precedent demonstrating how participatory forms of city-making can open up opportunities to implement the *buen vivir* agenda and facilitate access to rights to the city. However, the need to produce a land-management plan put a heavy burden on the community to mobilize and acquire the necessary political, social, and human assets. For example, supporting such a process needed strong partnership with the municipal government of Mejia because the regularization of Los Pinos could be perceived as encouragement for future occupations of vacant land, and the municipality's acceptance of responsibility for the housing problems generated by Quito Municipality's urban development patterns. It also required access to affordable and socially sensitive technical skills so the land-management plan developed both met official land-use planning regulations and also responded to the participatory efforts of the community. Furthermore, it required building and drawing on social assets to bring the community together, rather than intensifying existing divisions and tensions in the community.

Throughout this long-term trajectory of social mobilization and grassroots-led city-making, the Los Pinos development committee has been able to expand their **agency** to advance their aspiration for the right of permanence. Alliances with political representatives from the provincial government guaranteed the political commitment of the municipality of Mejia. Continuous collaboration with Universidad Politécnica Salesiana lecturers and students, and the participatory planning process led by ASF-UK, facilitated the development of a set of principles and guidelines to address diverse needs and aspirations. These principles were extremely important in enabling the planning process to respond to some of the internal tensions while producing a document that illustrated methods for facilitating participatory city-making processes to advance the *buen vivir* agenda. In addition, the community used their collective savings to hire an architect (registered to produce official land-management plans) to develop a technical report based on the results of the participatory planning process that would meet the requirements of MAGAP and the municipality of Mejia's land-use regulations. In 2015, MAGAP transferred the ownership of the Los Pinos land to the municipality of Mejia, which is expected to transfer ownership of the land to the Los Pinos development committee in due course. This achievement was recognized by the award of the 2017 Social Production of Habitat Award, given by the international CoHabitat network to recognize inspiring community-driven habitat solutions.[1]

While the participatory planning process has contributed to the expansion of agency to affect change related to the local scale, addressing issues related to the wider city scale has been more challenging. For example, the aspiration to promote better responsible management of natural resources requires metropolitan action to address the environmental and social effects of the current mode of urbanization and peripheralization, in which the settlements in the foothills of the Pichincha and Atacazo mountains are being developed.

Another example of the need for wider and strategic collective action was around the demands for the Ministry of Housing and Urban Development (MIDUVI) to develop housing programmes based on collective forms of housing production and management. The participatory planning process highlighted that government initiatives provide incentives for the delivery of housing to be carried out through subsidies and loans to individual households while, at the same time, creating conditions for large-scale private developers to engage in the production of low-income housing. This approach does not create the necessary mechanisms for communities to access a variety of the assets crucial for the implementation of collective forms of housing production, such as support in the formation and running of local groups and collectives, access to collective forms of financing or land management and ownerships, and access to meaningful technical and social assistance. MIDUVI is reproducing a market-driven approach to housing production that is not in line with national *buen vivir* development principles (Frediani et al., 2013). It is approaching housing purely as a commodity, rather than as a right and a process through which capabilities are negotiated and produced. However, addressing this gap, which is crucial to advancing the Los Pinos aspirations to promote socially inclusive processes and strengthen community organization through neighbourhood development, requires alliances and actions involving a network of stakeholders.

The initial objective of this participatory planning process was defined with the Confederación Nacional de Barrios del Ecuador (Confederation of Neighbourhoods of Ecuador) and aimed at addressing some of these city dynamics. The Los Pinos experience was to enhance collective agency by setting a precedent for participatory implementation of the *buen vivir* agenda which could be replicated to other localities. But, through the participatory planning process, it became clear that precedent-setting for more participatory process of developing local plans was not enough to address city-wide dynamics. These precedents run the risk of not directly challenging projects driving peripheralization and unequal forms of urban development, such as the new underground system (proposed for the inner city at the time of the workshop). To address the aspirations of Los Pinos residents it was necessary to expand collective agency to influence planning processes, policy, and programmes having city-wide impacts, and the market-driven approach of the national government's housing policy. (For a more detailed reflection about the city-wide impacts of this participatory process in Los Pinos, see De Carli and Frediani, 2021.) The experience in Los Pinos illustrates that, for city-making to foster human development, there is a fundamental need for participatory processes to promote forms of agency that can affect not only local but also wider structural processes of urban development.

Reflections on trajectories

The case of Los Pinos illustrates how the capability approach can be applied to make sense of and inform trajectories of city-making. Figure 9.1 summarizes the trajectory of Los Pinos, explained through the elements of the capability approach.

This case also highlights that the relationship between city-making and capabilities is being constantly negotiated and shaped by the conditions of urban development. In this sense, the agency of collectives such as the Los Pinos development committee to bring about meaningful change in the city is shaped by various factors influencing their bargaining power. This relational approach to city-making is at the core of conceptions of communicative planning theory (e.g. Forester, 1999; Innes, 1995); the just city approach (e.g. Fainstein, 2011); and approaches focused on issues of cultural differences and recognition of diversities (e.g. Sandercock, 1998). These collaborative understandings of planning have emerged as responses to the growing

Figure 9.1 Trajectory diagram

number of challenges for democratic governance of urban development and as proposals for normative approaches that can address the reproduction of urban inequalities and injustices. Collaborative planning emphasizes the unquestionable limitations of existing positivist, centralized, and (usually) top-down planning tools, through approaches that give 'priority to the process through which decisions are made and stresses the significance of undistorted speech, [allowing] the relation of group identities and the explicit recognition of difference ... to define a desirable set of social relations' (Fainstein, 1999: 259–260).

The current critiques of collaborative planning theory point to its limitations which are 'due to [their] inability to re-negotiate power imbalances in the planning processes and to provide responses to urban challenges in extremely unequal urban contexts' (Frediani and Cociña 2019: 144). Collaborative planning efforts have been criticized for prioritizing local actions, potentially leaving structural processes unchallenged. 'There is a tendency in some of the communicative literature to privilege communication at the expense of its wider social and economic contexts' (Huxley and Yiftachel, 2000: 333). These critiques also point to the tendency for collaborative planning approaches to focus on consensus-building, while obscuring social complexities and leading to limited recognition of social diversity.

> [D]ecades of professional planning practice that advocates inclusion through participation have shown that its conception within liberal ideals obscures, and at best is unable to address, complex layers of conflict, oppressive power, and imposition ... Inclusive planning through citizen participation has, indeed, often served as an alibi for elitist, private-sector-driven decision, or as cheat compensation for state withdrawal from public and social services. (Miraftab, 2018: 277)

Notions such as insurgent planning (Miraftab, 2009), post-collaborative planning (Brownill and Parker, 2010), movement-initiated co-production (Watson, 2014), participation as political (Legacy, 2017) and agonistic practices (Gunder, 2003; Mouat et al., 2013; Yamamoto, 2016; Thorpe, 2017) are examples of approaches that respond to these critiques and deepen the relational approach to planning, engaging with issues of power, conflict, and productive tensions. Conflict in planning is not seen as synonymous with violent confrontation, but 'as a constitutive element of social relations and as a source of their strength and ability to innovate' (Gualini, 2015). Conflict 'is neither physical nor violent, but a friction that emerges on a content and production level, a conflict played out within the remit of the democratic arena' (Miessen, 2010: 101).

Concerns with acts of cooperation and conflict that are at the core of current debates about planning resonate with the notion of cooperative conflict that Sen articulated to explore gender relations within households. He argues that analyses of family poverty that do not take into account gender relations can be 'misleading in terms of both causation and consequences' and calls for an analysis of the gender dynamics within households, seeing them as resources and opportunities that can be distributed unevenly between household members. He reflects on the bargaining processes among household members, recognizing the conditions shaping the agency of women when engaging in such negotiations. Importantly, Sen's work recognizes the complexities of the trade-offs taking place within household: the gains that can be made on the one hand, and the compromises on the other. Cooperative conflict acknowledges the delicate and constant trade-offs embedded in household relationships of oppression and liberation (Sen, 1990).

From a planning perspective, Sen's concept of cooperative conflict is important for two reasons. Firstly, Sen makes a spatial point by arguing that bargaining within the household needs to be analysed.

> Conflicts of interest between men and women are unlike other conflicts, such as class conflicts. A worker and a capitalist do not typically live together under the same roof – sharing concerns and experiences and acting jointly. This aspect of 'togetherness' gives the gender conflict some very special characteristics. (Sen, 1990: 147)

Secondly, Sen's focus on acts of cooperation and conflict develops an analytical lens that does not necessarily explain conditions and situations but does examine people's trajectories. The notion of cooperative conflict explains how collective decisions are being made, how priorities are valued, and how social norms shape the conditions of decision-making processes. In this way, cooperative conflict can be a conceptual entry point for using Sen's work to not only develop a framework for evaluating people's wellbeing but also to feed into discussions on projective thinking and practice associated with the field of planning.

Sen (1990: 147) calls for an understanding of bargaining processes, taking into account three key influences: '1) the respective wellbeing levels in the case of breakdown of cooperation ... 2) the perception (including illusions) about personal interests in a family setting, and 3) the perception of "contributions" made respectively by different members and the "claims" arising from these contributions'.

Box 9.1 Cooperative conflict

Cooperative conflict is a concept used by Amartya Sen (1990) to explore gender relations within households. The concept describes gender-based bargaining processes among household members, shedding light on the nature and consequences of trade-offs associated with the acts of cooperation and conflict. This notion of cooperative conflict makes an important contribution to gender studies and feminist economics, as it portrays women affected by intra-household oppressions not as passive household members, but as careful agents considering when and how to contest power asymmetries, given their room for manoeuvre and the potential consequences of their acts.

The first influence refers to who bears the cost of a breakdown of cooperation. As women are more likely to suffer (including physically) from the breakdown of cooperation, they have less bargaining power. It is possible to argue that similar influences affect bargaining processes taking place at other scales of negotiation in the city. The breakdown position in conflicts over land can mean forced evictions and state violence towards marginalized urban groups that may even result in the loss of lives, as in the case of Lagos (see Chapter 3).

The second influence refers to perceptions of personal interests. 'A person would get a worse collusive solution if his or her perceived interest takes little notice of his or her wellbeing' (Sen, 1990: 136). Sen here is alluding to collaborations that mis-recognize the interest of more marginalized groups and do not take into account their wellbeing motivations; these will tend to result in unfair outcomes. Stigmas and prejudices can influence bargaining processes and, if solutions are driven by prejudices rather than wellbeing outcomes, the result will tend to favour more powerful actors (Sen, 1990). In a similar fashion, dominant groups in urban conflicts tend to criminalize informal practices of the poor, arguing the practices are driven by opportunism, by those who do not want to contribute to the state's revenue, or by criminal organizations exploiting the poor for their own financial interests. Los Pinos residents and the occupants of the São Manoel building in São Paulo (Chapter 8) constantly experience this type of threat. For both communities, it was crucial that collective action involved an attempt to change misperceptions of the interests associated with the act of occupation.

The third key factor influencing a bargaining process is perceptions of the contributions made by different household members and the claims that originate from them (Sen, 1990). Women's contributions to the household economy are often substantially and systematically under-recognized, and this results in men having more favourable outcomes in negotiations A similar type of influence can be seen to affect bargaining processes at a wider urban scale. Many arguments favouring evictions and displacement of the urban poor are based on financial logic, arguing that attracting investment for large-scale developments would generate greater overall benefits for the city than the 'potential' risks of displacement they cause to local communities. Many scholars and activists have argued that this type of cost–benefit analysis does not recognize the depth and variety of contributions that lower-income neighbourhoods make to the overall economy and development of the city, nor does it capture the negative impacts of displacement. From Sen's perspective, this lack of recognition of the contribution of the urban poor to overall urban development would be a crucial factor compromising their bargaining power in situations where they are under threat of eviction and displacement as a result of large-scale developments, as in Quito. In response, many international studies have documented the contributions of the poor, revealing how the informal economy contributes to municipal revenues; how waste picking and recycling contribute to wider urban sustainability; and how urban agriculture by the poor safeguards important flood plains, reducing risks of flooding and making cities more resilient.

There is a lot more work to be done in applying the notion of cooperative conflict to the bargaining processes taking place at different urban scales. In future work, it would be important to explore how the three influences outlined above are conditioned by intersecting social identities experienced at different urban scales. For example, in Los Pinos, women's ethnicity, economic condition, and marital status were key factors influencing their bargaining power and ability to participate in various processes of collective action. A more substantial use of the notion of cooperative conflict would require an examination of such intersections and how they are embedded in and affect planning processes.

This chapter aimed to demonstrate the potential of Sen's writing in discussions about collaborative and agonistic planning. The notion of cooperative conflict illustrates Sen's approach to agency, recognizing the oppressive conditions within which bargaining processes take place while at the same time appreciating the ability of marginalized groups to navigate ways through and around these conditions. Cooperative conflict recognizes that grassroots practices constantly balance the tension between collusion and breakdown, are constantly driven by efforts of collaboration and agonism, and are conditioned by social and political contexts as well as strategic and tactical intentions. In different geographies and in different times, trade-offs will be negotiated in a variety of ways because a breakdown position will have particular risks in a particular place at a particular time. For planning practice and theory, the central question is not the choice between collaborative or agonistic planning but rather what capabilities people and groups have to navigate trajectories through collaboration and conflict.

Note

1. For more information on the award, see <https://psh.urbamonde.org/#/en/community/223> [accessed 19 May 2021].

CHAPTER 10
Learning: Expanding capabilities through knowledge co-production about city-making in Freetown, Sierra Leone

Abstract

Since 2016, the Sierra Leone Urban Research Centre (SLURC) has been running a series of research and capability development activities aimed at improving the wellbeing of residents living in informal settlements in Freetown. The core of SLURC's strategy is to focus on learning as a means of expanding the agency and capabilities of people living informal settlements while, at the same time, researching factors contributing to their wellbeing. This chapter explores how the capability approach has been applied in this situation as a heuristic device to enable learning and to facilitate collective and situated approaches to city-making. This book concludes by identifying ways to continue advancing the idea of cities as engines of human development.

Keywords: Freetown, institutional capabilities, learning, heuristic device

Introduction

In 2016 the Sierra Leone Urban Research Centre (SLURC) was established with the objective of engaging with the growing urban development challenges in Sierra Leone by undertaking a series of research, capacity-building, and advocacy activities. SLURC was founded as a result of a partnership between the Institute of Geography and Development Studies (IGDS) of Njala University and the Bartlett Development Planning Unit (DPU) of University College London. Since then, SLURC has carried out activities focused on the areas of urban health, urban livelihoods and city economies, land and housing, urban vulnerability and resilience, and urban mobility. Since 2019, SLURC has been operating as an autonomous entity, running a variety of research projects in partnership with community groups from informal settlements, NGOs, and government authorities.

At its second national conference in July 2019, SLURC's influence was recognized by the mayor of Freetown, Yvonne Aki-Sawyerr, who publicly acknowledged the importance of the centre's work in directly informing the implementation of the Freetown city council's Transform Freetown framework. Dr Alphajoh Cham of the national Ministry of Lands and Country Planning highlighted the key role that SLURC is playing in the development of the

Photo 10.1 Residents from the informal settlement of Dwarzack, Freetown (photograph by author)

Sierra Leone National Urban Policy. Representatives of NGOs and community groups from informal settlements have also emphasized that SLURC is raising awareness of the needs and aspirations of people living in Freetown's informal settlements, and building their capacities to influence policy and planning processes (SLURC, 2019).

From 2015 to 2019, I have worked with my colleagues from Njala University and DPU to conceive, set up, and support the running of SLURC. This extremely enriching experience has led to many lessons on how to approach city-making in ways that expand human development. Firstly, the SLURC case described in this chapter, like the other engagements examined in this book, illustrates the role that processes of knowledge co-production can play in addressing unequal distributions of capabilities in cities. SLURC demonstrates that partnerships between universities, civil society, and government authorities can create a powerful entry point to influence city-making in ways that expand the agency and capabilities of marginalized groups. Secondly, SLURC's research projects making use of the capability approach demonstrate its potential as a heuristic device, informing the practice of knowledge co-production initiatives. And thirdly, the SLURC journey has generated reflections about how the concepts and practice of the capability approach can contribute to the implementation of global and local development agendas related to city-making.

In this concluding chapter, reflections on the SLURC case summarize some of the main arguments of the book and support the argument that city-making from a capability perspective would require fostering more emancipatory urban learning processes, influencing the ways urban institutions and groups learn and interact with the city (Clark et al., 2019). This final chapter calls for city-making from a capability perspective to explicitly engage in dialogues questioning the power structures and neo-colonial relationships implicit in the ways that knowledge and practices of city-making circulate. In this sense, this book has reflected on the application of the capability approach to 'Southerning' urban theory and practice. The chapter concludes by pointing out the potential contribution of this book to urban development policy and practice.

The case of the Sierra Leone Urban Research Centre

After the opening remarks by the executive director of SLURC, Dr Joseph Macarthy, at the Urban Transformations in Sierra Leone Conference in Freetown in June 2019, Fatmata Shour, a young actress and dancer who grew up in the Freetown informal settlement of Akram Bomeh, was invited to come on stage. Fatmata stood in front of more than 100 attendees, including community representatives from informal settlements, Sierra Leonean and international academics, national government ministers, the mayor of Freetown, government officers, NGO workers, and journalists from local media. She read a poem that was a powerful depiction of the harshness of living in informal settlements as well as expressing her determination for transformation. Fatmata finished her speech by saying:

> I am a strong woman and I can rise up to the top; powerful leaders of tomorrow wake up, wise up! Don't let our future break up; let our voices be heard. We care about our future; we want to move on to fulfil our dreams and ambitions. It is our vision that makes us visible. My greatest hope today is to go back to my slum communities and help them to stand strong, work with them to change that page, and make a better life for all of us. Life in the slum, still we rise.

The conference was followed by a series of presentations and discussions reflecting on the findings and contributions of the research activities implemented by SLURC since its inception in 2016. However, Fatmata conveyed something that none of the other presentations were able to share so meaningfully: the urgency to do things differently, to 'wake up, wise up' by acknowledging citizens' agency to bring about transformations. Fatmata's poem was a plea to listen to the voices and experiences of those marginalized in the city and recognize their aspirations for a better future.

This moment of the conference encapsulated the values and ambition of the SLURC partnership. The story of SLURC starts with Dr Joseph Macarthy, a planner and Njala lecturer specializing in urban disaster and risk reduction.

Dr Macarthy was interested in setting up an urban studies centre at the university to address the limited and unreliable data available about informal settlements in Freetown. In 2014, colleagues from Njala University and DPU[1] developed a proposal to establish a research centre in Freetown and submitted it to Comic Relief (a UK charity). We were awarded a three-year grant to set up an internationally connected urban research centre capable of building the research and analysis capacities of urban stakeholders; making knowledge available to those who need it, prioritizing informal settlement dwellers and their organizations; and delivering world-leading research in order to influence urban policy and practice in Sierra Leone.

In 2019, at the end of the Comic Relief project, we were able to make SLURC a financially and administratively autonomous institution to conduct research, training, and policy-related work funded by different sources. The SLURC experience has generated two key lessons associated with understanding city-making from a capability perspective: first, the importance of enhancing institutional capabilities for producing cities that expand human development (Frediani et al., 2020); and second, from a methodological perspective, the potentials of the capability approach to inform processes of knowledge co-production.

The story of SLURC illustrates how a research and capacity-building organization can affect the institutional landscape shaping the processes of city-making. In particular, it highlights the importance of expanding **institutional capabilities** to produce cities that are more socially and environmentally just. The starting point for SLURC was a recognition of the lack of opportunities for institutions to develop relationships and collaborations focused on the upgrading of informal settlements and urban development more generally. Drawing on the initial set of partnerships with the Comic Relief guarantors in Freetown (Restless Development, Youth Development Movement, BRAC Sierra Leone, CODOHSAPA and Young Men's Christian Association), SLURC began to implement training, events, exchange visits, teaching activities, and participatory research projects aimed at expanding the set of practices available for building institutional capacities, relationships, and opportunities to affect city-making processes. Those participating in these activities approached these learning spaces as public arenas in which to discuss and debate visions and aspirations of city-making, especially in relation to how improvements to informal settlements should take place.

Box 10.1 Institutional capabilities

Institutional capabilities refer to the range of practices, abilities, and opportunities institutions have to advance values associated with human development. By applying the capability lens to examine and support institutions, this concept sheds light on the resources, systems, relationships, values, and organizational culture that shape the capabilities of institutions to promote human development (Frediani et al., 2020).

For example, in a workshop related to neighbourhood planning, representatives of informal settlements across Freetown worked with government and NGO officers to generate a charter of principles for participatory planning to make the city more inclusive (Frediani et al., 2018b). In 2019, SLURC involved key urban stakeholders in setting up the City Learning Platform. The team has collaboratively generated a set of principles and aspirations for the remit of their actions. The platform is a 'space for learning and sharing, in which different actors can gather to discuss experiences, current urban issues and identify solutions, coordinate and develop proposals for the upgrading of informal settlements in the city of Freetown' (City Learning Platform 2019: 2). Through the platform, the urban stakeholders hope to create a democratic platform on which to discuss and debate policies relating to informal settlement upgrading, to share community-led practices for the dissemination, institutionalization, and scaling-up of participatory initiatives, and to enable the development of concrete actions to improve living conditions in informal settlements.

SLURC's work also recognizes that the creation of particular spaces of dialogue and collaboration would not, in and of itself, enable the achievement of these outcomes. The institutional landscape is profoundly unequal, reproducing deep asymmetries of power in the processes of city-making in Freetown. The national government is a key urban development stakeholder. It focuses its attention on large-scale infrastructural issues and real-estate development concerns, making decisions in close partnership with major international private companies and other urban development agencies. Freetown city council has often been marginalized in decision-making processes and required to deal with new administrative and service-delivery responsibilities without the necessary financial and human resources. At the same time, local elites and decision-makers regard residents of informal settlements as obstacles to, and problems for, urban development. Many NGOs operate in the gap in this context, trying to respond to the local needs of residents living in informal settlements while having little traction to address wider structural issues reproducing inequalities in the city.

In response to this situation, SLURC prioritized enhancing the capabilities of marginalized groups to influence urban development processes. SLURC has promoted this by, firstly, contributing to changing the mind-set of government officials, encouraging them to move from a slum-clearance approach towards building capacities for incremental upgrading solutions to improve living conditions in informal settlements. SLURC has played a key role in helping urban stakeholders understand the call from community groups and wider civil-society actors to 'pull slums from people, not people from the slums' (this is a translation of the Krio slogan *'pul slum pan pupil, nor to pipul from the slum'*[2]). Secondly, SLURC has conducted a series of capacity-building activities directly targeting community groups and their support networks, enhancing their ability to engage with policy and planning documents, conduct urban development studies, and develop strategic local action plans and projects.

An important partnership for SLURC has been with the Federation of the Urban and Rural Poor of Sierra Leone (FEDURP-SL), a city-wide network of informal settlement dwellers mobilized around savings and community enumeration that is part of the network of Slum/Shack Dwellers International. Since our first feasibility study, the partnership with FEDURP-SL (and its support NGO, Centre of Dialogue on Human Settlement and Poverty Alleviation) has been central to identifying the ways a research centre could contribute to and strengthen community-led processes of knowledge production. SLURC had to learn to recognize and support the agency of informal settlement communities in the production and control of local data while, at the same time, learning to identify how its research could complement these initiatives without compromising them. In this way, SLURC was able to consolidate its community relationships while building collaborations with other important urban stakeholders and creating pathways for participatory and community-led research to influence policy and planning practices. The 2019 external evaluation of SLURC noted that:

> One of its [SLURC] biggest impacts to date has been its role in acting as a facilitator of dialogue. Both between national and local government policymakers, civil-society organizations and residents of informal settlements and cross-nationally, by bringing key urban stakeholders on knowledge-exchange visits to other African contexts. Already this approach has seen a shift in some government departments and local authorities thinking about informal settlements, with slum upgrading specifically mentioned ahead of forced evictions in the Mayor's Transform Freetown agenda. (Hitchen, 2019: iii)

In addition to working on the institutional set-up of SLURC, I also collaborated with the research team on two projects, making use of the **capability approach as a heuristic device** to facilitate processes of knowledge co-production. My first research engagement was exploring the role of empowerment in urban humanitarian responses in Freetown (Macarthy et al., 2017). In initial discussions with the Comic Relief guarantors' network after the Ebola crisis, many organizations highlighted the importance of research on the role of community groups in responding to humanitarian crises in cities. These civil-society organizations felt that it was strategically important to generate knowledge to inform their advocacy strategy which aimed to raise the recognition of community-led initiatives in the eyes of governmental and international development actors. In order to address this research need, we developed a project focusing on one particular informal settlement community (Portee-Rokupa) to explore how different urban humanitarian responses affected the empowerment capabilities of different community groups in the settlement.

My second project with SLURC was an action-research initiative, which included working with Architecture Sans Frontières – UK to apply the Change by Design (CbD) participatory planning and design methodology (see Chapter 9) to develop Community Action Area Plans for two informal settlements in Freetown (SLURC and ASF-UK, 2019a; 2019b). In this project, we documented the experiences of different people who participated in the CbD workshops, including local residents and urban development actors. We explored how participatory planning and design affected the capabilities of marginalized groups to participate in city-making processes (Macarthy et al., 2019).

In both projects, the analytical lens of the capability approach was extremely relevant and useful in guiding the development of the research and its implementation. Firstly, the capability approach, as articulated in this book, offered flexibility, which allowed values, aspirations, needs, abilities, and opportunities to be researched in a situated manner. Secondly, the framework outlined a series of analytical elements that emphasized the importance of unpacking the relationship between agency and structure in cities. It helped to connect micro and localized practices to wider structuring processes driven by environmental and political economy relations. And thirdly, capabilities and human development values associated with people-centredness, participation, and inclusion helped to navigate ethical deliberations around knowledge co-production.

To activate the use of capability approach, we made use of a worksheet (Macarthy et al., 2017: 13) that reflects the capability map shown in Figure 10.1. It illustrates the different elements of the capability approach analysed in this book and aims to highlight the relationships between them. The capability elements are listed in Table 1.1 (see Chapter 1), which sets out and explains the terms used in the diagram.

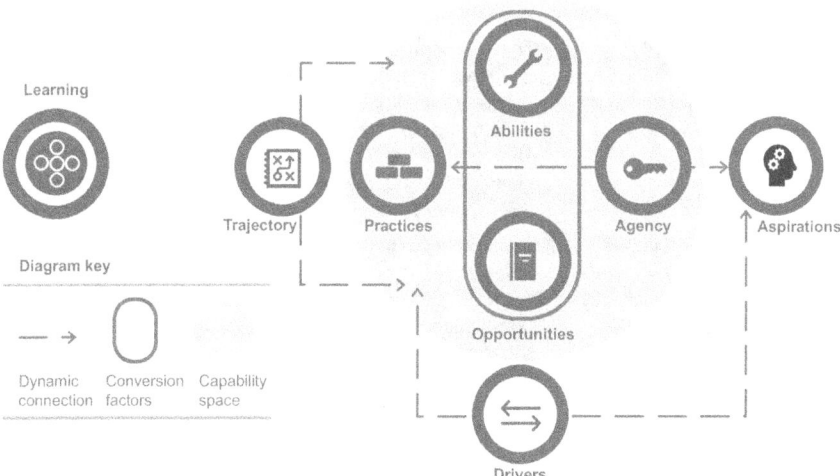

Figure 10.1 Capability map

Table 10.1 Capability-oriented urban learning

Principles Interrogating and advancing city-making from a capability perspective requires forms of learning that:	Guidelines
1. Deepen and reframe diagnoses of city-making, revealing wider trends and processes as well as opportunities for expansion of capabilities.	This reframing positions learning from and through the condition of urban marginality, focusing on the experiences of all the diverse and disparate groups living on urban peripheries and margins. 'Periphery' here does not only refer to a physical location, but also includes conditions of precarity and mis/mal-recognition in the city (Caldeira, 2017). This reframing links the wider structural shaping of city-making with the experiences of everyday lives, revealing freedoms and unfreedoms, agency, and alienations. This reframing engages with historical accounts of oppressions and struggles for freedom and liberation in cities.
2. Promote collective analytical capacities to engage with diverse socio-spatial conditions and imaginaries.	This collective analytical capacity seeks to decentre epistemic positions and destabilize dominant and exclusionary ways of seeing city-making. This collective analytical capacity recognizes the importance of approaching intersections of social identities as entry points for more emancipatory knowledge production. The collective analytical capacity requires mechanisms that approach the production, use, and appropriation of space as drivers of freedoms and mindsets as well as sites of manifestation of power relations. (For more on this, see debates on spatial justice in Chapter 2 and spatial agency in Chapter 8.)
3. Re-examine the role, purpose, scope, and nature of planning practice and interventions.	This re-examination recognizes various sites, agents, and relations of planning practice. This re-examination reveals the power relations embedded in planning practice, ideals, and instruments. This re-examination questions, reformulates, and reorients planning towards the expansion of capabilities and human development.
4. Co-produce situated strategies of city-making that recognize the agency of urban marginalized groups and collective action.	Supporting co-produced and situated strategies seeks to foster action-oriented engagement, driven, led, and promoted by embedded actors and relationships. Co-produced and situated strategies are enabled in situations of negotiation and contestation over current and future ways of making cities. Co-produced and situated strategies are results of the encounter of 'conflicting rationalities' (Watson, 2003) with the potential to destabilize existing epistemic prejudices and silences, enabling more emancipatory outcomes.

Table 10.1 *Continued*

5. Facilitate a reflexive and empowering ethos of city-making practice and collaboration.	An ethos of city-making recognizes the importance of supporting the capabilities of grassroots urban actions. This ethos of city-making generates awareness of power imbalances embedded in various forms of collaborative urban engagements. This ethos of city-making promotes relations of equivalence, recognizing diverse needs, capabilities, and aspirations associated with processes of city-making.

Work with SLURC partners revealed the following key points about the application of a capability approach and use of this diagram. First, these elements of the capability approach cannot be addressed in isolation; they relate to each other, and the particular power of the capability approach is to reveal, discuss, and act through these relations. Secondly, this visualization must not be seen as a linear or prescriptive map for the expansion of capabilities: quite the opposite. Its objective is to recognize that there are various different ways and entry points for the expansion of capabilities through city-making practices. Thirdly, the visualization aims to support the application of the capability approach as a heuristic device, as an instrument to facilitate collective forms of reflection on how capabilities are negotiated, and to develop actions to intervene in the city-making processes that shape capabilities. Finally, while the elements identified are intended to help the exploration of particular issues and relationships (see element definitions in Table 1.1, Chapter 1), the hope is that the diagram will enable and nurture grounded and situated understandings of the relationships between city-making and human development. The proposed set of elements and potential links between them have been used to recognize marginalized knowledges and practices of city-making.

The experience with SLURC demonstrates that the openness and depth of the capability approach can be developed to disrupt dominant and exclusionary epistemologies, stimulating the recognition of marginalized practices of city-making and enabling articulations of more emancipatory urban trajectories and imaginaries.

Reflections on learning

The importance of learning in triggering social change in cities is brought to the fore by the experience in Freetown, as well as by the other cases explored in this book. Learning is not only related to educational or capacity development initiatives and their outcomes, but is also embedded in experiencing, planning, producing, and researching the city. Critical research in urban studies, planning, and design has highlighted the potentials of advancing emancipatory urban transformation by reconfiguring the way we learn about the city.

> Learning has the potential to challenge and transform the ways of knowing and seeing the city that we inherit, sometimes take for granted, and routinely put to work ... As a form of wayfinding (Ingold, 2000) and struggle, the form and politics of learning in the city cannot simply be restricted to the domain of specialist and expertise knowledge and their effects, as important as these are. We need alongside this to repeatedly ask who 'we' – critical urban researchers, planners and so on – learn from, with, for what ends and under what conditions of power and inclusion. (McFarlane, 2018: 323–324)

McFarlane's work on critical urban learning (2011; 2018) is an important contribution to wider debates around Southerning urban theory and practice. These approaches critique currently dominant pedagogies and systems of learning about cities that privilege agendas and urban processes associated with the commodification of urban spaces and services. The urban imaginaries that underpin these agendas emerge from the circulation of knowledge between international consultancy firms and global urban professionals, and take no account of the aspirations and aesthetics produced in place by experiences of everyday urban life. Current debates about smart cities have privileged technical and professional knowledge while continuing to marginalize and disregard the expertise of urban inhabitants. As a result, inequalities in the distribution of opportunities for learning about the city have been reproduced, deepening the asymmetries of power over access to knowledge about the city and urban decision-making. This uneven landscape of urban learning, and the proliferation of large multinational private corporations producing and managing data about cities, marks a new era of urban politics. In efforts to decolonize city-making, 'there is a struggle ahead in both critically exposing whose learning is prioritized in depictions of the urban future, and in developing alternative urban visions foregrounded in more socially and ecologically just concerns and learning' (McFarlane, 2018: 331).

The core motivation for bringing debates on city-making into the capability approach is not only to call for more and better knowledge of cities, but also to rethink and democratize the politics of learning about cities. This critical approach to learning as a means to democratize city-making is also at the core of existing debates about knowledge co-production and its applications to the advancement of epistemic and social justice in the field of urban development (Simon et al., 2018; Osuteye et al., 2019; Mitlin et al., 2020). As this chapter shows, the capability approach is a constructive heuristic device enabling collaborative and critical urban learning. The case study of Freetown and the experience of SLURC highlight the importance of putting the capability approach into practice through partnerships that strive to make learning more democratic and emancipatory. This resonates directly with the concept of 'empowered learning systems' that stress the 'interactions and linkages between individual and collective capabilities, human agency and learning processes' (Clark et al., 2019: 395).

Drawing on these debates about learning, and the experiences outlined in this book, Table 10.1 outlines a set of principles and guidelines to advance learning journeys towards making cities engines of human development. These principles are based on encounters between experiences of practice and elaborations of the capability approach in relation to urban development. They aim to contribute to the practice of urban learning in ways that generate reflection and action on capabilities in cities.

Concluding remarks: implications for urban policy and planning

The argument and supporting cases in this book hope to promote a field of research and practice applying the capability approach to the examination of, and intervention in, urban development processes. Drawing on relevant debates and research, the book has proposed a series of concepts that offer productive entry points to approaching city-making from a capability perspective.

I have argued that, for city-making to expand capabilities, it is crucial to interrogate and respond to the structural drivers shaping capabilities in the city. This requires understanding the history of places, the factors affecting the production of space, and their implications for human development. City-making from a capability perspective has to address the discriminatory and exclusionary nature of particular spatial development trends, highlighting, for example, the relationship between land dynamics and social-spatial segregation (such as the ones in Lagos and Cape Town explored in Chapters 3 and 5), or patriarchal and racialized ideologies perpetuated in urban planning and design which continue to make assumptions about physical features of space and their functions and outcomes without taking into account the diverse experiences, needs, and aspirations of people in cities. Therefore, approaching city-making from a capability perspective involves approaching drivers that operate at various scales, establishing the links between localized experiences of everyday lives with municipal, regional, and global dynamics. In this sense, capability-oriented city-making needs both local and global actions, for example, targeting the frameworks regulating transnational corporations involved in real-estate development as well as producing new ways of learning about urban planning and design (such as the work of SLURC described in this chapter).

City-making that expands capabilities needs to enlarge the choices people have in terms of how to produce and manage goods and services in the city. This involves recognizing that city-making practices take place in different ways, including collective and insurgent forms of producing and using spaces, cooperative models as well as private-sector or state-led practices. Instead of closing down people's choices about how to make cities, a capability-oriented approach to city-making is concerned with revealing and expanding people's portfolios of options. If we approach housing as an example, high-rise buildings in the outskirts of cities cannot be the only option promoted by public housing programmes targeting low-income groups. Housing policies need to diversify their housing practices, recognizing the potentials for participatory *in situ* upgrading and neighbourhood improvements as well as for rehabilitation and re-appropriation of vacant buildings and land located in proximity to social facilities and livelihood opportunities. At the same time, housing choice is about diversifying tenure options beyond individual home ownership; reaching out to the poorest involves the provision of truly affordable or social rent homes, or supporting community-led housing options.

A capability approach to city-making puts people's valued dimensions of wellbeing at the core of urban policy and planning. Instead of purely focusing on productivity or competitiveness, urban development and planning needs to be concerned with securing and promoting a set of principles associated with the notion of the good life. This calls for democratization of urban governance in ways that recognize people's diverse aspirations, while at the same time connecting these with existing rights-based commitments and obligations. In practice, this means, for example, promoting participatory planning processes, such as the one in Los Pinos (examined in Chapter 9), which connected the community's diverse aspirations with notions articulated in Ecuador's Good Living National Plan.

Crucially, making cities in ways that expands capabilities means not being content with the simple provision and availability of a particular good or service in the city. It requires going further, making sure that conditions are in place so that people in all of their diversity can make use of these goods and services in ways that expand wellbeing equitably. The capability approach calls these conditions conversion factors and, in this book, I have illustrated how they are shaped by people's abilities and opportunities to pursue their valued aspirations. In Chapter 6, I have shown how the capability outcomes of the informal settlement upgrading project in Salvador were compromised by the physical characteristics of the intervention as well as the consultative nature of the participatory process put in place. This example highlights how the cycle of city-making, which includes the design, production, and appropriation of space, affects people's abilities to pursue the life they want and have the right to live. Meanwhile, Chapter 7's examination of the delegated management model (DMM) in Kisumu highlights that enhanced abilities are not enough to make sure city-making expands capabilities. Urban policy and planning need to recognize and intervene in the asymmetries of power embedded in the way spatial production is regulated and managed. Otherwise, as in the case of Kisumu, city-making can lead to unfavourable inclusions which devolve more burdens and risks, rather than meaningful opportunities, to vulnerable communities.

Meanwhile, an agenda of city-making that prioritizes human development over economic growth recognizes people as agents of change. This book captures various stories of agency as grassroots groups and their support networks are striving to make cities more socially and environmentally just. Chapter 8, exploring the experience of Ocupação Marconi, demonstrated in more detail how city-making can support people's agency to bring about change. The occupation's personal and collective spatial practices deepened critical awareness, nurtured collective abilities to act together, and strengthened the bargaining power of marginalized groups to influence policy and planning processes. If urban policy and planning is to take agency as a core concern in its practice, it needs to stop criminalizing this type of collective experience of city-making, and start supporting and nurturing the potentials that it creates to expand capabilities in cities. This involves, for example, working through principles of incrementality and community action-planning (Hamdi and Goethert, 1997), which starts from what is already going on and is focused on cultivating opportunities rather than delivering predetermined plans and projects (Hamdi, 2010: 16).

This focus on agency in city-making opens up the discussion about the different trajectories that bring about human development in cities. This book does not prescribe a starting point, as experiences in different places utilize different entry points to equitably expand wellbeing in cities. Chapter 9 argued that urban policy and planning that approaches city-making from a capability perspective needs to learn how to 'dance with conflict' (Hamdi, 2010: 33), encouraging trajectories that recognize diverse needs and aspirations as well as possibilities for change. Urban planning from this perspective embraces conflict as a mechanism to identify and expand the possibilities for change. Therefore, trajectories to expand capabilities through city-making are made up of bargaining encounters, generating acts of cooperation and conflict. Here, Sen's concept of cooperative conflict makes a substantial contribution to planning practice, highlighting the need for policy and planning to make the conditions of bargaining fairer. For example, in the case of the residents of Los Pinos, members of the Los Pinos development committee deployed a series of grassroots tactics to make the conditions of bargaining fairer: challenging the misconceptions and stigmas associated with the act of occupation of the vacant land; and demonstrating to government officials the innovation potentials of democratizing urban governance through participatory process of designing and planning neighbourhood development.

Finally, by bringing all these elements together, this capability approach to city-making helps to explain how capabilities can be expanded in cities. Beyond the identification and measurement of capabilities, this book articulates a series of conceptual elements that helps to interrogate and support the ways within which capabilities are pursued, generated, and expanded in cities. The cases, capability elements, and diagrams are focused on the acts, relationships, processes, and strategies that define and enlarge the possibilities of change. In this sense, this approach to capabilities in cities is, most of all, a heuristic device aimed at supporting critical learning which advances socially and environmentally just urban development. The various experiences of city-making reflected in this book highlight the strategic potential of learning experiences situated in the interfaces between the tensions shaping city-making: reflection and action, past and future, resistance and reform, cooperation and conflict, the collective and the personal, agency and structure, the local and the global. The capability approach is a productive device to engage with these interfaces and tensions, liberating analysis and strategies that have the potential to build pathways for a radical as well as progressive politics in the city.

Fundamentally, I argue that the capability approach can be used to advance what Mouffe (2019) calls 'radical reformism', which sheds light on the possibilities of engaging with 'existing political institutions in view of transforming them through democratic procedures' (2019: 45). For me, the transformative potential of the capability approach lies precisely in its subversive potential to pursue concrete reforms to city-making in ways that open up possibilities for more profound changes in the relations of power governing spatial production. A capability approach to city-making starts with what is possible; in light of the ideal, it recognizes the particular; without denying the universal and structural, it mobilizes notions of freedom and wellbeing in ways that promote equality and justice.

In the quest of advancing this potential of the capability approach to bring about radical and progressive transformations to city-making, this book identifies an emerging agenda for research and practice focused on the evidence, pedagogies, and practices of city-making. Generation of empirical evidence about the relationship between city-making and capabilities is necessary for a better understanding of inequalities and injustice in cities. A capability perspective can investigate processes of spatial production and highlight the ways through which these processes constrain or enable capabilities and human development. In Chapter 6, I shared some of the empirical findings from my PhD research, which explores how a squatter settlement upgrading programme affected the capabilities of local residents. Further research along similar lines is needed, unpacking how spaces are perceived, conceived, and lived affects people's choices, opportunities, aspirations, and agency. Some interesting studies in this direction include the work of Mella Lira (2019), which explores the relationship between access to transport opportunities and people's capabilities in Santiago, and that of Jones (2021), which has documented how access to energy shapes people's capabilities in informal settlements in Dhaka. While my work and these examples address city-making practices from the experiences and initiatives of marginalized groups in the city, further research could explore the urban operations of privileged and dominant groups and document their impact on the uneven distribution of capabilities in the city.

This book also highlights the importance of generating capability-centred urban pedagogies. The capability approach can support the design of urban pedagogical processes and instruments to bring together notions of emancipatory processes and outcomes. There is a growing amount of research in the field of human development and the capability literature reflecting on participatory methodologies and their relationships to people's capabilities. In a similar vein, this book draws on action-research experiences that have applied a variety of methods to understand capabilities in cities in participatory ways. These include: participatory video in Lagos (Chapter 3); participatory design and planning in London, Cape Town and Quito (Chapters 4, 5 and 9); focus-group discussions and semi-structured interviews in Salvador and Kisumu (Chapters 6 and 7); and participatory mapping in São Paulo (Chapter 8). We need further work that adapts and applies participatory methodologies to address city-making from a capability perspective. In this, it would be crucial to focus on a wider project of developing urban pedagogical processes, instruments, and conditions that engage with the concepts and debates emerging from the capability approach.

Finally, a capability perspective can support the advancement and development of city-making practices that strive for social and environmental justice. A capability-informed approach to city-making contributes to existing policy and practices to advance the right to the city. From a capability perspective, efforts to support and design city-making practices need to start by recognizing the ongoing struggles of marginalized groups. The capability perspective joins forces with calls to shed light on the subaltern practices that play a central role in the production of cities. Chapter 8 illustrates how the practice of occupying vacant buildings in São Paulo can be understood as enhancing agency and capabilities through collective forms of appropriation and management of urban spaces. A capability-informed theory of change can support grassroots groups, NGOs, and government authorities to identify strategic areas of intervention and entry points for leverage. Chapter 7, in exploring the DMM of water delivery in informal settlements in Kisumu, highlights precisely this potential of the capability approach to inform the practices of an NGO to advance wellbeing while also considering long-term urban development and real-estate market trends affecting people's capabilities. By exploring the ways in which the relationship between agency and structure is shaping people's capabilities, the framework allows strategies and tactics to recognize and strengthen trajectories of change. Chapter 9 reveals the capability trajectory of a community in search of security of tenure in the outskirts of Quito. The case illustrates how, by recognizing such a trajectory, the framework can inform the development of future pathways for change. Its multidimensionality forces urban practices to break from sectorial silos and design actions that are driven by their purpose rather than by predefined fields of operation and expertise. This was one of the lessons of the debates about urban regeneration in Cape Town, explored in Chapter 5, in which participatory processes debating regeneration aspirations for the neighbourhood of Woodstock unlocked a series of intersectorial dialogues and development strategies.

However, there are various areas of implementation of the right to the city agenda that could benefit from further application of the capability approach. For example, it would be productive to explore the potential contributions of the capability perspective to the practices of commonning and building solidarity in the city. The COVID-19 pandemic has brought to light the need to explore social determinants of urban health which the capability perspective could help to articulate in more detail. It would be also useful to explore ways in which securing the social function of property and land could build capabilities and agency in the long term.

Applying the capability perspective to engagement with city-making, this book has aspired to contribute examples of evidence, pedagogies, and practices with potentials for producing fairer, more sustainable, and emancipatory cities. What if we understood cities not as places of growth but as generators of human development? What if we saw cities not for what they *are* in form and function but for what they *do* to people and nature? A capability response would start with condemning violations of human rights, recognizing the collective agency of urban dwellers, and calling for public actions and interventions that address uneven distributions of opportunities and burdens while promoting democratic processes in which to imagine and create the cities we value.

Notes

1. The setting up of SLURC was led by Joseph Macarthy and Braima Koroma from Njala University, together with Andrea Rigon and myself from UCL.
2. This slogan was coined by Chief Kabenpa from Kroo Bay informal settlement, during a visit of Comic Relief staff in 2013. Following that visit, the network of civil-society organisations involved in the Comic Relief Urban Slums Initiative in Freetown became known as 'Pull Slum Pan Pupil Partnership' (SLURC, 2016: 5).

References

Alkire, S. (2002) *Valuing Freedoms: Sen's Capability Approach and Poverty Reduction*. Oxford: University Press, Oxford UP (Oxford scholarship online) <http://dx.doi.org/10.1093/0199245797.001.0001>.

Alkire, S. (2006) 'Structural injustice and democratic practice: the trajectory in Sen's writings', in Deneulin, S., Nebel, M. and Sagovsky, N. (eds), *Transforming Unjust Structures: The Capability Approach*. Dordrecht: Springer (Library of Ethics and Applied Philosophy), pp. 47–61.

Alkire, S. (2013) 'Choosing dimensions: the capability approach and multidimensional poverty', in Kakwani, N. and Silber, J. (eds), *The Many Dimensions of Poverty*. New York: Palgrave Macmillan, pp. 89–119.

Allen, A. (2013) 'Water provision for and by the peri-urban poor: public-community partnerships or citizens coproduction', in Vojnovic, I. (ed.), *Urban Sustainability: A Global Perspective*. East Lansing: Michigan State University Press, pp. 309–340.

Allen, A., Dávila, J. D., Hofmann, P. (2006) *Governance of Water and Sanitation Services for the Peri-Urban Poor: A Framework for Understanding and Action in Metropolitan Regions*. London: The Bartlett Development Planning Unit, UCL: London.

Alova, G. and Burgess, G. (2017) 'Housing poverty in Ecuador: challenges to eradication', *Survey Review*, 49(353), pp. 117–133 <http://dx.doi.org/10.1080/00396265.2015.1133519>.

Alsop, R., Bertelsen, M. and Holland, J. (2006) *Empowerment in Practice: From Analysis to Implementation*. Washington DC: World Bank (Directions in Development). Available at: <https://openknowledge.worldbank.org/handle/10986/6980> [accessed 19 May 2021].

Alvaredo, F., Chancel, L., Piketty, T., Saez, E., Zucman, G. (2018) *World Inequality Report 2018*. Cambridge, MA: Harvard University Press.

Ambode, A. (2016) 'Lagos state government confirms release of pupils and teachers of Igbonla kidnap' <https://akinwunmiambode.com/lagos-state-government-confirms-release-of-pupils-and-teachers-of-igbonla-kidnap/> (posted 12 October 2016) [accessed 21 June 2021].

Amin, A. (2013) 'Telescopic urbanism and the poor', *City*, 17(4), pp. 476–492 <http://dx.doi.org/10.1080/13604813.2013.812350>.

Anand, P. B. (2007) 'Capability, sustainability, and collective action: an examination of a river water dispute', *Journal of Human Development*, 8(1), pp. 109–132 <http://dx.doi.org/10.1080/14649880601101465>.

Anand, P. B. (2018) 'Cities and the capability approach', in Comim, F., Anand, P. B., and Fennell, S. (eds), *New Frontiers of the Capability Approach*. Cambridge: Cambridge University Press, pp. 519–546 <http://dx.doi.org/10.1017/9781108559881.022>.

Appadurai, A. (2004) 'The capacity to aspire: culture and the terms of recognition', in Rao, V. and Walton, M. (eds), *Culture and Public Action*. Stanford, California: Stanford University Press, pp. 59–84.

Arantes, O., Vainer, C. and Maricato, E. (eds) (2002) *A Cidade do Pensamento Único: Desmanchando Consensos*. Petrópolis: Editora Vozes.

Asfour, L., De La Parra, A. M., Faghiri, O., Huerta, M., Lara, V. and Ulcica, I. (2015) 'HS2 untangled: your guide to accountability', in Frediani, A. A., Monson, T., and Butcher, S. (eds), *Reclaiming Regeneration: Negotiating a Citizens Charter for Euston Area*. London: The Bartlett Development Planning Unit, University College London (MSc Social Development Practice Student Report), pp. 36–44.

Awan, N., Schneider, T. and Till, J. (2011) *Spatial Agency: Other Ways of Doing Architecture*. Abingdon: Routledge.

Bainbridge, E., Bennett, J., Campkin, B., De Carli, B., Frediani, A. A., French, M., Macedo, C. and Walker, J. (2015) *Change by Design: Re-imagining Regeneration through Participatory Design in Cape Town*. London, UK: Architecture Sans Frontières UK. Available at: <https://issuu.com/asf-uk/docs/cbd2015_cape_town> [accessed 18 May 2021].

Barbosa, B. R. (2014) *Protagonism dos movimentos de moradia no centro de São Paulo: trajetória, lutas e influencias nas políticas habitacionais*. Masters dissertation. Universidade Federal do ABC.

Bartlett Development Planning Unit (Bartlett DPU) (2017a) *Participatory video workshop – the right to work* [video] <https://www.youtube.com/watch?v=JS9vi_Ccf_A> [accessed 18 May 2021].

Bartlett DPU (2017b) *Participatory video workshop – save the waterfront* [video] <https://www.youtube.com/watch?v=tM6CER4w5Rw> [accessed 18 May 2021].

Basta, C. (2016) 'From justice in planning toward planning for justice: a capability approach', *Planning Theory*, 15(2), pp. 190–212 <http://dx.doi.org/10.1177/1473095215571399>.

Bayat, A. (1997) 'Un-civil society: the politics of the "informal people"', *Third World Quarterly*, 18(1), pp. 53–72 <https://www.jstor.org/stable/3992901> [accessed 28 June 2021].

Beebeejaun, Y. (2017) 'Gender, urban space, and the right to everyday life', *Journal of Urban Affairs*, 39(3), pp. 323–334 <http://dx.doi.org/10.1080/07352166.2016.1255526>.

Belda-Miquel, S., Blanes, J. P. and Frediani, A. A. (2016) 'Institutionalization and depoliticization of the right to the city: changing scenarios for radical social movements', *International Journal of Urban and Regional Research*, 40(2), pp. 321–339 <http://dx.doi.org/10.1111/1468-2427.12382>.

Bhan, G. (2019) 'Notes on a Southern urban practice', *Environment and Urbanization*, 31(2), pp. 639–654.

Biggeri, M. and Ferrannini, A. (2014) *Sustainable Human Development: A New Territorial and People-centred Perspective*. Basingstoke: Palgrave Pivot.

Biggeri, M. and Libanora, R. (2011) 'From valuing to evaluating: tools and procedures to operationalise the capability approach', in Biggeri, M., Ballet, J., and Comim, F. (eds), *Children and the Capability Approach*. Basingstoke, UK: Palgrave Macmillan UK (Studies in Childhood and Youth), pp. 79–106 <http://dx.doi.org/10.1057/9780230308374>.

Biggeri, M., Ballet, J. and Comim, F. (eds) (2011) *Children and the Capability Approach*. Basingstoke, UK: Palgrave Macmillan UK (Studies in Childhood and Youth) <http://dx.doi.org/10.1057/9780230308374>.

Biggeri, M., Ferrannini, A. and Arciprete, C. (2018) 'Local communities and capability evolution: the core of human development processes', *Journal of Human Development and Capabilities*, 19(2), pp. 126–146 <http://dx.doi.org/10.1080/19452829.2017.1411896>.

Biggeri, M., Libanora, R., Mariani, S. and Menchini, L. (2006) 'Children conceptualizing their capabilities: results of a survey conducted during the first Children's World Congress on Child Labour', *Journal of Human Development*, 7(1), pp. 59–83 <http://dx.doi.org/10.1080/14649880500501179>.

Blečič, I., Cecchini, A. 'Bibo' and Talu, V. (2013) 'The capability approach in urban quality of life and urban policies: towards a conceptual framework', in Serreli, S. (ed.), *City Project and Public Space*. Dordrecht: Springer Netherlands (Urban and Landscape Perspectives), pp. 269–288 <http://dx.doi.org/10.1007/978-94-007-6037-0_17>.

Boni, A. and Frediani, A. A. (2020) 'Expanding capabilities through participatory action research', in Chiappero-Martinetti, E., Osmani, S., and Qizilbash, M. (eds), *The Cambridge Handbook of the Capability Approach*. Cambridge, UK: Cambridge University Press, pp. 477–496.

Bourdieu, P. (1977) *Outline of a Theory of Practice*. Cambridge: Cambridge University Press.

Brenner, N., Marcuse, P. and Mayer, M. (2012) *Cities for People, Not for Profit: Critical Urban Theory and the Right to the City*. Abingdon: Routledge.

Brickell, K., Arrigoitia, M. F. and Vasudevan, A. (eds) (2017) *Geographies of Forced Eviction: Dispossession, Violence, Resistance*. UK: Palgrave Macmillan <http://dx.doi.org/10.1057/978-1-137-51127-0>.

Brownill, S. and Parker, G. (2010) 'Why bother with good works? The relevance of public participation(s) in planning in a post-collaborative era', *Planning Practice & Research*, 25(3), pp. 275–282 <http://dx.doi.org/10.1080/02697459.2010.503407>.

Burgess, R., Carmona, M. and Kolstee, T. (eds) (1997) *The Challenge of Sustainable Cities: Neoliberalism and Urban Strategies in Developing Countries*. London: Zed.

Butcher, S. (2016) 'The "everyday water practices" of the urban poor in Kisumu Kenya', in Wilson Center (ed.), *Urban Solutions: Metropolitan Approaches, Innovation in Urban Water and Sanitation, and Inclusive Smart Cities: A New Generation of Ideas*. Washington DC: Wilson Center Urban Sustainability Laboratory. Available at: <https://www.wilsoncenter.org/sites/default/files/media/documents/publication/usl_150623_urban_solutions_report_web.pdf> [accessed 7 October 2020].

Butcher, S. (2019) 'The everyday politics of water: services and citizenship for the urban poor in Kathmandu, Nepal', PhD thesis, University College London. Available at: <https://discovery.ucl.ac.uk/id/eprint/10071506/> [accessed 21 September 2020].

Byskov, M. F. (2017) 'Democracy, philosophy, and the selection of capabilities', *Journal of Human Development and Capabilities*, 18(1), pp. 1–16 <http://dx.doi.org/10.1080/19452829.2015.1091809>.

Caldeira, T. P. (2017) 'Peripheral urbanization: autoconstruction, transversal logics, and politics in cities of the global south', *Environment and Planning D: Society and Space*, 35(1), pp. 3–20 <http://dx.doi.org/10.1177/0263775816658479>.

Cardoso, A. L. (ed.) (2013) *O Programa Minha Casa Minha Vida e seus Efeitos Territoriais*. Rio de Janeiro: Letra Capital (Série Habitação e Cidade).

Carey, H. F. (Chip) (2019) 'Urban unrest propels global wave of protests', *The Conversation*. Available at: <http://theconversation.com/urban-unrest-propels-global-wave-of-protests-126306> [accessed 31 August 2020].

Carrington, D. (2017) 'London breaches annual air pollution limit for 2017 in just five days', *The Guardian*, 6 January. Available at: <https://www.theguardian.com/environment/2017/jan/06/london-breaches-toxic-air-pollution-limit-for-2017-in-just-five-days> [accessed 18 May2021].

Carrión, F. and Erazo Espinosa, J. (2012) 'La forma urbana de Quito: una historia de centros y periferias', *Bulletin de l'Institut français d'études andines*, 41(3), pp. 503–522 <http://dx.doi.org/10.4000/bifea.361>.

Carvalho, E. T. (2002) *Os Alagados da Bahia: intervenções públicas e apropriação informal fo espaço urbano*. Universidade Federal da Bahia (UFBA).

de Certeau, Michel (1984) *The Practice of Everyday Life*. Berkeley: University of California Press.

Chattopadhyay, S. (2012) *Unlearning the City: Infrastructure in a New Optical Field*. Minneapolis: University of Minnesota Press.

Chiappero-Martinetti, E., Budd, C. H. and Ziegler, R. (2017) 'Social innovation and the capability approach – introduction to the special issue', *Journal of Human Development and Capabilities*, 18(2), pp. 141–147 <http://dx.doi.org/10.1080/19452829.2017.1316002>.

Chicaiza, A. E. M. (2016) *Perspectivas acerca de la participación comunitaria de las mujeres del barrio 'Los Pinos' enfocada a la vida cotidiana*. Graduate dissertation. Universidad Politécnica Salesiana.

City Learning Platform (2019) *Practitioner Brief 1#: Principles of Engagement for the City Learning Platform*. 1. Freetown: Sierra Leone Urban Research Centre (SLURC) <https://www.slurc.org/uploads/1/0/9/7/109761391/cilp_pb_web.pdf> [accessed 18 May 2021].

City Mayors (2018) 'The largest cities in the world by land area, population and density' in City Mayors Statistics [website] <http://www.citymayors.com/statistics/largest-cities-density-125.html> [accessed 18 May 2021].

Clark, D. A. (2002) *Visions of Human Development: A Study of Human Values*. Cheltenham, UK: Edward Elgar.

Clark, D. A. (2012) *Adaptation, Poverty and Development: The Dynamics of Subjective Well-Being*. Basingstoke: Palgrave Macmillan.

Clark, D. A. (2014) 'Defining and measuring human well-being', in Freedman, B. (ed.), *Global Environmental Change*. Dordrecht: Springer Netherlands (Handbook of Global Environmental Pollution), pp. 833–855 <http://dx.doi.org/10.1007/978-94-007-5784-4_66>.

Clark, D. A. and Qizilbash, M. (2008) 'Core poverty, vagueness and adaptation: a new methodology and some results for South Africa', *The Journal of Development Studies*, 44(4), pp. 519–544 <http://dx.doi.org/10.1080/00220380801980855>.

Clark, D., Biggeri, M. and Frediani, A. A. (eds) (2019) *The Capability Approach, Empowerment and Participation: Concepts, Methods and Applications*. London: Palgrave Macmillan (Rethinking international development series). Available at: <https://ebookcentral.proquest.com/lib/ucl/detail.action?docID=5776019> [accessed 31 August 2020].

Colenbrander, S. (2016) 'Cities as engines of economic growth', *IIED Working Paper*. IIED, London. Available at: <https://pubs.iied.org/pdfs/10801IIED.pdf> [accessed 18 May 2021].

Comaroff, J. and Comaroff, J. L. (2015) *Theory from the South: Or, How Euro-America is Evolving Toward Africa*. New York: Routledge <http://dx.doi.org/10.4324/9781315631639>.

Connell, R. (2007) *Southern Theory: The Global Dynamics of Knowledge in Social Science*. Cambridge and Malden, MA: Polity.

Connolly, J. and Steil, J. (2009) 'Introduction: Finding justice in the city', in Marcuse, P., Connolly, J., Novy, J., Olivo, I., Potter, C. and Steil, J. (eds), *Searching for the Just City: Debates in Urban Theory and Practice*. Abingdon: Routledge, pp. 1–16 <http://dx.doi.org/10.4324/9780203878835>.

Conradie, I. and Robeyns, I. (2013) 'Aspirations and human development interventions', *Journal of Human Development and Capabilities*, 14(4), pp. 559–580 <http://dx.doi.org/10.1080/19452829.2013.827637>.

Crocker, D. (2008) *Ethics of Global Development: Agency, Capability, and Deliberative Democracy*. Cambridge, UK: Cambridge University Press.

Crompton, A. (2015) 'Runaway train: public participation and the case of HS2', *Policy & Politics*, 43(1), pp. 27–44 <http://dx.doi.org/10.1332/030557312X655963>.

Dagnino, E. (2007) 'Citizenship: a perverse confluence', *Development in Practice*, 17(4/5), pp. 549–556 <https://www.jstor.org/stable/25548252>.

Datta, A. (2016) 'The intimate city: violence, gender and ordinary life in Delhi slums', *Urban Geography*, 37(3), pp. 323–342 <http://dx.doi.org/10.1080/02723638.2015.1096073>.

Davis, M. (2006) *Planet of Slums*. London: Verso.

Davoudi, S. (2018) 'Spatial planning: the promised land or rolled-out neoliberalism?', in Gunder, M., Madanipour, A., and Watson, V. (eds), *The Routledge Handbook of Planning Theory*. Abingdon: Routledge, pp. 15–27.

De Carli, B. and Frediani, A. A. (2016) 'Insurgent regeneration: spatial practices of citizenship in the rehabilitation of inner-city São Paulo', *GeoHumanities*, 2(2), pp. 331–353 <http://dx.doi.org/10.1080/2373566X.2016.1235984>.

De Carli, B. and Frediani, A. A. (2021) 'Situated perspectives on the city: a reflection on scaling participation through design', *Environment and Urbanization*, 33(2). <https://doi.org/10.1177/09562478211028066>

De Carli, B., Frediani, A. A., Barbosa, R. B., de Assis Comarú, F., and de Sousa Moretti, R. (2015) 'Regeneration through the 'pedagogy of confrontation': exploring the critical spatial practices of social movements in inner city São Paulo as avenues for urban renewal', *Dearq Revista de Arquitectura / Journal of Architecture*, (16), pp. 146–161 <http://dx.doi.org/10.18389/dearq16.2015.10>.

Deneulin, S. (2008) 'Beyond individual freedom and agency: structures of living together in Sen's capability approach to development', in Alkire, S., Flavio Comim, and Qizilbash, M. (eds), *The Capability Approach: Concepts, Measures and Application*. Cambridge: Cambridge University Press, pp. 105–124. Available at: <https://researchportal.bath.ac.uk/en/publications/beyond-individual-freedom-and-agency-structures-of-living-togethe> [accessed 2 September 2020].

Deneulin, S. (2014) 'Creating more just cities: the right to the city and capability approach combined'. Working paper no. 32. Bath: Centre for Development Studies, University of Bath. Available at: <https://research-portal.bath.ac.uk/en/publications/creating-more-just-cities-the-right-to-the-city-and-capability-ap> [accessed 2 September 2020].

Deneulin, S., Nebel, M. and Sagovsky, N. (eds) (2006) *Transforming Unjust Structures: The Capability Approach.* Dordrecht: Springer (Library of Ethics and Applied Philosophy) <http://dx.doi.org/10.1007/1-4020-4432-1>.

Dong, A. (2008) 'The policy of design: a capabilities approach', *Design Issues*, 24(4), pp. 76–87.

Doshi, S. (2017) 'Embodied urban political ecology: five propositions', *Area*, 49(1), pp. 125–128 <http://dx.doi.org/10.1111/area.12293>.

Drèze, J. and Sen, A. (1991) *Hunger and Public Action.* Oxford: Oxford University Press. Available at: <https://oxford.universitypressscholarship.com/view/10.1093/0198283652.001.0001/acprof-9780198283652> [accessed 11 September 2020].

Drèze, J. and Sen, A. (2013) *An Uncertain Glory: India and its Contradictions.* Princeton: Princeton University Press. Available at: <https://press.princeton.edu/books/hardcover/9780691160795/an-uncertain-glory> [accessed 30 September 2020].

Duque Franco, I., Ortiz, C., Samper, J. and Millan, G. (2020) 'Mapping repertoires of collective action facing the COVID-19 pandemic in informal settlements in Latin American cities', *Environment and Urbanization*, 32(2), pp. 523–546. <http://dx.doi.org/10.1177/0956247820944823>.

Durand-Lasserve, A. (2006) 'Market-driven evictions and displacements: implications for the perpetuation of informal settlements in developing cities', in Huchzermeyer, M. and Karam, A. (eds), *Informal Settlements: A Perpetual Challenge.* Cape Town: Cape Town Press, pp. 207–227.

Earle, L. (2012) 'From insurgent to transgressive citizenship: housing, social movements and the politics of rights in São Paulo', *Journal of Latin American Studies*, 44(1), pp. 97–126 <http://dx.doi.org/10.1017/S0022216X11001118>.

Earle, L. (2017) *Transgressive Citizenship and the Struggle for Social Justice: The Right to the City in São Paulo.* London: Palgrave Macmillan (Studies of the Americas) <http://dx.doi.org/10.1007/978-3-319-51400-0>.

Euston Community Representatives Group (ECRG) (2016) *Corrected Minutes of Meeting on 7 December 2016.* Available at: <https://s3-eu-west-1.amazonaws.com/commonplace-cloudfront/resources/projects/hs2ineuston/Corrected+minutes+of+ECRG+meeting+2016+12+07.pdf> [accessed 18 May 2015].

Fainstein, S. S. (1999) 'Can we make the cities we want?', in Beauregard, R. A. and Body-Gendrot, S. (eds), *The Urban Moment: Cosmopolitan Essays on the Late-20th-Century City.* Thousand Oaks, CA: Sage Publications, pp. 249–272.

Fainstein, S. S. (2000) 'New directions in planning theory', *Urban Affairs Review*, 35(4), pp. 451–478 <http://dx.doi.org/10.1177/10780874000 3500401>.

Fainstein, S. S. (2009) 'Planning and the just city', in Marcuse, P., Connolly, J., Novy, J., Olivo, I., Potter, C. and Steil, J. (eds), *Searching for the Just City: Debates in Urban Theory and Practice.* Abingdon: Routledge, pp. 19–39.

Fainstein, S. S. (2011) *The Just City*. Cornell University Press.
Falú, A. (ed.) (2009) *Mujeres en la ciudad: de violencias y derechos*. Santiago de Chile: Ediciones SUR.
Fancello, G. (2011) 'A survey of applications of CA on urban quality of life', in *8th Annual Conference of the Human Development and Capability Association*, The Hague.
Ferguson, C., Moser, C. O. N. and Norton, A. (2007) 'Claiming rights: citizenship and the politics of asset distribution', in Moser, C. O. N. (ed.), *Reducing Global Poverty: The Case for Asset Accumulation*. Washington, DC: Brookings Institute, pp. 273–288.
Ferreira, J. S. W. F. (ed.) (2012) *Produzir casas ou construir cidades? Desafios para um novo Brasil urbano*. São Paulo: FAUUSP / FUPAM.
Figueiredo, G. C. dos S., Estévez, B. and Rosa, T. T. (2020) 'The black city: modernisation and fugitives in Salvador, Bahia, Brazil', *Radical Housing Journal*, 2(2). Available at: <https://radicalhousingjournal.org/2020/the-black-city/> [accessed 30 June 2021].
Fleming, A. (2011) 'Making a place for the rich? Urban poor evictions and gentrification in Woodstock, South Africa'. MSc dissertation. London School of Economics.
Foot, T. (2013), '"Our HS2 plan saves hundreds of homes" – rail lords pledge to push forward with alternative "Euston Cross" scheme', *Camden New Journal*, 23 May. Available at: <http://camdennewjournal.com/article/our-hs2-plan-saves-hundreds-homes-rail-lords-pledge-push-forward-alternative-eusto?sp=20&sq=Hs2> [accessed 18 May 2021].
Ford Foundation (2004) *Building Assets to Reduce Poverty and Injustice*. New York, NY: Ford Foundation. Available at: <https://www.fordfoundation.org/work/learning/research-reports/building-assets-to-reduce-poverty-and-injustice/> [accessed 6 October 2020].
Forester, J. (1985) 'Designing: making sense together in practical conversations', *Journal of Architectural Education*, 38(3), pp. 14–20.
Forester, J. (1999) *The Deliberative Practitioner: Encouraging Participatory Planning Processes*. MA: MIT Press.
Foster, J. E. and Handy, C. (2008) 'External capabilities', *Oxford Poverty & Human Development Initiative (OPHI) Working Paper*, 8. Available at: <https://ora.ox.ac.uk/objects/uuid:35f220d1-fa80-410f-8851-31f0ff48a994> [accessed 2 September 2020].
Fraser, N., (1997) *Justice Interruptus: Critical Reflections on the Postsocialist Condition*. New York: Routledge.
Frediani, A. A. (2007) 'Housing freedom, Amartya Sen and urban development policies: squatter settlement upgrading in Salvado da Bahia, Brazil'. PhD thesis. Oxford Brookes University. Available at: <https://ethos.bl.uk/OrderDetails.do?uin=uk.bl.ethos.491185> [accessed 6 October 2020].
Frediani, A. A. (2009) *Freedom in the Urban Arena: The World Bank, Turner and Sen*. 136. London: The Bartlett Development Planning Unit, University College London.
Frediani, A. A. (2010) 'Sen's capability approach as a framework to the practice of development', *Development in Practice*, 20(2), pp. 173–187 <http://dx.doi.org/10.1080/09614520903564181>.
Frediani, A. A. (2015) 'Space and capabilities: approaching informal settlement upgrading through a capability perspective', in Lemanski, C. and Marx, C.

(eds), *The City in Urban Poverty*. Basingstoke, UK: Palgrave Macmillan (EADI Global Development), pp. 64–84.

Frediani, A. A. (2016) 'Re-imagining participatory design: reflecting on the ASF-UK change by design methodology', *Design Issues*, 32(3), pp. 98–111 <http://dx.doi.org/10.1162/DESI_a_00403>.

Frediani, A. A. (2019a) 'Participatory research methods and the capability approach: researching the housing dimensions of squatter upgrading initiatives in Salvador da Bahia, Brazil', in Clark, D., Biggeri, M., and Frediani, A. A. (eds), *The Capability Approach, Empowerment and Participation: Concepts, Methods and Applications*. London: Palgrave Macmillan, pp. 261–288.

Frediani, A. A. (2019b) 'The "Right to the City" as an ethos of engagement: lessons from civil society experiences in the global South', in Garcia-Chueca, E. and Vidal, L. (eds), *Advancing Urban Rights. Equality and Diversity in the City*. Barcelona: CIDOB edicions (Monografías CIDOB, 76), pp. 127–136.

Frediani, A. A. and Boano, C. (2012) 'Processes for just products: the capability space of participatory design', in Oosterlaken, I. and van den Hoven, J. (eds), *The Capability Approach, Technology and Design*. London: Springer (Philosophy of Engineering and Technology 5), pp. 203–221.

Frediani, A. A. and Boieras, G. (2007) *Ferida Aberta / Open Wound* [documentary film]. Available at: <https://youtu.be/LxM0OtjSVuI> [accessed 18 May 2021].

Frediani, A. A. and Cociña, C. (2019) '"Participation as planning': strategies from the south to challenge the limits of planning', *Built Environment*, 45(2), pp. 143–161 <http://dx.doi.org/10.2148/benv.45.2.143>.

Frediani, A. A. and Hirst, L. (2016) 'Critical urban learning through participatory photography', in Campkin, B. and Duijzings, G. (eds), *Engaged Urbanism: Cities & Methodologies*. London: IBTauris, pp. 131–138. Available at: <http://ebookcentral.proquest.com/lib/ucl/detail.action?docID=4890560> [accessed 7 October 2020].

Frediani, A. A., Boni, A. and Gasper, D. (2014a) 'Approaching development projects from a human development and capability perspective', *Journal of Human Development and Capabilities*, 15(1), pp. 1–12.

Frediani, A. A., Butcher, S. and Hirst, L. (2014b) *Regeneration Aspirations for Euston: Local Perspectives on the High Speed Two Rail Link*. London: The Bartlett Development Planning Unit, University College London. Available at: <https://www.ucl.ac.uk/bartlett/development/sites/bartlett/files/sdp_euston_report_2014.pdf> [accessed 19 May 2021].

Frediani, A. A., Clark, D. and Biggeri, M. (2019a) 'Human development and the capability approach: the role of empowerment and participation', in Clark, D., Biggeri, M., and Frediani, A. A. (eds), *The Capability Approach, Empowerment and Participation: Concepts, Methods and Applications*. London: Palgrave Macmillan, pp. 3–35.

Frediani, A. A., Monson, T. and Butcher, S. (2015) *Reclaiming Regeneration: Negotiating a Citizen's Charter for Euston Area*. London: The Bartlett Development Planning Unit, University College London. Available at: <https://www.ucl.ac.uk/bartlett/development/sites/bartlett/files/2015_report_reclaiming_regeneration_euston_0.pdf> [accessed 19 May 2021].

Frediani, A. A., Peris, J. and Boni, A. (2019b) 'Notions of empowerment and participation: contributions from and to the capability approach', in

Clark, D. A., Biggeri, M., and Frediani, A. A. (eds), *The Capability Approach, Empowerment and Participation: Concepts, Methods and Applications*. Basingstoke: Palgrave Macmillan, pp. 101–124.

Frediani, A. A., De Carli, B., Nuñez Ferrera, I., Shinkins, N. (2013) *Change by Design: New spatial imaginations for Los Pinos*. Workshop report. London, UK: Architecture Sans Frontières UK.

Frediani, A. A., De Carli, B., Barbosa, B. R., de Assis Comarú, F. and de Sousa Moretti, R. (2018a) 'São Paulo: occupations – a pedagogy of confrontation – informal building occupations in São Paulo's central neighborhoods', in Rocco, R. and van Ballegooijen, J. (eds), *The Routledge Handbook on Informal Urbanization*. Oxon, UK: Routledge, pp. 259–269 <http://dx.doi.org/10.4324/9781315645544-24>.

Frediani, A. A., Koroma, B., Sesay, O., Morley, S. and Wright, S. (2018b) *Change by Design: Participatory Design and Planning. How Can Neighbourhood Planning Bring About Inclusive City-making in Freetown?* Workshop report. Freetown: SLURC and ASF-UK. Available at: <https://www.slurc.org/uploads/1/0/9/7/109761391/slurc_cbd_report_final.pdf> [accessed 19 May 2021].

Frediani, A. A., Cociña, C., Bhan, G., Lwasa, S., Peña Díaz, J. and Levy, C. (2020) 'Institutional capabilities towards urban equality: reflections from KNOW Programme in Bangalore, Kampala and Havana'. Working paper no. 4. London: Bartlett DPU, University College London. Available at: <https://45279888-944b-4def-99e5-22ea75128921.filesusr.com/ugd/623440_5a6f1a77a80d49f59ad6c857cfcb4351.pdf> [accessed 19 May 2021].

Frediani, A. A., De Carli, B., Shinkins, N., Kinnear, M., Morley, S. and Powis, A. (2014c) *Change by Design: Collective Imaginations for Contested Sites in Euston*. London: Architecture Sans Frontières UK. Available at: <https://issuu.com/asf-uk/docs/cbd_london_report_> [accessed 19 May 2021].

Freire, P. (1968) *Pedagogia do Oprimido*. Rio de Janeiro: Paz e Terra.

Freire, P. (1970) *Cultural Action for Freedom*. Harvard: Harvard Educational Review.

Freire, P. (1996) *Pedagogia da Autonomia*. São Paulo: Cortez.

Friedmann, J. (1987) *Planning in the Public Domain: From Knowledge to Action*. Princeton, NJ: Princeton University Press.

Friedmann, J. (2000) 'The good city: in defense of utopian thinking', *International Journal of Urban and Regional Research*, 24(2), pp. 460–472 <http://dx.doi.org/10.1111/1468-2427.00258>.

Friedmann, J. (2013) 'Why do planning theory?', *Planning Theory*, 2(1), pp. 7–10 <http://dx.doi.org/10.1177/1473095203002001002>.

Fukuda-Parr, S. (2003) 'The human development paradigm: operationalizing Sen's ideas on capabilities', *Feminist Economics*, 9(2–3), pp. 301–317 <http://dx.doi.org/10.1080/1354570022000077980>.

Garside, J. (1993) 'Inner city gentrification in South Africa: the case of Woodstock, Cape Town', *GeoJournal*, 30(1), pp. 29–35 <https://www.jstor.org/stable/41145712v>.

Gasper, D. (2002) 'Is Sen's capability approach an adequate basis for considering human development?' *Review of Political Economy*, 14(4), pp. 435–461 <https://doi.org/10.1080/0953825022000009898>.

Giraud, G., Renouard, C., L'Huillier, H., de la Martinière, R. and Sutter, C. (2013) 'Relational capabilities: a multidimensional approach', *ESSEC Working Paper*

1306. ESSEC Business School, Cergy-Pontoise Cedex. Available at: <https://hal-essec.archives-ouvertes.fr/hal-00815586/document> [accessed 31 May 2021].

Global Platform for the Right to the City (2020) *Cities for Dignity, not for Profit! Social Function of the City and the Right to the City*. Available at: <https://www.right2city.org/wp-content/uploads/2020/10/WHD-and-WD-for-the-Right-to-the-City-Statement.pdf> [accessed on 31 May 2021].

Gualini, E. (ed.) (2015) *Planning and Conflict: Critical Perspectives on Contentious Urban Developments*. New York: Routledge (RTPI library series) <http://dx.doi.org/10.4324/9780203734933>.

Gunder, M. (2003) 'Passionate planning for the others' desire: an agonistic response to the dark side of planning', *Progress in Planning*, 60(3), pp. 235–319 http://dx.doi.org/10.1016/S0305-9006(02)00115-0.

Hamdi, N. (2010) *The Placemaker's Guide to Building Community*, London: Earthscan.

Hamdi, N. and Goethert, R. (1997) *Action Planning for Cities: A Guide for Community Practice*. Chichester: Wiley & Sons.

Hamza, M. and Zetter, R. (eds) (2004) *Market Economy and Urban Change: Impacts in the Developing World*. London: Earthscan.

Harvey, D. (1973) *Social Justice and the City*. Baltimore: John Hopkins University Press.

Harvey, D (2003) *The New Imperialism*. New York, NY: Oxford University Press

Harvey, D. (2008) 'The right to the city', *New Left Review*, 53(September–October), pp. 23–40.

Harvey, D. (2009) *Cosmopolitanism and the Geographies of Freedom*. New York: Columbia University Press.

Hayes-Conroy, J. and Hayes-Conroy, A. (2013) 'Veggies and visceralities: a political ecology of food and feeling', *Emotion, Space and Society*, 6, pp. 81–90 <http://dx.doi.org/10.1016/j.emospa.2011.11.003>.

Heynen, N. (2017) 'Urban political ecology III: the feminist and queer century', *Progress in Human Geography* <http://dx.doi.org/10.1177/0309132517693336>.

Hitchen, J. (2019) *External Evaluation of the Sierra Leone Urban Research Centre*. Freetown: Sierra Leone Urban Research Centre. Available at: <https://www.slurc.org/uploads/1/0/9/7/109761391/slurc_evaluation_report_final.pdf> [accessed 19 May 2021].

Hodgett, S. and Clark, D. (2011) 'Capabilities, well-being and multiculturalism: a new framework for guiding policy', *International Journal of Canadian Studies / Revue internationale d'études canadiennes*, (44), pp. 163–184 <https://doi.org/10.7202/1010086ar>.

Holston, J. (2008) *Insurgent Citizenship: Disjunctions of Democracy and Modernity in Brazil*. Princeton: University Press (In-fomation series).

HS2 (2021) *ECRG* [website] HS2 Ltd <https://hs2ineuston.commonplace.is/schemes/happening-now/ecrg/details> [accessed on 7 June 2021].

HS2 Euston Action Group (2015a) *Petition: High Speed Rail (London – West Midlands) Bill (Additional Provision 3)*, in Parliament House of Commons, Session 2015–16, AP3: 053. Available at: <https://publications.parliament.uk/pa/cmhs2/addpetitions3/AP300053.pdf> [accessed 7 June 2021].

HS2 Euston Action Group (2015b), *HS2 – The Drummond Street Traders have a Problem* [film]. Available at: <https://www.youtube.com/watch?v=gAUaT-BeCxtE> [accessed 18 May 2021].

Huxley, M. and Yiftachel, O. (2000) 'New paradigm or old myopia? Unsettling the communicative turn in planning theory', *Journal of Planning Education and Research*, 19(4), pp. 333–342 <http://dx.doi.org/10.1177/0739456X0001900402>.

Iaione, C. (2016) 'The CO-City: sharing, collaborating, cooperating, and commoning in the city', *American Journal of Economics and Sociology*, 75(2), pp. 415–455 <https://doi.org/10.1111/ajes.12145>.

Ibrahim, S. S. (2006) 'From individual to collective capabilities: the capability approach as a conceptual framework for self-help', *Journal of Human Development*, 7(3), pp. 397–416 <http://dx.doi.org/10.1080/14649880600815982>.

Ibrahim, S. (2008) 'The self-help initiatives of the poor: the road to sustainable poverty reduction in Egypt'. PhD dissertation. University of Cambridge.

Ibrahim, S. (2014) 'Introduction: The capability approach: from theory to practice – rationale, review and reflections', in Ibrahim, S. and Tiwari, M. (eds), *The Capability Approach: From Theory to Practice*. Basingstoke: Palgrave Macmillan, pp. 1–28.

Ingold, T. (2000) *The Perception of the Environment: Essays in Livelihood, Dwelling and Skill*. London, UK: Routledge.

Innes, J. E. (1995) 'Planning theory's emerging paradigm: communicative action and interactive practice', *Journal of Planning Education and Research*, 14(3), pp. 183–189 <http://dx.doi.org/10.1177/0739456X9501400307>.

International Alliance of Inhabitants (2005) *The World Charter for the Right to the City*. Available at: <https://www.right2city.org/wp-content/uploads/2019/09/A1.2_World-Charter-for-the-Right-to-the-City.pdf> [accessed 31 May 2021].

Jacobs, J. (1962) *The Death and Life of Great American Cities*. London: Jonathan Cape.

Jacques, P. B. (2001) 'Estetica das Favelas', *Vitruvius*. Available at: <https://vitruvius.com.br/revistas/read/arquitextos/02.013/883> [accessed 17 August 2021].

Jenkins, P., Smith, H. and Wang, Y. P. (eds) (2007) *Planning and Housing in the Rapidly Urbanising World*. London: Routledge (Housing, planning, and design series).

Jones, M. L. G. (2021) 'Energy justice in Dhaka's slums'. PhD thesis. University College London.

Justice & Empowerment Initiatives (JEI) (2017) *Context Analysis for Research Project Assessing the Role of Participatory Well-Being Assessment in Supporting the Capacity of Informal Settlement Dwellers to Resist Evictions*. London: Bartlett DPU, University College London.

Kabeer, N. (1999) 'Resources, agency, achievements: reflections on the measurement of women's empowerment', *Development and Change*, 30(3), pp. 435–464 <https://doi.org/10.1111/1467-7660.00125>.

Kallus, R. (2001) 'From abstract to concrete: subjective reading of urban space', *Journal of Urban Design*, 6(2), pp. 129–150 <http://dx.doi.org/10.1080/13574800120057818>.

Kern, L. (2020) *Feminist City: Claiming Space in a Man-made World.* London: Verso.

Khader, S. J. and Kosko, S. J. (2019) '"Reason to value": process: opportunity, and perfectionism in the capability approach', in Keleher, L. and Kosko, S. J. (eds), *Agency and Democracy in Development Ethics.* Cambridge: Cambridge University Press, pp. 178–204.

Khosla, R. (2002) *Removing Unfreedoms: Citizens as Agents of Change. Background Support Project Document,* UN-Habitat Brussels Liaison Office. Available at: <https://www.ucl.ac.uk/~ucftwww/freedom/Removing_Unfreedoms.pdf> [accessed 31 March 2021].

Kisumu Water and Sewerage Company (2007) *Kisumu Water and Sewerage Company Strategic Plan 2007–2012.* Nairobi, Kenya.

Kleine, D. (2010) 'ICT4WHAT? – Using the choice framework to operationalise the capability approach to development', *Journal of International Development,* 22(5), pp. 674–692 <https://doi.org/10.1002/jid.1719>.

Kleine, D. (2013) *Technologies of Choice? ICTs, Development, and the Capabilities Approach.* Cambridge, MA: MIT Press.

Kohara, L. T. (2013) 'As Contribuições dos Movimentos de Moradia do Centro para as Políticas Habitacionais e do Desenvolvimento Urbano do Centro da Cidade de São Paulo'. Postdoctoral thesis. Faculty of Architecture and Urbanism, Universidade de São Paulo.

Kowarick, L. and Marques, E. (eds) (2011) *São Paulo: Novos Percursos e Atores.* São Paulo: Editora 34 Ltd.

Kuek, S. C., Paradi-Guilford, C. M., Fayomi, T., Imaizumi, S., Ipeirotis, P. (2015) *The Global Opportunity in Online Outsourcing.* World Bank Other Operational Studies 22284. The World Bank. Available at: <http://documents.worldbank.org/curated/en/138371468000900555/The-global-opportunity-in-online-outsourcing> [accessed 31 August 2020].

Lagos State High Court (2016), *Ruling of 4 November 2016 in Akakpo Agemu & Others v. A.G. Lagos State & Others (Suit No. LD/4232MFHR/16).* Available at: <https://static1.squarespace.com/static/535d0435e4b0586b1fc64b54/t/5824bbf0bebafb37e4e6f159/1478802426166/Injunction+Order+from+Lagos+State+High+Court+%287+Nov+2016%29+-+Nov+10+2016+-++12-48+PM.pdf> [Accessed 18 May 2021].

Lagos State High Court (2017), *Ruling of 26 January 2017 in Akakpo Agemu & Others v. A.G. Lagos State & Others (Suit No. LD/4232MFHR/16).* Available at: <https://static1.squarespace.com/static/535d0435e4b0586b1fc64b54/t/58947fc686e6c0558d87e37e/1486127074123/170126+Ruling+-+Akakpo+Agemo+%26+Ors+v+LASG+%26+Ors.pdf> [accessed 18 May 2021].

Lees, L. (2004) 'The emancipatory city: urban (re)visions', in *The Emancipatory City? Paradoxes and Possibilities.* London: Sage Publications, pp. 3–20.

Lefebvre, H. (1968) *Le Droit à la ville.* Paris: Anthropos.

Lefebvre, H. (1971) *Everyday Life in the Modern World.* London: Penguin.

Lefebvre, H. (1991a) *Critique of Everyday Life.* Vol. 1. Introduction. London: Verso.

Lefebvre, H. (1991b) *The Production of Space.* Oxford: Blackwell.

Lefebvre, H. (1996) *Writings on Cities.* Malden, MA: Blackwell.

Lefebvre, H. (2003) *The Urban Revolution*. Minneapolis; London: University of Minnesota Press. Available at: <http://UCL.eblib.com/patron/FullRecord.aspx?p=1637302> [accessed 1 September 2020].

Legacy, C. (2017) 'Is there a crisis of participatory planning?', *Planning Theory*, 16(4), pp. 425–442 <http://dx.doi.org/10.1177/1473095216667433>.

Levy, C. (1996) *The Process of Institutionalising Gender in Policy and Planning: the 'Web' of Institutionalisation*. 74. London: Bartlett DPU, University College London. Available at: <https://discovery.ucl.ac.uk/id/eprint/34/1/wp74.pdf> [accessed 19 May 2021].

Lewis, F. (2012) 'Auditing capability and active living in the built environment', *Journal of Human Development and Capabilities*, 13(2), pp. 295–315 <http://dx.doi.org/10.1080/19452829.2011.645028>.

te Lintelo, D., Gupte, J., McGregor, J.A., Lakshman, R., Jahan, F. (2017) 'Wellbeing and urban governance: who fails, survives or thrives in informal settlements in Bangladeshi cities?', *Cities*, 72(B), pp. 391–402 <https://doi.org/10.1016/j.cities.2017.10.002>.

Lokko, L. N. N. (ed.) (2000) *White Papers Black Marks: Architecture, Race, Culture*. Minneapolis: University of Minnesota Press.

Macarthy, J. M., Frediani, A. A., Foday Kamara, S., Morgado, M. (2017) *Exploring the Role of Empowerment in Urban Humanitarian Responses in Freetown*. London, UK: International Institute for Environment and Development. Available at: <https://pubs.iied.org/10845IIED> [accessed 19 May 2021].

Macarthy, J. M., Frediani, A. A. and Kamara, S. F. (2019) *Report on the Role of Community Action Area Planning in Expanding the Participatory Capabilities of the Urban Poor*. Freetown: Sierra Leone Urban Research Centre. Available at: <https://www.slurc.org/uploads/1/0/9/7/109761391/caap_research_report_final__web_quality_.pdf> [accessed 19 May 2021].

Macfarlane, A. and Frediani, A. A. (2018) *Wellbeing Narratives Against Evictions: Participatory Video on the Waterfronts of Lagos*. London: Bartlett DPU, University College London.

Madden, D. and Marcuse, P. (2016) *In Defense of Housing: The Politics of Crisis*. London and New York: Verso Books.

Martínez Cure, F. A., Montero Prieto, M. and Richardson, A. (2013) 'Delegated management model. Water kiosk, Manyatta B', in Frediani, A. A., Walker, J., and Butcher, S. (eds), *Participatory Informal Settlement Upgrading and Well-Being in Kisumu*. London: Bartlett DPU, University College London (MSc Social Development Practice Student Report), pp. 25–35. Available at: <https://www.ucl.ac.uk/bartlett/development/sites/bartlett/files/sdp_kisumu_report.pdf> [accessed 19 May 2021].

Maslow, A. H. (1943) 'A theory of human motivation', *Psychological Review*, 50, pp. 370–396.

Massey, D. (1994) *Space, Place and Gender*. Cambridge, UK: Polity Press.

Massey, D. (2005) *For Space*. London: SAGE.

Massey, D. (2013) *World City*. Hoboken: Wiley.

Matrix (1984) *Making Space: Women and the Man-made Environment*. London: Pluto Press.

Mbembe, A. and Nuttall, S. (2004) 'Writing the world from an African metropolis', *Public Culture*, 16(3), pp. 347–372 <https://doi.org/10.1215/08992363-16-3-347>.

McDowell, L. (1999) *Gender, Identity and Place: Understanding Feminist Geographies*. Cambridge, UK: Polity Press.

McFarlane, C. (2011) *Learning the City: Knowledge and Translocal Assemblage*. Oxford, UK: Wiley-Blackwell.

McFarlane, C. (2018) 'Learning from the city: a politics of urban learning in planning', in Gunder, M., Madanipour, A., and Watson, V. (eds), *The Routledge Handbook of Planning Theory*. London, UK: Routledge, pp. 323–333.

Medina, L. and Schneider, F. (2019) *Shedding Light on the Shadow Economy: A Global Database and the Interaction with the Official One*. SSRN Scholarly Paper ID 3502028. Rochester, NY: Social Science Research Network. Available at: <https://papers.ssrn.com/abstract=3502028> [accessed 31 August 2020].

Mele, C. (2013) 'Neoliberalism, race and the redefining of urban redevelopment', *International Journal of Urban and Regional Research*, 37(2), pp. 598–617 <https://doi.org/10.1111/j.1468-2427.2012.01144.x>.

Mella Lira, B. (2019) '16 - Using a capability approach-based survey for reducing equity gaps in transport appraisal: Application in Santiago de Chile', in Lucas, K., Martens, K., Di Ciommo, F. and Dupont-Kieffer, A. (eds), *Measuring Transport Equity*. Amsterdam, Netherlands: Elsevier, pp. 247–264 <http://dx.doi.org/10.1016/B978-0-12-814818-1.00016-0>.

Miessen, M. (2010) *The Nightmare of Participation*. Berlin: Sternberg Press.

Mignolo, W. (2011) *The Darker Side of Western Modernity: Global Futures, Decolonial Options*. Durham, NC; London, Durham: Duke University Press (Latin America otherwise). <http://dx.doi.org/10.1215/9780822394501>.

Miraftab, F. (2009) 'Insurgent planning: situating radical planning in the global south', *Planning Theory*, 8(1), pp. 32–50 <http://dx.doi.org/10.1177/1473095208099297>.

Miraftab, F. (2018) 'Insurgent practices and decolonization of future(s)', in Gunder, M., Madanipour, A., and Watson, V. (eds), *The Routledge Handbook of Planning Theory*. London, UK: Routledge, pp. 276–288.

Mitlin, D., Bennett, J., Horn, P., King, S., Makau, J. and Masimba Nyama, G. (2020) 'Knowledge matters: the potential contribution of the coproduction of research', *The European Journal of Development Research*, 32(3), pp. 544–559 <http://dx.doi.org/10.1057/s41287-020-00277-w>.

Moore, S. A., Wilson, J., Kelly-Richards, S. and Marston, S. A. (2015) 'School gardens as sites for forging progressive socioecological futures', *Annals of the Association of American Geographers*, 105(2), pp. 407–415 <http://dx.doi.org/10.1080/00045608.2014.985627>.

Moser, C. O. N. (1993) *Gender Planning and Development: Theory, Practice and Training*. London: Routledge.

Moser, C. O. N. (1998) 'The asset vulnerability framework: reassessing urban poverty reduction strategies', *World Development*, 26(1), pp. 1–19 <http://dx.doi.org/10.1016/S0305-750X(97)10015-8>.

Moser, C. O. N. (2006) 'Asset-based approaches to poverty reduction in a globalized context', Global Economy and Development Working Paper no. 1. Washington, DC: The Brookings Institute, <http://dx.doi.org/10.2139/ssrn.1011176>.

Moser, C. O. N. and Felton, A. (2007) 'The construction of an asset index measuring asset accumulation in Ecuador'. Chronic Poverty Research Centre Working Paper no. 87. Washington, DC: The Brookings Institution.

Mouat, C., Legacy, C. and March, A. (2013) 'The problem is the solution: testing agonistic theory's potential to recast intractable planning disputes', *Urban Policy and Research*, 31(2), pp. 150–166 <http://dx.doi.org/10.1080/08111146.2013.776496>.

Mouffe, C. (2005) *On the Political*. London: Routledge (Thinking in action) <http://dx.doi.org/10.4324/9780203870112>.

Mouffe, C. (2019) *For a Left Populism*. London: Verso.

MUDA_coletivo (2013) *Café na Rua - Ocupação Marconi* [film]. Available at: <https://www.youtube.com/watch?v=_FwQDtJYDd0> [accessed 1 June 2016].

Nieves Rico, M. and Segovia, O. (eds) (2017) *¿Quién cuida en la ciudad? Aportes para políticas urbanas de igualdad*. Santiago de Chile: CEPAL.

Nussbaum, M. C. (2000) *Women and Human Development: The Capabilities Approach*. Cambridge: Cambridge University Press (The Seeley Lectures) <http://dx.doi.org/10.1017/CBO9780511841286>.

Oosterlaken, I. (2009) 'Design for development: a capability approach', *Design Issues*, 25(4), pp. 91–102.

Orderson, K. (2018) *Not in My Neighbourhood*. New Days Films. Available at: <https://www.notinmyneighbourhood.com/> [accessed 19 May 2021].

Organisation for Economic Co-operation and Development (OECD) (no date) *OECD affordable housing database* [webpage] <http://www.oecd.org/social/affordable-housing-database/> [accessed 6 May 2021].

Ortiz, H. (2003) 'Social production of habitat: marginal option or reality-transforming strategy?' *TRIALOG*, 78, pp. 39–43. Available at: <https://www.trialog-journal.de/wp-content/uploads/2016/04/TRIALOG-78-Social-Production-of-Habitat-in-Latin-America-Vol.-3_2003-IKO-OD0B81.pdf> [accessed 15 June 2021].

Ortiz, H. (2010) 'The construction process towards the right to the city in Latin America', in Sugranyes, A. and Mathivet, C. (eds), *Cities for All: Proposals and Experiences towards the Right to the City*. Santiago: Habitat International Coalition, pp. 113–120.

Ossul Vermehren, M. I. (2019) 'The politics of home-making: the case of informal settlements in Viña del Mar, Chile'. PhD thesis. University College London. Available at: <https://discovery.ucl.ac.uk/id/eprint/10066816/> [accessed 21 September 2020].

Osuteye, E., Ortiz, C., Lipietz, B., Castán Broto, V., Johnson, C. and Kombe, W. (2019) *Knowledge Co-production for Urban Equality*. 1. London: Bartlett DPU, University College London. Available at: <https://www.urban-know.com/no-1-know-working-paper> [accessed 19 May 2021].

Patnaik, P. (1998) 'Amartya Sen and the theory of public action', *Economic and Political Weekly*, 33(45), pp. 2855–2859.

Payne, G., Durand-Lasserve, A. and Rakodi, C. (2009) 'The limits of land titling and home ownership', *Environment and Urbanization*, 21(2), pp. 443–462 <http://dx.doi.org/10.1177/0956247809344364>.

Pellicer-Sifres, V., Belda-Miguel, S., López-Fogués, A. and Boni Aristizábal, A. (2017) 'Grassroots social innovation for human development: an analysis of alternative food networks in the city of Valencia (Spain)', *Journal of Human Development and Capabilities*, 18(2), pp. 258–274 <http://dx.doi.org/10.1080/19452829.2016.1270916>.

Petrescu, D. (2017) 'Being-in-relation and reinventing the commons', in Schalk, M., Kristiansson, T., and Mazé, R. (eds), *Feminist Futures of Spatial Practice: Materialism, Activism, Dialogue, Pedagogies, Projections*. Baunach: AADR – Art Architecture Design Research, pp. 101–110.

Petrescu, D. and Gibson, K. (2017) 'Diverse economies, ecologies and practices of urban commoning', in Frichot, H., Gabrielsson, C., and Runting, H. (eds), *Architecture and Feminisms: Ecologies, Economies, Technologies*. London: Routledge, pp. 218–230 <http://dx.doi.org/10.4324/9780203729717-24>.

Petrescu, D., Petcou, C., Safri, M. and Gibson, K. (2020) 'Calculating the value of the commons: generating resilient urban futures', *Environmental Policy and Governance*, n/a(n/a), pp. 1–16 <https://doi.org/10.1002/eet.1890>.

Pillay, S. (2016) 'The displacement phenomenon: Woodstock and Salt River', *News24*. Available at: <https://www.news24.com/news24/southafrica/news/the-displacement-phenomenon-woodstock-and-salt-river-20160922-2> [accessed 29 September 2020].

Pillay, S., Russell, S., Sendin, J., Sithole, M., Budlender, N. and Knoetze, D. (2017) *I Used to Live Here: A Call for Transitional Housing for Evictees in Cape Town*. Cape Town: Ndifuna Ukwazi. Available at: <http://www.ngopulse.org/sites/default/files/attachments/TransitionalHousingwithCorrections.pdf> [accessed 2 December 2020].

Pløger, J. (2004) 'Strife: urban planning and agonism', *Planning Theory*, 3(1), pp. 71–92. <http://dx.doi.org/10.1177/1473095204042318>.

Ponsford, M. (2017) 'Lagos court demands state halt slum demolitions, consult residents', *Reuters*, 27 January. Available at: <https://www.reuters.com/article/us-nigeria-slums-court-idUSKBN15B1P0> [accessed 3 September 2020].

Prada-Trigo, J. (2017) 'Governance and territorial development in Ecuador: the Plan Nacional del Buen Vivir in Zaruma, Piñas and Portovelo', *Journal of Latin American Studies*, 49(2), pp. 299–326 <http://dx.doi.org/10.1017/S0022216X16001474>.

Purcell, M. (2003) 'Citizenship and the right to the global city: reimagining the capitalist world order', *International Journal of Urban and Regional Research*, 27(3), pp. 564–590 <http://dx.doi.org/10.1111/1468-2427.00467>.

Purcell, M. (2006) 'Urban democracy and the local trap', *Urban Studies*, 43(11), pp. 1921–1941.

Qizilbash, M. (1996) 'Capabilities, well-being and human development: a survey', *The Journal of Development Studies*, 33(2), pp. 143–162 <http://dx.doi.org/10.1080/00220389608422460>.

Quijano, A. (2007) 'Coloniality and modernity/rationality', *Cultural Studies*, 21(2–3), pp. 168–178 <http://dx.doi.org/10.1080/09502380601164353>.

Railway Technology (2012) 'UK HS2 plans approved' [webpage] <https://www.railway-technology.com/news/newsuk-high-speed-rail-2-plans-approved> [accessed 18 May 2015].

Rakodi, C. and Lloyd-Jones, T. (eds) (2002) *Urban Livelihoods: A People-centred Approach to Reducing Poverty*. London: Earthscan.

Republic of Kenya (2011) *Urban Areas and City Act*, National Council for Law Reporting: Nairobi. Available at: <http://www.parliament.go.ke/sites/default/files/2017-05/UrbanAreasandCitiesAct_No13of2011.pdf> [accessed 15 June 2021].

Republic of Kenya (2012) *County Government Act*, National Council of Law Reporting: Nairobi. Available at: <http://www.parliament.go.ke/sites/default/files/2017-05/CountyGovernmentsAct_No17of2012_1.pdf> [accessed 15 June 2021].

República del Ecuador (2008) *Constitucion de la República del Ecuador*. Last updated on 13 July 2011. Available at: <https://www.cec-epn.edu.ec/wp-content/uploads/2016/03/Constitucion.pdf> [accessed 16 June 2021].

Rigon, A., Abah, S., Dangoji, S., Walker, J., Frediani, A. A., Ogunleye, O., and Hirst, L. (2015) *Well-being and Citizenship in Urban Nigeria*. London: ICF International.

Robeyns, I. (2003) 'Sen's capability approach and gender inequality: selecting relevant capabilities', *Feminist Economics*, 9(2–3), pp. 61–92 <http://dx.doi.org/10.1080/1354570022000078024>.

Robeyns, I. (2005) 'The capability approach: a theoretical survey', *Journal of Human Development*, 6(1), pp. 93–117 <http://dx.doi.org/10.1080/146498805200034266>.

Robeyns, I. (2017) *Wellbeing, Freedom and Social Justice. The Capability Approach Re-examined*. Cambridge, UK: Open Book Publishers.

Robinson, J. (2006) *Ordinary Cities: Between Modernity and Development*. Abingdon: Routledge.

Roy, A. (2009) 'The 21st-century metropolis: new geographies of theory', *Regional Studies*, 43(6), pp. 819–830 <http://dx.doi.org/10.1080/00343400701809665>.

Roy, A. and Ong, A. (eds) (2011) *Worlding Cities Asian Experiments and the Art of Being Global*. Hoboken: Wiley (Studies in Urban and Social Change).

Samuels, J. (2005) *Removing Unfreedoms: Citizens as Agents of Change in Urban Development*. Rugby, UK: ITDG.

Sandbrook, R. (2000) 'Globalization and the limits of neoliberal development doctrine', *Third World Quarterly*, 21(6), pp. 1071–1080 <http://dx.doi.org/10.1080/01436590020012052>.

Sandercock, L. (1998) *Towards Cosmopolis: Planning for Multicultural Cities*. Chichester: John Wiley & Sons.

Santos, M. (2000) *Por uma outra globalização: do pensamento único à consciência universal*. Rio de Janeiro: Record.

Sassen, S. (2014) *Expulsions: Brutality and Complexity in the Global Economy*. Cambridge, MA: Belknap Press of Harvard University Press.

Scheba, A. and Turok, I. (2020) 'Informal rental housing in the south: dynamic but neglected', *Environment and Urbanization*, 32(1), pp. 109–132 <http://dx.doi.org/10.1177/0956247819895958>.

Schiller, N. G. and Çağlar, A. (eds) (2011) *Locating Migration: Rescaling Cities and Migrants*. 1st edn. Ithaca: Cornell University Press. Available at: <http://www.jstor.org/stable/10.7591/j.ctt7zh6v> [accessed 20 March 2021].

Schlosberg, D. (2007) *Defining Environmental Justice: Theories, Movements, and Nature*. Oxford: Oxford University Press.

Schwartz, K. and Sanga, A. (2010) 'Partnerships between utilities and small-scale providers: delegated management in Kisumu, Kenya', *Physics and Chemistry of the Earth, Parts A/B/C*, 35(13), pp. 765–771 <http://dx.doi.org/10.1016/j.pce.2010.07.003>.

Select Committee on the High Speed Rail (London–West Midlands) Bill (2017), *Special Report of Session 2016–17 – published 15 December 2016 – HL Paper*

83. Available at: <https://publications.parliament.uk/pa/ld201617/ldselect/ldhs2/83/8302.htm> [accessed 18 May 2021].

Sen, A. (1981) *Poverty and Famines: An Essay on Entitlement and Deprivation*. Oxford: Oxford University Press.

Sen, A. (1985) 'Well-being, agency and freedom: the Dewey Lectures 1984', *The Journal of Philosophy*, 82(4), pp. 169–221.

Sen, A. (1987) *The Standard of Living*. Cambridge, UK: Cambridge University Press.

Sen, A. (1990) 'Gender and cooperative conflict', in Tinker, I. (ed.), *Persistent Inequalities*. Oxford: Oxford University Press, pp. 123–148.

Sen, A. (1992) *Inequality Re-examined*. Oxford: Clarendon Press.

Sen, A. (1993) 'Capability and well-being', in Nussbaum, M. C. and Sen, A. (eds), *The Quality of Life*. Oxford: Clarendon Press, pp. 30–53.

Sen, A. (1999a) *Commodities and Capabilities*. Oxford: Oxford University Press.

Sen, A. (1999b) *Development as Freedom*. Oxford: Oxford University Press.

Sen, A. (2000) *Social Exclusion: Concept, Application, and Scrutiny*. Manila: Asian Development Bank (Social Development Paper, 1). Available at: <https://www.adb.org/publications/social-exclusion-concept-application-and-scrutiny> [accessed 11 September 2020].

Sen, A. (2009) 'Capability: reach and limit', in Chiappero Martinetti, E. (ed.), *Debating Global Society: Reach and Limits of the Capability Approach*. Milan: Fondazione Giangiacomo Feltrinelli, pp. 15–28.

Sennett, R. (1989) 'The civitas of seeing', *Places: A Quarterly Journal of Environmental Design*, 5, pp. 82–85.

SENPLADES (2013) *National Development Plan / National Plan for Good Living, 2013–2017*. Quito, Ecuador: National Secretariat of Planning and Development.

Simon, D., Palmer, H. Riise, J., Smit, W. and Valencia, S. (2018) 'The challenges of transdisciplinary knowledge production: from unilocal to comparative research', *Environment and Urbanization*, 30(2), pp. 481–500 <http://dx.doi.org/10.1177/0956247818787177>.

Simone, A. (2004) *For the City Yet to Come: Changing African Life in Four Cities*. Durham, NC: Duke University Press.

Simonsen, K. (2013) 'In quest of a new humanism: embodiment, experience and phenomenology as critical geography*', *Progress in Human Geography*, 37(1), pp. 10–26 <http://dx.doi.org/10.1177/0309132512467573>.

Sierra Leone Urban Research Centre (SLURC) (2016) 'Hitting the road running: The Sierra Leone Urban Research Centre (SLURC) coordinates the Pull Slum Pan Pipul (PSPP) Partnership', *Sierra Leone Urban Research and Development News*, vol. 1, pp. 5. SLURC: Freetown. Available at: <https://www.slurc.org/uploads/1/0/9/7/109761391/slurc_newsletter_draft_v.1_1.pdf> [accessed 17 June 2021].

SLURC (2019) *Urban Transformations in Sierra Leone: Lessons from SLURC's Research in Freetown*. Conference Report. Freetown: SLURC. Available at: <https://www.slurc.org/uploads/1/0/9/7/109761391/urban_transformations_in_sierra_leone_conference_report_web.pdf> [accessed 19 May 2021].

SLURC and Architecture Sans Frontières-UK (ASF-UK) (2019a) *Change by Design: Dworzark Community Action Area Plan*. SLURC: Freetown. Available at: <https://www.slurc.org/uploads/1/0/9/7/109761391/dworzark_caap_final_web_quality.pdf> [accessed 25 June 2021].

SLURC and ASF-UK (2019b) *Change by Design: Cockle Bay Community Action Area Plan*. SLURC: Freetown. Available at: <https://www.slurc.org/uploads/1/0/9/7/109761391/cockle_bay_caap_final_web_quality.pdf> [accessed 25 June 2021].
Smith, A. (1759) *The Theory of Moral Sentiments*. Oxford, UK: Clarendon Press.
Snow, D. A. and Trom, D. (2002) 'The case study and the study of social movements', in Klandermans, B. and Staggenborg, S. (eds), *Methods of Social Movement Research*. Minneapolis: University of Minnesota Press, pp. 146–172.
Soares, A. M. de C. and Espinheira, C. G. D. (2006) 'Conjuntos habitacionais em Salvador-Ba e a transitória inserção social', *Risco – Revista de Pesquisa em Arquitetura e Urbanismo*, (3), pp. 57–65 <http://dx.doi.org/10.11606/issn.1984-4506.v0i3p57-65>.
Soja, E. W. (2010) *Seeking Spatial Justice*. Minneapolis: University of Minnesota Press.
Stavrides, S. (2016) *Common Space: The City as Commons*. London: Zed Books.
Stewart, F. and Deneulin, S. (2002) 'Amartya Sen's contribution to development thinking', *Studies in Comparative International Development*, 37(2), pp. 61–70 <https://doi.org/10.1007/BF02686262>.
Stop HS2 (2017) 'Camden residents continue to resist HS2's green space destruction' [webpage], 14 May <http://stophs2.org/news/16954-camden-residents-continue-resist-hs2s-green-space-destruction> [accessed 18 May 2021].
Sverdlik, A. (2020) 'Emerging lessons from community-led COVID-19 responses in urban areas', *International Institute for Environment and Development*, 25 June. Available at: <https://www.iied.org/emerging-lessons-community-led-covid-19-responses-urban-areas> [accessed 4 September 2020].
Swyngedouw, E. (2004) *Social Power and the Urbanization of Water: Flows of Power*. Oxford, UK: Oxford University Press.
Swyngedouw, E. (2010) 'Apocalypse forever? Post-political pluralism and the spectre of climate change', *Theory, Culture and Society*, 27, pp. 213–232.
Swyngedouw, E. (2011) *Designing the Post-Political City and the Insurgent Polis*. London: Bedford Press.
Swyngedouw, E. and Heynen, N. C. (2003) 'Urban political ecology, justice and the politics of scale', *Antipode*, 35(5), pp. 898–918. <https://doi.org/10.1111/j.1467-8330.2003.00364.x>
Talu, V. and Blečič, I. (2012) 'Pedestrian mobility as a fundamental urban right: the possible contribution of children to urban walkability', in De Montis, A., Pira, C., Campagna, M., Zoppi, C., Isola, F. and Lai, S. (eds), *Planning Support Tools: Policy Analysis, Implementation and Evaluation. Proceedings of the Seventh International Conference on Informatics and Urban and Regional Planning INPUT2012: Proceedings of the Seventh International Conference on Informatics and Urban and Regional Planning INPUT2012*. Milano: FrancoAngeli.
Tatagiba, L., Paterniani, S. Z. and Trindade, T. A. (2012) 'Ocupar, reivindicar, participar: sobre o repertório de ação do movimento de moradia de São Paulo', *Opinião Pública*, 18(2), pp. 399–426 <http://dx.doi.org/10.1590/S0104-62762012000200007>.
Thorpe, A. (2017) 'Rethinking participation, rethinking planning', *Planning Theory & Practice*, 18(4), pp. 566–582 <http://dx.doi.org/10.1080/14649357.2017.1371788>.

Till, J. (2005) 'The negotiation of hope', in Blundell Jones, P., Petrescu, D., and Till, J. (eds), *Architecture and Participation*. London, UK: Spon Press, pp. 23–41.

Tonon, G. (2018) 'Communities and capabilities', *Journal of Human Development and Capabilities*, 19(2), pp. 121–125 <http://dx.doi.org/10.1080/19452829.2018.1454288>.

Totaro, P. and Ponsford, M. (2016) 'Demolitions of Lagos waterfront communities could leave 300,000 homeless – campaigners', *Reuters*, 12 November. Available at: <https://www.reuters.com/article/uk-nigeria-slum-demolition-idUKKBN1370OU> [accessed 5 June 2021].

Turner, J. F. (1972) 'Housing as a verb', in Turner, J. F. and Fichter, R. (eds), *Freedom to Build: Dweller Control of the Housing Process*. New York: Macmillan.

United Nations (UN) (no date) *Sustainable Development Goals, Goal 11: Make cities inclusive, safe, resilient and sustainable* [webpage] <https://www.un.org/sustainabledevelopment/cities/> [accessed 6 May 2021].

UN (2005) 'Report of the Special Rapporteur on adequate housing as a component of the right to an adequate standard of living', Economic and Social Council, Commission on Human Rights, 61st session, item 10. Available at: <https://undocs.org/E/CN.4/2005/48> [accessed 25 June 2021].

UN (2015) *World Urbanization Prospects: The 2014 Revision*. New York: Department of Economic and Social Affairs, Population Division.

UN (2017) *New Urban Agenda*. Conference on Housing and Sustainable Urban Development (Habitat III). Quito, Ecuador.

UN (2019) *Sustainable Development Goals Review, Goal 11: Make cities inclusive, safe, resilient and sustainable* [webpage] <https://unstats.un.org/sdgs/report/2019/goal-11/> [accessed 6 May 2021].

United Nations Development Programme (UNDP) (1990) *Human Development Report 1990*. Oxford: Oxford University Press.

Urson, R. (2019) 'Reclaiming the spatial imaginary: a photovoice study of resistance to displacement in Woodstock, Cape Town'. MA thesis. University of Cape Town. Available at: <https://open.uct.ac.za/handle/11427/30836> [accessed 2 December 2020].

Uyan-Semerci, P. (2007) 'A relational account of Nussbaum's list of capabilities', *Journal of Human Development*, 8(2), pp. 203–221 <http://dx.doi.org/10.1080/14649880701371034>.

Visagie, J. and Turok, I. (2020) 'Getting urban density to work in informal settlements in Africa', *Environment and Urbanization*, 32(2), pp. 351–370 <http://dx.doi.org/10.1177/0956247820907808>.

Walker, J., Berekashvili, N. and Lomidze, N. (2014) 'Valuing time: time use survey, the capability approach, and gender analysis', *Journal of Human Development and Capabilities*, 15(1), pp. 47–59 <http://dx.doi.org/10.1080/19452829.2013.837033>.

Walker, J., Frediani, A. A. and Trani, J.-F. (2013) 'Gender, difference and urban change: implications for the promotion of well-being?', *Environment and Urbanization*, 25(1), pp. 111–124 <http://dx.doi.org/10.1177/0956247812468996>.

Walker, M. and Boni, A. (eds) (2020) *Participatory Research, Capabilities and Epistemic Justice*. Cham: Springer Nature.

Wallman, S. (2011) *Capability of Places: Methods for Modelling Community Response to Intrusion and Change*. London: Pluto Press.

Walsh, C. (2010) 'Development as buen vivir: institutional arrangements and (de)colonial entanglements', *Development*, 53(1), pp. 15–21 <http://dx.doi.org/10.1057/dev.2009.93>.
Watkins, C. and Hagelman, R. R. (2011) 'Hurricane Katrina as a lens for assessing socio-spatial change in New Orleans', *Southeastern Geographer*, 51(1), pp. 110–132.
Watson, V. (2003) 'Conflicting rationalities: implications for planning theory and ethics', *Planning Theory & Practice*, 4(4), pp. 395–407 <http://dx.doi.org/10.1080/1464935032000146318>.
Watson, V. (2009) *Strategic Literature Assessment for Informal Rental Research Project*. Johannesburg: Social Housing Foundation. Available at: <https://www.suelourbano.org/wp-content/uploads/2018/03/small_scale_rental_report_watson_2010.pdf> [accessed 30 September 2020].
Watson, V. (2013) 'African urban fantasies: dreams or nightmares?', *Environment and Urbanization*, 26(1), pp. 215–231 <http://dx.doi.org/10.1177/0956247813513705>.
Watson, V. (2014) 'Co-production and collaboration in planning – the difference', *Planning Theory & Practice*, 15(1), pp. 62–76 <http://dx.doi.org/10.1080/14649357.2013.866266>.
Weinstein, L. (2020) 'Introduction: The spatiality of street protests before and during Covid-19', *IJURR: International Journal of Urban and Regional Research*. Available at: <https://www.ijurr.org/spotlight-on/urban-revolts/the-spatiality-of-street-protests-before-and-during-covid-19/> [accessed 20 October 2020].
Weisman, L. K. (1992) *Discrimination by Design: A Feminist Critique of the Man-made Environment*. Chicago: University of Illinois Press.
Wenz, L. (2012) 'Changing tune in Woodstock: creative industries and local urban development in Cape Town, South Africa', *Gateways: International Journal of Community Research and Engagement*, 5, pp. 16–34 <http://dx.doi.org/10.5130/ijcre.v5i0.2010>.
Woodcraft, S., Osuteye, E., Ndezi, T., and Mokoba, F. D. (2020) 'Pathways to the "good life": co-producing prosperity research in informal settlements in Tanzania', *Urban Planning*, 5(3), pp. 288–302 <http://dx.doi.org/10.17645/up.v5i3.3177>.
Yamamoto, A. D. (2016) 'Why agonistic planning? Questioning Chantal Mouffe's thesis of the ontological primacy of the political', *Planning Theory* <http://dx.doi.org/10.1177/1473095216654941>.
Yap, C. and McFarlane, C. (2020) 'Understanding and researching urban extreme poverty: a conceptual–methodological approach', *Environment and Urbanization*, 32(1), pp. 254–274 <http://dx.doi.org/10.1177/0956247819890829>.
Yiftachel, O. (2009) 'Theoretical notes on "gray cities": the coming of urban apartheid?', *Planning Theory* <https://doi.org/10.1177/1473095208099300>.
Young, I. M. (1990) *Justice and the Politics of Difference*. Princeton, NJ: Princeton University Press.
Zetter, R. and White, R. R. (eds) (2002) *Planning in Cities: Sustainability and Growth in the Developing World*. London: ITDG (Urban management series).

www.ingramcontent.com/pod-product-compliance
Lightning Source LLC
Chambersburg PA
CBHW070042120526
44589CB00035B/2253